To. Elsa Alexander

With Best Wishes

[signature] 24/4/86

FIRST·BABY
AFTER
THIRTY

FIRST·BABY
AFTER
THIRTY

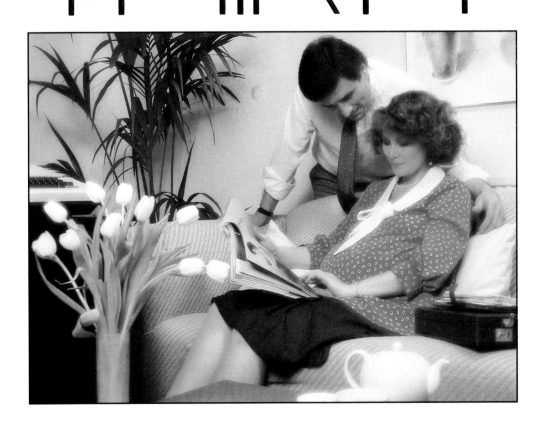

WINDWARD

Editor: Casey Horton
House Editor: Donna Wood
Designer: Gordon Robertson
Production: Richard Churchill

Published by Windward, an imprint owned by
W.H. Smith & Son Limited
Registered No. 237811 England
Trading as WHS Distributors,
St John's House, East Street, Leicester LE1 6NE

© Marshall Cavendish 1986

ISBN O-7112-0442-X

Typeset in Grotesque by Bookworm Typesetting.
Printed and bound by Jerez Industrial S.A. Spain.

CONTENTS

INTRODUCTION

THIS BOOK IS LARGELY ABOUT CHOICES.

We are particularly concerned with the woman who has made a conscious decision to postpone her first pregnancy until after the age of 30. Traditionally this has been regarded by doctors as dangerous, but the risks have been rather exaggerated. In the last hundred years the safety of childbearing has improved beyond expectation; if it has appeared to improve less for the older first-time mother it is because the statistics do not distinguish between choice and circumstance.

At the turn of the century pregnancy and childbirth were still hazardous. Six or seven women in every thousand died in the attempt to bear a child. One in 20 of the babies were stillborn and of those born alive, some 15% failed to reach their first birthday. Most women had their first child in their teens and were pregnant every two or three years for the rest of their lives; only a minority reached the menopause. In the first 50 years of the century priority was given to making reproduction safer; the major strides occurring in the 1940s and 50s with the introduction of the Blood Transfusion Service, the National Health Service and the discovery of antibiotics.

It was not until the Population Statistics Act of 1938 that birth registration data began to include the mother's date of birth. Since that time the statistics suggest that the safest time to have children is when the woman is in her 20s. The dangers seem to increase with age for women over 30. When the first baby is postponed until after 30, the trend is exaggerated.

Since 1950 the reproductive mortality rate for women aged 25 to 35 has fallen by 75%; in women of 35 to 44 there is a much smaller improvement of only about 20%. The risk to the mother aged 35 to 44 is approximately double that of younger women.

These statistics do not distinguish between the constituent elements of the older age group. For some the postponement will be of necessity; the necessity of social circumstance, of infertility or of recurrent miscarriage. For others the postponement will be by choice. It is this last group with whom we are most concerned.

The women in this group are likely to have had access to further and higher education and to have pursued a career before embarking upon pregnancy. As a group, they are highly motivated towards motherhood, and have a constructive and responsible attitude to ante-natal care. For the obstetrician, the women of this group make ideal patients.

If the woman of the 1980s is in a position to exercise choice about the timing of her reproduction and the conduct of her pregnancy it is precisely because major strides have been made in the direction of safety in the first half of the century; the second half has therefore been able to concentrate much more on the patient's own options – options which medical technology have made possible.

Since the 1950s, the choice of postponement of pregnancy has been more readily available. With modern methods of contraception, most women find it possible to delay the first pregnancy until their chosen time – their mothers and grandmothers often had the timing determined for them. Since 1968, women have had the further choice of terminating their pregnancy if they wish.

Choices are also available in parenting. No longer is it the rule or even the norm that all mothers are married and stay home whilst their husbands go to work. Chapter 4 deals with some of these issues.

The medical side of pregnancy is also subject to choice. The practice of midwifery – and even obstetrics – is now much less rigid than in my youth. Those of us who were trained in the 1950s have had to adapt to the consumer awareness of different techniques and options. In the first half of the century the doctor's concern was entirely for what he or she perceived as safety for mother and baby.

We are still concerned with these major issues, but have had to re-examine some of our cherished notions of normality. Most obstetric departments are now alert to the wishes of the parents in the conduct of pregnancy and labour; some of the choices available are dealt with in Chapter 3.

It has not been our aim to provide a rival to the many explanatory texts written for pregnant women. We have tried to concentrate on the particular issues that affect the older patient. In the paediatric section, the emphasis is on the development of the normal infant, with a few indications as to when medical advice may be necessary.

In concentrating on the element of choice, we have tried to illustrate the positive aspects of parenting after 30. There are, of course, special problems for a few patients; as the chapters on infertility and ante-natal screening rightly emphasize. If occasional disasters are to be avoided, it is essential to be aware of the risks. A sensible discussion with the health professionals will usually help to put these matters in perspective. It is the intention of this book to provide background information against which such constructive discussion can take place.

Roger V Clements FRCS (Ed), FRCOG

Chapter 1

COMING TO A DECISION

- Emotional factors
- Financial concerns
- Social attitudes
- Physical considerations

Fewer women are having children now than ten years ago. Over the last decade the overall birthrate has dropped from 68 births per 1000 women to 60. This downward trend is evident in all age groups except one. Among women aged 30 to 34, the fertility rate has risen from 60 births to 74 for every 1000 women in this group. Of course women have always had babies while in their 30s. The new phenomenon is the woman in this age group who has deliberately delayed starting a family, for whom this is a first birth.

The phenomenon exists because women in western societies have a real choice: medical science has given them the opportunity to decide if and when they should become, or remain, pregnant. Education, careers and job opportunities allow many women to be more than just a wife or a mother. Because women have a choice it is sensible for them to want to consider and discuss the advantages and disadvantages of childbearing – an event that will change their life.

There is nothing natural or loving about bringing a child into the world who is not truly welcome. Conversely, there is nothing un-natural or unloving about women who consider all the factors that will influence their ability to love, care for and enjoy a child. Discussion prior to decision-making enables women, or women and their partners, to make the best decision for all concerned.

It is a convention to think of pregnancy as something that is contemplated by couples

only, although it is true that most women who bring up children on their own are in this situation by default. Of the 900,000 single mothers in the United Kingdom, the majority are in this state because they have been widowed, abandoned by or separated from the father of their children. However, there is a small but growing number of women who make single parenthood a deliberate choice.

Some women, having reached a particular stage in their career or personal development, want to have a child but have no desire to accept marriage or partnership outside of marriage. Others genuinely want to be solely responsible for their child, or have not yet found a partner who they think would be suitable as a father.

Any woman contemplating single parenthood should be aware that in some areas she will be at a disadvantage: in matters of finance and child care she will lack the support of another adult; in the event of illness or even death the child might be left alone and might have to face enormous difficulties; and, although illegitimacy no longer carries the stigma it once attracted, the child to some extent would come under the social pressures put on any child who does not come from a 'normal' family. In addition, although there can be no doubt that a happy one-parent upbringing would be preferable to an unhappy traditional home, there is some evidence that children who lack two parents of different sexes are in some ways disadvantaged.

Whether pregnancy is considered by a woman with a permanent partner or by a woman on her own, whether the advantages and disadvantages of pregnancy are considered before conception or after conception has taken place, most of the elements to be taken into account are essentially the same. Anyone deciding whether or not to embark on pregnancy should consider whether emotionally, financially, physically and socially they are ready and able to cope with the stresses of pregnancy and parenthood and the changes it will inevitably bring. It would be unrealistic to claim that becoming a parent will not involve change. Wisdom lies in anticipating the changes that will occur and making allowances for them.

Motherhood was once viewed as an integral and inevitable part of a woman's life. Today, however, a woman has the opportunity to decide for herself whether she should have a child and at what stage in her life she will become a mother

EMOTIONAL FACTORS

Many reasons can be given for deciding to have a child, yet the best and perhaps the overriding reason is that the child is really wanted. However, it should be clear whether the desire for a child is a deep-felt need or an acceptance of some of the many myths that surround childbearing and parenthood. Many couples see parenthood as a means of obtaining family continuity and an investment in the future. Others see this continuity in far more specific and personal terms – in having a child they hope to raise a person who will achieve in all the areas where they have failed.

Parents who try to live vicariously through their children can make their own and their child's life a misery. Instead of appreciating the child as a person in their own right, and recognising and encouraging talents and interests, pressure is brought to bear on the child to perform as the parents would like. Parenthood under such terms can be frustrating and miserable for everyone.

Children may also be looked on as a type of insurance policy, where it is anticipated that the child will look after the parents in their old age. This was once a reasonable expectation when communities were more stable and children first took part in, and then inherited, their parents' lifestyle. However, to a greater extent, care is now shared by society as a whole, and children very rarely live in close contact with their parents after they have left full-time education and started a family of their own.

Many people seek love in the child-parent relationship. They either wish to create a person on whom to lavish their own affection, or hope they will create someone who will give them uncritical and unforced love. Problems can arise if expectations of emotional attachment are not met. Parents may find their child less loveable than they had hoped or feel that they do in fact need love to be returned for it to satisfy them. Children, especially when they are young, demand far more care and affection than they are able to express in reciprocation.

Some people regard childbearing as a rite of passage. Men may wish to father children as a way of proclaiming their masculinity, women their femininity, and both to acquire adult status. Men and women who reach their 30s without children can find that both friends and employers are unsure of their status. A person's age would suggest a certain level of experience and responsibility, but often those without children are viewed as young and pre-adult.

Pressure to conform to accepted behaviour is often behind childbearing. Couples can choose parenthood to avoid the stigma of being 'odd' and the only partnership in their social circle without children. In some cases, it is their parents who put pressure on the couple to provide them with grandchildren – either as a social asset or from a real desire to see a much-loved child produce much-loved children of his or her own.

Pregnancy as a solution
All the above are positive reasons for having children, given any disadvantages mentioned. However, some women become pregnant for far more destructive reasons. There are men who use pregnancy as a means of keeping their wives under control. This is based on the belief that while their wife is pregnant or occupied with childbearing and rearing, she cannot give her full attention to other matters. This may prevent a woman seeking another, happier relationship or finding a measure of independence in employment; or it may be a

Encouraging children to develop their talents and interests is an important aspect of parenting, but anyone who has a child in order to gain vicarious satisfaction for their own frustrated ambitions is in danger of damaging their own and their child's emotional life

means of preventing the woman from rising in her career to equal or overtake her husband in status or financial reward.

Similarly, there are women who use pregnancy as a means of exerting their own form of control. The woman may feel that the man may be prepared to pursue another woman or take risks with his career while his responsibility is only to another adult, but as a father he would be constrained to behave with more circumspection. Also, both sexes may see parenthood as a means of gaining some measure of power. A parent can command the obedience and respect of a child which neither employer or partner may be prepared to give.

Another reason for deciding to have a child is that many women near the age of 30 have an acute awareness of the biological clock, and perceive this age as a time for the last chance. The physical risks to mother and child increase after this age at the same time as fertility begins to wane. Some women therefore hurry the decision for fear that, if left much longer, they will either be unable to conceive, will produce a handicapped child, or be too old to share life fully with a growing child. The fear, in both men and women, of being too old to perform well, or of being mistaken for the child's grandparent, can lead couples to force the issue without full consideration.

Pregnancy can also be seen as a solution to an unrewarding partnership. It can be an expression of ultimate love and trust and a symbol of commitment to a relationship. Unhappily, couples sometimes take this step in an attempt to create this commitment rather than to reflect what is already there. Studies of parental satisfaction have found that marital happiness often decreases after the arrival of children and only rises again when the couple can return to a measure of independence. However, this reaction seems to be strongly dependent on the expectations of parenting. The more stable a relationship before having a child, and the more realistic the hopes, the better the chances are of finding the experience a happy one.

While discussing the reasons for wanting a child, it is wise to examine the state of the relationship and whether or not you and your partner differ widely in your views about parenthood. Having a baby in an attempt to improve a failing relationship may have superficial results. You could be forced to remain together because of your obligations to the child. The social and economic demands for this may be very strong. Many couples successfully sublimate the drawbacks of a dying relationship as lovers in a busy life as parents. Such marriages or partnerships can be suc-

cessful as long as both partners are aware of, and satisfied with, the fact that love and involvement with one another have been replaced, not enhanced, by the care they give to their children. If only one partner finds this arrangement satisfactory, the strain on the couple can be considerable.

Personality and lifestyle

Many people speak of having children as part of a settling down process that they equate with maturity. In such cases, both partners may agree that certain traits and activities belong to their younger, child-free state and are inappropriate to their status as parents. Others may feel that spontaneous pleasures are just as much a part of the life of parents as of younger couples who are childless. It might be worth considering whether you and your partner have the same idea about what parenthood should entail.

Mothers have a special place in our society and are sometimes seen as being above the realities of sexual activity. Some men find it difficult to relate sexually to their wives if they have given them this status. Others may see the child as a sexual rival. Women can find that the physical as well as the emotional demands of motherhood drain them of the

Women considering motherhood should be realistic about what this may entail; while some women are content to care for their child and home on a full-time basis, others may find that this experience is too restricting

energy to maintain both their sexual relationship with their partner as well as their maternal relationship with their child.

Just as the expectations of what parenthood will do to your relationship and your perceptions of yourselves can differ, so can your attitudes towards the role of each partner as parent. Will your partner be revealed as someone who wants the status of father but will decline to take part in the actual work of bringing up a child? Will you find yourself falling back on motherhood role models that make it difficult for you to share the special bond between nurturer and child with another person? However much you agree intellectually with shared child care, it might surprise you how much your partner's involvement could cause anxieties. Similarly, your partner may be unwilling to rid himself of his fears that any involvement in child caring and rearing is emasculating.

Part of becoming a parent is adjusting to the fact that a child's needs are usually demands rather than requests. From necessity, parents must be prepared to forego a very large area of self-determination and choice. It will no longer be possible for them to act on impulse, either in how they spend their time or their money. If they accept that such matters as impetuous outings will be that much more difficult, and that they cannot ask a child to starve until pay day, they will probably find parenting rewarding. But couples will need to discuss whether either of them will resent the child for imposing some restrictions on their lifestyle.

Children do take up a considerable amount of time. A recent survey estimated that the average time spent on tasks related to child care – that is, on both caring for children and the extra time required for other tasks such as shopping and housework – was approximate-

Women who wish to be totally involved in caring for their young infant and also return to work are actively seeking solutions to the problems this involves. For a fortunate few with understanding employers, the solution is to take the baby to work with them

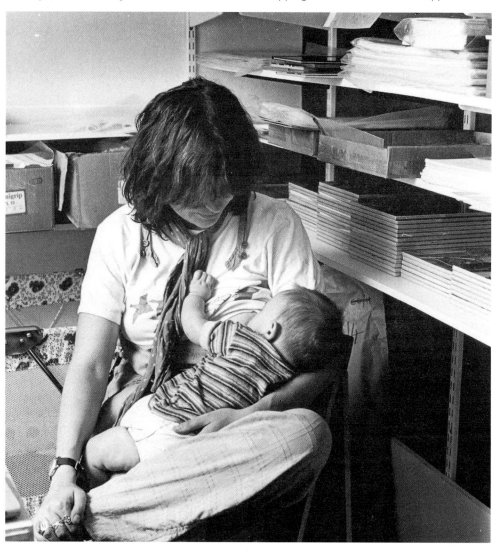

ly seven hours a day. Of the study sample, only 36 per cent of the women could report an entire hour during the day that was free from the demands and needs of their children. Being constantly on call to children can be a strain, especially on the sexual relationship of a couple.

A leading woman's magazine conducted a survey of their readers in 1983. Three in five of those with children under five years of age reported that their sexual life had suffered because of the children. The presence of older children was similarly inhibiting.

Ideally, couples should be able to portion out their time to leave both themselves and their child satisfied with the results. This may need prior discussion and planning. Parents should not feel that because parenting can be a joyful and absorbing undertaking, they are somehow unnatural or failing in their task by wishing to spend personal or private time away from their children. Full-time parenthood does not need to occupy the major portion of a parent's life.

Neglecting your own personality and private relationship can reduce you to the single role of mother or father – a role that can leave you without identity or without a relationship when the children grow up and leave home. An inability or refusal to relinquish this role is often the cause of bitter conflict between parents and children in later years as the young adults seek to become independent.

Being a parent largely requires you to be unselfish and giving. If you view parenthood more in terms of what you will get from the experience rather than what you can bring to it, you may find it disappointing. As a couple, do either of you feel the need to be the primary focus for the care and protection of your partner – care and protection that would have to be offered first to a child if you become parents? If so, you may need to reassess your decision in this light.

The question of a career

Working women contemplating a first pregnancy should discuss with their partners how the baby will affect their working lives in the future. Some women will want to continue with their job or career shortly after the baby is born; others may want to stay at home with the child, at least during the first few years. While the male partner may take it for granted that if anyone is to give up their job it is the woman who should do so, this does have an unfortunate consequence that more and more men find limiting – the partner who has the greatest share of contact with the child also has the strongest emotional bond. If the father would like to be more involved with child care, the couple could consider sharing

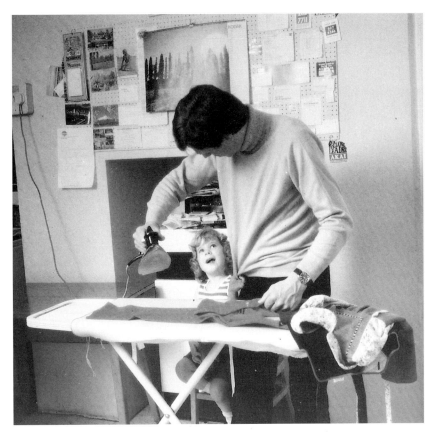

child care equally between them.

In Sweden, in the first six months of the child's life, leave from work can be shared between father and mother, in whatever proportion they choose. In Britain, while maternity leave is now a woman's right in many circumstances, it is only enlightened firms who will offer the same facility to the father. And while some firms who employ a larger number of women have been persuaded to offer a crèche, firms with a predominately male workforce do not seem to see the need for such a facility. However, couples might like to explore between them the possibility of sharing the responsibility for the welfare of the child. In some cases, for example, both partners may be able to negotiate part-time employment, or it may be possible to set up a business together until the child begins to attend school.

In discussing these options, it may become evident that the woman's career or job might not have been as exciting or fulfilling as expected. There can be a real danger that motherhood seems appealing, not on its own merits, but as a refuge from dissatisfaction with employment. Similarly, men can be attracted to fatherhood as a distraction from a stagnating career and a means of revitalising their life.

In some cases, women may only be able to return to work if their partner is willing to take part in sharing child care and domestic duties

FINANCIAL CONCERNS

Babies are expensive. It has been estimated that the cost of having a first child is some £10,000. This includes maternity clothes, food, basic baby clothes and equipment and loss of earnings in the first year. However, if less basic but by no means less essential purchases such as a washing machine, tumble drier, baby carriage and a larger car and safety seats are included, the costs can be even higher. A one-year-old baby will probably take up about eight per cent of its parent's income. By the age of 17 this will be about 26 per cent. The total bill, including loss of earnings, may be well over £70,000.

Benefits and tax allowances

The largest single item in all of these calculations is the loss of earnings by the mother, which will need to be taken into account when the decision is made about how a couple will arrange their lives after the birth. Yet remaining at work almost always means that someone will have to be paid to look after the child. The payment to a nanny, minder or nursery will be inflated by the extra costs to enable the mother or father to fit their schedule into that of the childminder's. In real terms, all this could take up an entire salary. State benefits replace only a small proportion of this loss.

BENEFITS FOR WHICH PARENTS MAY BE ELIGIBLE		
Benefit	**Who can claim**	**How to claim**
Supplementary Benefit		
The most elastic of all benefits. It aims to fill the gap between the money you have coming in and what you realistically have to pay out, including all sorts of extras you might be eligible for. You automatically can receive free school meals, free milk and vitamins and free NHS dental treatment, glasses and prescriptions	People 16 or over who are not in full-time work or education and do not have enough money to live on, and have no more than £2,500 in total savings and investments. Some people have to sign on at an Unemployment Benefit Office and be available for work. Check whether you are in this category	Unemployed people get a form from the Unemployment Office. Everyone else fills in the claim form in leaflet SB 1 from the Post Office or Social Security Office. You will have to show how much money you have coming in, and how much you spend out on food, fuel, rent, buying and maintaining clothes, essential household expenses and leisure items. Also extra costs incurred through your own or a dependent relative's disability
Family Income Supplement		
Claimed by people in full-time work who don't have enough money to live on. Also free meals etc., as above	People bringing up children, and are in full-time work that doesn't pay their expenses. Self-employed people can claim too as long as they work more than 24 hours a week (single parent) or 30 hours a week (couple)	Use the claim form on the leaflet FIS 1 from the Post Office or Social Security Office, and send the completed form to the address on the forms using a pre-paid envelope from the Post Office
Child Benefit		
A basic allowance for people with a dependent child under 19, with extras for some single parents	People with dependent children in the right age bracket – however much the parent(s) earn	Basic benefit: form CH 2 from the Social Security Office. One-parent benefit: form CH 11
Maternity Grant		
A lump sum for each baby expected	A pregnant woman who applies between 14 weeks before the birth, and three months after	Form BM 4 from the Social Security Office or maternity clinic
Maternity Allowance		
A weekly sum for up to 18 weeks, plus, sometimes, a bit extra for dependent children	A pregnant woman who has paid full rate National Insurance contributions for the year preceding the birth of the baby. Women who have not worked for up to 2 years before the birth may also be eligible	Form BM 4 from the Social Security Office or maternity clinic

All pregnant women are entitled to a lump sum, called the maternity grant. At present, this is set at £25. The only qualification for this is that the mother has been resident in the United Kingdom for the greater part of the pregnancy. The grant is payable after the woman has been pregnant for 29 weeks.

Women who have paid full national insurance contributions, whether they were employed or self-employed, might also be eligible for maternity allowance. Eligibility is calculated on the contributions for the tax year preceding the birth of the baby. For instance, for a baby due before 23 March 1987, contributions in the tax year 1984/85 will be counted. The basic maternity allowance at present is £29.15 a week, and is payable for 18 weeks starting 11 weeks before the birth.

Women who have worked during pregnancy may also be entitled to paid maternity leave. If they have been with the same employer continuously for two years, if they work full-time (or five years if it is a part-time job), they can ask for this entitlement. As long as they continue to work until 11 weeks before the baby is due, and let their employer have written confirmation of their plans 21 days before they stop work, they must then be given maternity pay for six weeks. This sum will be 90 per cent of the normal salary, less the standard rate of maternity allowance, tax and national insurance contributions. Time off to attend antenatal classes must also be paid by the employer. Paid paternity leave is not a right and is at the discretion of the individual employer.

Expectant mothers and mothers with babies are also entitled to free dental treatment and free prescriptions.

If a woman has a stillborn baby after the 28th week of pregnancy, she should allow herself time to recuperate; she will still be entitled to all these payments as well as maternity leave.

There are no additional tax allowances for a couple when the baby arrives. Single people and married women have a tax allowance of £2005, while a married man's allowance is £3155. If an unmarried couple has a child, either of them can add the personal allowance of £1150 to their single person's claim.

For each child, there is a tax free sum called child benefit of £7 a week. This is usually paid to the mother in weekly or monthly amounts.

In the majority of cases, the decision whether or not to have a child, and, if the decision is to become pregnant, whether the woman will remain at work, will largely rest on emotional rather than financial matters. However, it is worth realising that quarrels and worries about money are at the bottom of most marital disputes.

Finance and the single woman

For the single woman deciding to bring up a child on her own, the financial picture is more fraught. With only one salary on which to rely, the choice between working and staying at home is more difficult. Single parents receive an extra £4.55 a week for their first child – this is called one-parent benefit. They can of course also add the additional personal allowance to their single person's tax allowance.

If the father does not agree voluntarily to pay maintenance for the child's upkeep, the courts can be asked to order him to do so. This will involve taking out an affiliation order. (See also p111.) Such an order does not jeopardise the mother's sole rights over the child. If the father does make regular payments these would be subtracted from any additional benefits claimed, such as supplementary benefit or family income supplement. Even if the woman is employed, she could be entitled to either or both of these benefits. They can be paid to couples or to single women who are working part-time or are receiving a low wage for full-time work, or whose essential costs, such as transport and child care, take up a large part of a low salary. Women receiving such payments might also be eligible for single payments. A single lump sum can be made to cover clothing, nappies, feeding equipment, cots and blankets, prams, baby baths, high chairs and safety gates for the home. Milk tokens and vitamins can also be obtained.

Prospective parents who want information about their rights and benefits can obtain relevant pamphlets and leaflets from the DHSS, Citizen's Advice Bureaux or libraries

SOCIAL ATTITUDES

However you reconcile your own view of yourself as parent or individual, having become a mother or father you will find that society is likely to make demands on you and pass judgements that are different to those imposed on people without children.

The same people who would have urged you to have a child and admired your baby in its pram may complain if you bring a toddler into a library, shop or restaurant. Unlike many continental countries, children in this country are often rigorously excluded or frowned upon in many public places. Public buildings, and private ones, are very rarely designed with children in mind. Motherhood is applauded and indeed often almost insisted upon, but neither in building design nor in career structure is it allowed for. The simplest task, such as taking public transport into town to shop, or manoeuvering a pram along busy streets, is full of obstacles for a woman with a pram or a small child.

Women may find themselves denied promotion on the grounds that they will leave to have children – and having done so, will find the complex administrative and managerial experience they gain through motherhood will count for nothing on their return to employment. Women who return to work while their children are still young may come under pressure. In spite of evidence to the contrary, there is still a strong feeling that working mothers are bad mothers, neglecting their children or at least putting their own selfish desires before the needs of the child. Yet, any necessary time off to care for a sick child will often be met with disproportionate disapproval from colleagues and employers. In this society, parenthood and work are felt to be incompatible – in spite of the fact that the majority of working men are fathers. Motherhood, it would appear, is a respected and supported occupation – as long as it remains in its proper place, in the home.

Despite the many obvious, and sometimes subtle, pressures on women to become mothers, children are frequently seen as a nuisance and an inconvenience, especially in public places

Our society offers mothers with small children very little in the way of adequate facilities outside the home. Even a short journey on public transport can become something of an obstacle course for a mother with a young child

PHYSICAL CONSIDERATIONS

Two centuries ago obstetricians first noted that older women had an increased risk of developing fatal complications in pregnancy. Today, however, serious maternal complications are rare and the main focus of attention is the health of the baby. Surveys in the 1950s showed that older women had an increased chance of losing their babies during pregnancy or just after delivery, and because of this the International Federation of Obstetricians and Gynaecologists decided in 1958 that women over 35 years of age were a 'high-risk' group.

Recently, doubts have been raised about the seriousness of this risk. It has been suggested that the older surveys might have been biased – for example, by including a large proportion of women whose childbearing was delayed by illness or infertility. Women today who choose to delay childbearing are generally healthy and have an above-average standard of living, and therefore the risks calculated from older surveys may no longer be applicable. How can we assess the physical risks to older mothers in the 1980s?

Assessing risks
The simplest way for a doctor to assess risk is by clinical experience – having seen similar cases a doctor builds up a picture of the probable outcome. However, individual experience is subjective and a more accurate assessment is gained by looking at large numbers of cases, such as the work-load of a large hospital. Here again, there are pitfalls; for example, only women with problems may be admitted to a specialist hospital, while those with a straightforward pregnancy may deliver in a small hospital or GP unit, or at home.

Better information therefore comes from more comprehensive surveys, two of which are of particular importance. The *British Perinatal Mortality Survey* and *British Births 1970* attempted to include all babies born in Britain during one particular week, in 1958 and 1970 respectively. About 1700 births were included in each survey, and information was collected about the babies' health and the mothers' background.

These studies showed a significant improvement in the safety of pregnancy between 1958 and 1970, and there has been further overall improvement since then, but no further comparable surveys have been carried out. For a more up-to-date assessment of risks hospital surveys must be relied on, many of which come from abroad and in many cases may not be directly applicable to British women.

Fertility

Fertility is discussed in detail in the next chapter, and only a few points will be made here. Female fertility appears to be maximal about the age of 24, and declines noticeably after the age of 30. Of normal young couples, 50 per cent take three months to conceive and 90 per cent achieve conception in a year, but for couples in the 35-44 age group conception is likely to take twice as long. This delay may be due to a reduction in the male's fertility, the frequency of intercourse, the regularity of ovulation, or other factors.

The importance of the woman's age is seen most clearly in clinics undertaking artificial insemination by donor (AID) or in-vitro ferti- lization (IVF), where semen quality and timing of insemination are controlled. In an AID clinic in France, 74 per cent of women under 30 conceived after 12 cycles of treatment, compared with 62 per cent of woman aged 31-35, and 57 per cent of those over 35. A leading English IVF centre has reported that although egg cells, or ova, from older women can be fertilized satisfactorily, the success of reimplantation declines slightly after the age of 35 and considerably after 40. This suggests that some factor within the uterus alters as women grow older.

Miscarriage

The same English IVF centre reported an increasing risk of miscarriage as maternal age rises. A similar increase seems to occur among pregnancies conceived naturally. In younger age groups the overall risk of miscar- riage is relatively lower than it is in women over 30.

Perinatal mortality

The perinatal period extends from a short time before birth until shortly after – from the time the foetus is about 28 weeks old until the infant is about 1 month old. Stillbirths and young infant, or neonatal, deaths in this period account for the perinatal mortality rate.

In 1970 the overall risk of a stillbirth or neonatal death in Britain was 1 in 50. Fifteen years later the risk has been halved, to about 1 in 100. In both the 1958 and 1970 British surveys, the risk of perinatal death was lowest in the 20-24 age group, and was roughly 50 per cent higher in the 35-plus age group. Almost all hospital surveys between 1970 and 1980 have confirmed a similarly higher peri- natal mortality among women over 35, and a slightly greater increase among women over 40. However, among 243 women over 35 having first babies in a Californian hospital during 1981-1983, there was no increase in perinatal mortality, perhaps because of good obstetric care.

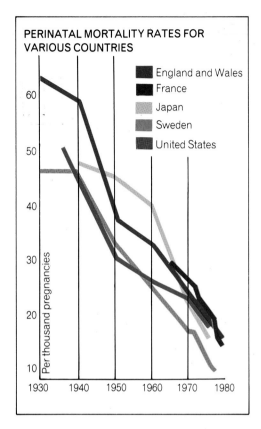

PERINATAL MORTALITY RATES FOR VARIOUS COUNTRIES

- England and Wales
- France
- Japan
- Sweden
- United States

Per thousand pregnancies

Complications of pregnancy

The higher perinatal mortality rate among women over 35 is not explained by the increased incidence of congenital abnormali- ties (*see* below, and *pp 28-31*), and seems to be due to a variety of pregnancy complica- tions. There is some uncertainty about which complications are more common in the first pregnancies of older women, because inves- tigations of the effect of maternal age have not always differentiated between first and subsequent pregnancies, which have diffe- rent patterns of complications.

Some, but not all, surveys report an in- creasing risk of low-birthweight babies and premature babies, from the maternal age of 30 onwards. *British Births 1970* found that pregnancy was on average three days shorter in women over 35, and in some hospital surveys the prematurity rate in women over 40 was approximately doubled, to over 10 per cent. The risk of a small-for-dates baby (a baby born at term but with a lower than average birthweight) in the over-35s may also be doubled, at 1 in 10, although some studies have failed to confirm this. At the opposite extreme, it is believed that prolonged preg- nancy is also more common in women over 35, but this is difficult to confirm as labour is now usually induced soon after term in the older woman.

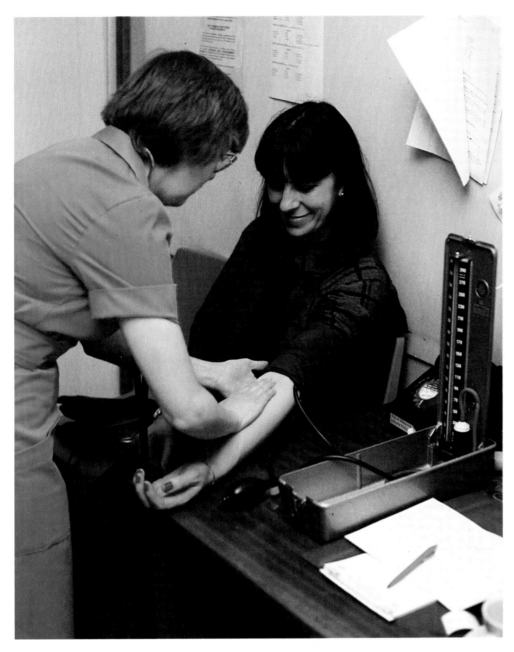

Since 1930, deaths from the 28th week of pregnancy until one month after birth – the perinatal mortality – have dropped dramatically (far left). Improved health care for pregnant women, including routine monitoring of blood pressure (left) has contributed to this decline

There is also some lack of consensus about the finding that women over 35 have an increased risk of pre-eclampsia (a disorder involving high blood pressure in late pregnancy). In several studies pre-eclampsia affected about one-third of women over 35 and up to 50 per cent of women over 40, but recent hospital surveys have not confirmed these high rates. Its severest form, which can endanger maternal health, is more common in younger women, but moderate pre-eclampsia, which can impair foetal growth, is the form that seems more common in older women, and this explains their higher risk of giving birth to small-for-dates babies.

Some studies have reported that the incidence of maternal diabetes also rises with age, from two per cent in younger women to four per cent in women over 35 and seven per cent in those over 40. Most of these cases were already diabetic before becoming pregnant. Diabetes is associated with a variety of risks in pregnancy and needs careful supervision. Older women are also more likely to have fibroids, which can obstruct labour and necessitate Caesarean section, but these will usually be detected on vaginal examination before pregnancy.

Labour

Although it is often stated that labour lasts about 25 per cent longer in older women, a careful study carried out as long ago as 1965 showed that age does not affect the duration of labour except for a lengthening of the second stage, which begins when the cervix is fully dilated. This stage is 45 minutes longer in women of 40 than in girls of 16. This means only a relatively small increase in the total duration of labour, but because concern for the baby's well-being is greatest at this time, delay in the second stage increases the chance of a forceps delivery or even Caesarean section.

There is undoubtably an increased chance of operative delivery among older women, and Caesarean section rates of 30-50 per cent have been reported from some hospitals in the United States, although in general rates in Britain are lower. The main reason for operative delivery is concern about the safety of the baby, for example because of maternal diabetes or high blood pressure, or because of fears that the placenta may have less functional reserve in older women due to diminished uterine blood flow. Perhaps also, obstetricians are more ready to intervene because of an understandable feeling that a pregnancy is more precious in an older woman. (For a full discussion of the management of labour in the older woman, *see also* Chapter 3, Labour complications.)

The puerperium

In the past, it has been accepted that older women have a higher risk of venous thrombosis after delivery, but recent studies have not confirmed this. Caesarean section increases the risks of thromboembolism, but it is doubtful whether maternal age *per se* does so. Thrombosis requiring treatment occurs after 0.15 per cent of normal deliveries and after about one per cent of Caesarean sections. As far as breastfeeding is concerned, *British Births 1970* showed very little effect of maternal age on the decision to breastfeed.

Maternal health in later life

If a woman enters pregnancy in good health and does not suffer complications her long-term health will not be compromised. Forceps delivery or Caesarean section should not have long-term serious after-effects. High blood pressure is not permanently worsened by pregnancy. Gestational diabetes disappears after pregnancy and pre-existing diabetes worsened by pregnancy always improves again soon after delivery.

Epidemiologists have discovered subtle effects of pregnancy on subsequent maternal health. Pregnancy may reduce the risk of subsequent breast cancer, but this protective effect steadily diminishes as first pregnancy is delayed, and disappears around the age of 35. Age at first pregnancy is of course only one of a large number of factors influencing a

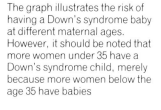

The graph illustrates the risk of having a Down's syndrome baby at different maternal ages. However, it should be noted that more women under 35 have a Down's syndrome child, merely because more women below the age 35 have babies

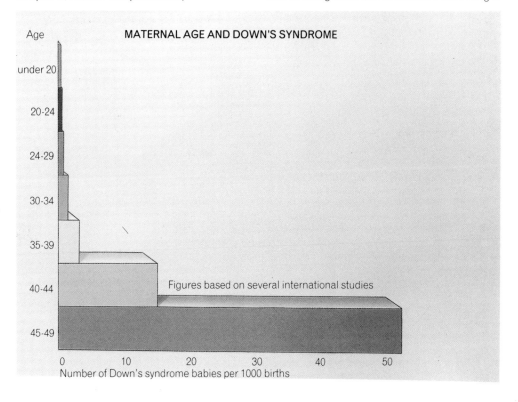

MATERNAL AGE AND DOWN'S SYNDROME

Figures based on several international studies

Number of Down's syndrome babies per 1000 births

woman's risk of breast cancer. Reports that an early first pregnancy has a similar protective effect on ovarian and colon cancer remain unconfirmed.

The child's health

The main hazard of increasing maternal age is the risk that the baby may suffer from chromosomal abnormalities, the most important of which is Down's syndrome. The risk of Down's syndrome is related to the mother's age, not the father's, because a woman's ovaries release eggs but do not make new ones; they contain their lifetime supply of eggs at the time of the woman's birth. By contrast, a man's testes are continuously making new spermatozoa, so when conception occurs to an older couple, a young sperm fertilizes an old egg-cell or ovum, whose chromosomes may fail to divide accurately. Any woman may have a baby with Down's syndrome, but the risk increases with age. (Methods of antenatal diagnosis of Down's syndrome are discussed in Chapter 3.)

Because children with Down's syndrome are susceptible to other diseases such as leukaemia or Alzheimer's disease (a form of dementia), several studies have attempted to assess whether these conditions are commoner among normal children born to older women. The results are contradictory, and there is no clear indication that the children have an increased risk of these rare condi-

tions. The suggestion that children of older mothers are at higher risk of lung cancer later in life is also unproved, and a report of an increased risk of breast cancer was not confirmed by a recent large study in England. However, the child may have a 50 per cent higher risk of juvenile-onset diabetes, a condition which affects 1 in 600 children.

Children of older mothers have a decreased risk of certain problems. Child abuse (baby battering) is no more frequent among older mothers, and on the contrary is commoner among teenage mothers, who tend to have more difficulty than older mothers in coping with their babies. Similarly, the risk of sudden infant death (cot death) is greater in younger women than older women.

Summary

Many of the risks discussed here are of little practical importance. Even with a 50 per cent increase in perinatal mortality an older woman has less risk of losing her baby than the 25-year-old had 15 years ago. Reduced fertility is a significant problem only to women over the age of 40. Some problems, such as fibroids, can be diagnosed – or ruled out – at a pre-pregnancy examination. The most important risk in numerical terms is the increased likelihood of obstetrical interference, and recent studies indicate that if older women are prepared to pay this price, they have a good chance of having a healthy baby.

While it is true that women over 30 have an increased risk of complications during pregnancy and labour, the majority enjoy good health during pregnancy and have a perfectly normal baby

THE PLANNED PREGNANCY

For the majority of women, contraception is very effective; discontinuing its use is normally the result of a decision to have a child. Modern contraceptive methods have therefore given rise to the concept of the planned pregnancy – women now have more freedom to plan when the desired pregnancy should occur and time to consider how they will manage it when it does.

There are many advantages in planning pregnancy: the woman and her partner can choose to have a child when financial, emotional and other personal circumstances are most favourable and make plans for their future life together as a family; and the woman has the opportunity to physically prepare herself for childbearing. Naturally, the opportunity to plan a pregnancy is not unique to women over the age of thirty, but for women in their thirties and forties the planned pregnancy has the additional advantage of providing them with the time to consider and resolve any age-related gynaecological or other problems affecting pregnancy and birth that might arise.

As far as this chapter is concerned, the specific problems that may apply to women in the age groups we are considering concern the increased risk of genetic disorders such as Down's syndrome and the possibility of problems relating to fertility. Genetics and genetic counselling, conception and infertility are therefore discussed in the following pages. The section on termination of pregnancy has been included for those women and their partners who, either through necessity or informed and deliberated choice, are considering terminating a pregnancy and wish to have information on the legal, emotional and medical factors involved.

CARE BEFORE PREGNANCY

Pre-pregnancy exercises (right) to strengthen the back and abdominal muscles and improve posture: Lie flat on your back (a), legs straight, arms at sides. Slowly raise one knee at a time towards the chest (b). Repeat 10 times. Lie with head supported on a folded towel (c), knees bent, feet flat on the ground. Gently raise and lower your bottom (d). Repeat 10 times. Stand upright (e) with arms loosely by your sides and with shoulders back. Bend slightly from the waist (f) letting head and arms fall forward. Continue movements by reaching gently towards your toes (g). Repeat 10 times

A woman who has decided to have a baby should discuss her intention to become pregnant with her general practitioner. The GP, with his or her knowledge of the woman's past medical history, is in an ideal position to give advice. If there are problems requiring specialist attention he should make the appropriate referral. He will also know what facilities are available at local hospitals and be able to give his patient relevant information about their organisation.

Birthing techniques, such as self-control in labour and the use of Leboyer, Odent, La Maze and related methods, vary from one obstetric unit to another, and it will be helpful for the woman to know what the range of choice is in her area.

In some areas, pre-pregnancy, or pre-conception clinics have been established for those women and their partners who may have particular problems or needs. These may include anxieties about an inherited disease in the family of either partner, or chronic illness in the woman – such as certain types of heart disease and blood disorders, multiple sclerosis and diabetes – which might make pregnancy a risk to her health. Problems such as these should be fully discussed before conception so that the optimum conditions can prevail during pregnancy and birth.

Weight and exercise

It is important for women to maintain or achieve their correct body weight through good nutrition before they become pregnant. Women who are very overweight or underweight have a tendency to be less fertile and may have difficulties in conceiving.

A woman is considered to be underweight if she is ten per cent or more below the standard weight for her height and age. Underweight mothers are more likely to give birth to a baby with a low birthweight and they are significantly more likely to have a haemorrhage during pregnancy or to develop toxaemia. The total amount of energy expended during pregnancy is about 75,000 calories; generally this should be provided for by increasing caloric intake to 300 calories per day throughout pregnancy. Therefore, a woman who is very underweight when she begins a pregnancy is at some disadvantage and she may be putting herself and her baby at risk.

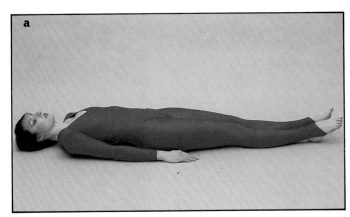

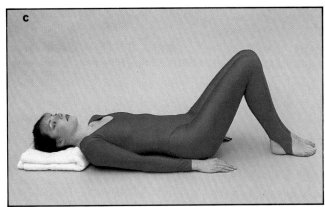

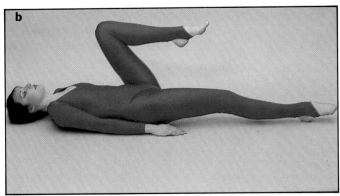

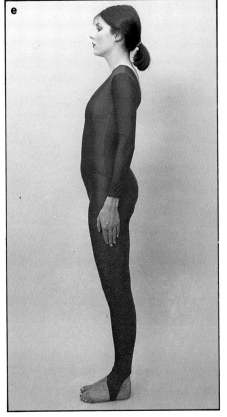

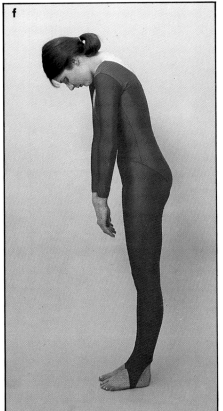

CORRECT WEIGHT FOR HEIGHT

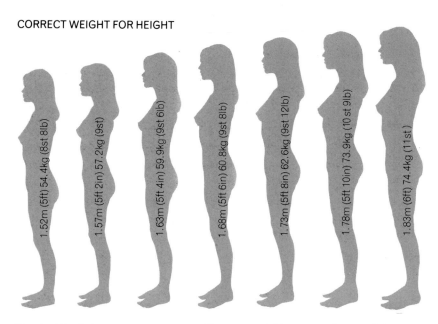

1.52m (5ft) 54.4kg (8st 8lb)

1.57m (5ft 2in) 57.2kg (9st)

1.63m (5ft 4in) 59.9kg (9st 6lb)

1.68m (5ft 6in) 60.8kg (9st 8lb)

1.73m (5ft 8in) 62.6kg (9st 12lb)

1.78m (5ft 10in) 73.9kg (10 st 9lb)

1.83m (6ft) 74.4kg (11st)

The chart illustrates average weights for women aged 30-39 years, of medium build and at varying heights. Height alone, however, does not determine ideal weight – the basic body type is also important, as is the individual's age

The overweight woman (or man) is more likely to develop high blood pressure, coronary artery disease or diabetes; any of these conditions may be aggravated by pregnancy or give rise to other problems during pregnancy. If a woman is overweight she should try to lose the excess before she becomes pregnant. Losing weight during pregnancy may adversely affect the intelligence of the foetus; the rapidly developing foetal tissues are very sensitive to the keytones (toxic substances that are produced when body fat is metabolized) in the bloodstream of a mother who is starving herself of nutrients.

Excessive exercise, particularly jogging, can also result in difficulties in conceiving. Women who are extremely fit and take more than the normal amount of regular exercise are usually slim and have low resting pulse rates. Any woman with a resting pulse rate of less than 40 beats per minute will probably not menstruate and will fail to ovulate. In such cases the cessation of menstrual periods continues until the woman becomes less athletic. Recently it has become known that certain substances, called endorphins, released in the brain play an important part in the control of the menstrual cycle, and that changes in endorphin release and breakdown occur during jogging, weight loss and depression.

Although it is unwise for a woman intent on pregnancy to take excessive and prolonged exercise, it is an excellent idea to try to become moderately fit and to strengthen muscles which will be put under strain as pregnancy progresses. Backache in pregnancy is a common problem and sometimes can be very severe; it can often be avoided or minimised by pre-pregnancy exercises which will improve the strength of the abdominal and back muscles, as well as the flexibility of the spine. Sit-ups and sports such as swimming are extremely beneficial as back and abdomen-strengthening techniques.

Smoking

It is well known that smoking is harmful to the developing foetus. Babies born to mothers who smoke heavily have a low birthweight, and the relationship between the two is dose dependent – that is, the heavier the smoking, the more foetal growth will be slowed down. This is due to a reduction in the levels of oxygen delivered to the foetal tissue during smoking. Smoking also increases the risk of premature births and of death in the newborn infant; cot death, or unexplained infant death, is more common in infants of mothers who smoke.

There is no evidence that a previous heavy smoking habit will damage a foetus – the effect is related to the amount of smoking during pregnancy. When planning a pregnancy, both the woman and her partner should seriously attempt to give up smoking (passive smoking can also be harmful). Nicotine chewing gum may be helpful in this situation, but its use should be discontinued by the woman if there is any possibility that she has become pregnant.

Drugs

The dangers of smoking to the unborn foetus are due simply to the effects of carbon monoxide and nicotine. Any drug taken by the mother must be viewed similarly with suspicion. Women who take any drug or medication, whether on a regular or occasional basis, should tell her medical attendants. Women being treated for epilepsy, for example, may need to have their treatment altered or adjusted when embarking on a pregnancy, and the situation may be similar for other conditions, such as diabetes, high blood pressure and asthma. The use of steroids in creams, aerosol inhalers and tablets will have to be carefully considered if a woman who normally uses these is considering pregnancy. Ideally, all steroids should be withdrawn, but this is not always possible; therefore a compromise must be reached. The minimum effective dose of the steroid should be used.

Given the enormous amount of publicity concerning the potential effects of drugs on the foetus since the thalidomide tragedy, it is surprising that so many women continue to take drugs during pregnancy, many of them prescribed by their doctors. In a recent study which looked at 168 pregnant women, it was found that the average number of drugs used during pregnancy was 11. All the women took at least two types of medication.

Almost all drugs that are absorbed by the pregnant woman cross the placental barrier and may reach quite high levels of concentration in the foetus. It is thought, however, that only between one and nine per cent of congenital abnormalities are caused by drugs or are related to other external environmental factors such as virus infections. Many drugs are entirely safe in pregnancy, but all should be viewed with suspicion, and a woman should not take any medication unless it is absolutely necessary. All new drugs are now screened in the laboratory for possible adverse effects on the foetus before women of child-bearing potential are exposed to them.

In the future it is likely that drugs will be given in pregnancy to treat the foetus rather than the mother – in some cases this is already being put into practise.

Alcohol consumption

Most pregnant women who enjoy an occasional alcoholic drink have no reason to be concerned about alcohol. It is thought that

two glasses of wine a day, or the equivalent, will not produce any ill-effects, and if a woman drinks a little more than this every now and again without becoming drunk it will not harm the baby.

Although it has been found that certain abnormalities are more likely to occur in babies of alcoholic mothers, severe damage to the foetus from grossly excessive alcohol consumption is very rare in Great Britain. However, heavy drinkers should certainly try to cut down on their consumption of alcohol before becoming pregnant and seek support if necessary. The GP should be able to give advice about this. Vitamin B and other nutrient supplements, including folic acid, may be given to women who are heavy drinkers to improve nutrition before conception, as well as advice about following a healthy diet.

Most women are aware of the possible dangers of smoking, excessive alcohol consumption and drugs in pregnancy, and the ill-effects they can have on the foetus, yet these substances should also be viewed with suspicion prior to pregnancy as well. Their avoidance will certainly improve the health of any woman planning to have a child – the healthier the woman, the better chance she will have of having a healthy baby

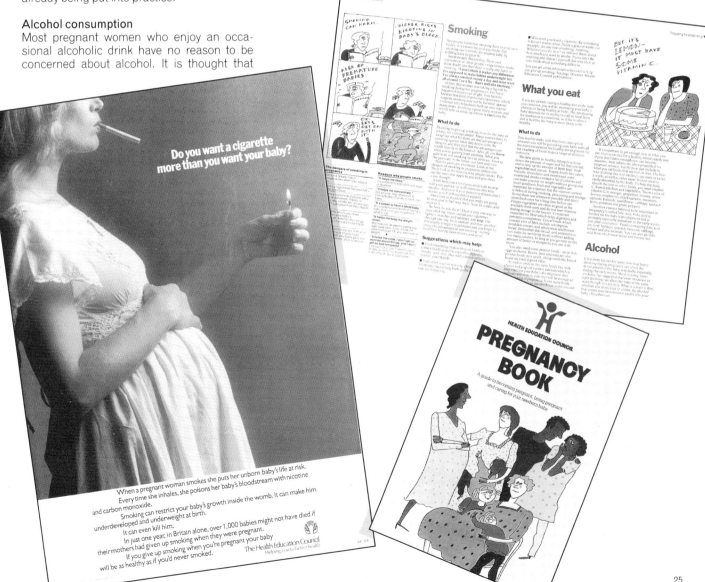

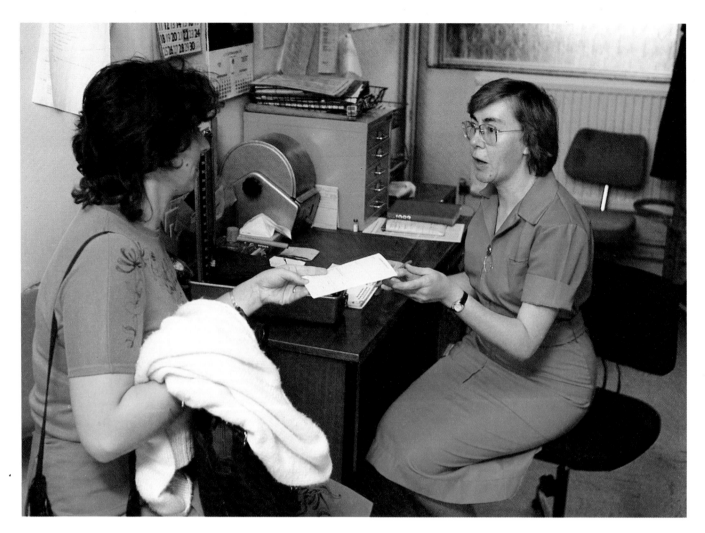

It is in the best interests of every woman planning a pregnancy to ensure that their health is sound before they conceive. For most women, a visit to the GP will be sufficient, but in some cases referral to a specialist will be necessary to clear up gynaecological or other problems that may affect the pregnancy

Gynaecological problems

During the pre-pregnancy visit to the GP, it is advisable to discuss previous gynaecological problems. A vaginal examination may be necessary and where there are any special problems the woman should be referred to a gynaecologist. Prolapse of the uterus and fibroids are two of the problems that may require specialist attention, as they may cause difficulties later. If a woman has had a previous termination of pregnancy or spontaneous miscarriage she may have anxieties about how this may affect a future pregnancy and she should take this opportunity to discuss these with her doctor.

One of the main problems affecting future pregnancy in a woman who has had a termination arises if the operation was followed by an infection. (Other problems may be premature labour or miscarriage in a subsequent pregnancy.) This is a rare complication of termination but it can have the serious effect of blocking one or both of the Fallopian tubes. Pelvic infection, or pelvic inflammatory disease (PID) can also occur unassociated with any operative procedure. A course of antibiotics is prescribed to treat it.

Women who have had a sexually transmitted disease, even if completely cured, should inform their doctor. Although this may give rise to feelings of guilt or anxieties about the pregnancy and the health of the baby, the medical attendants should know of any previous infection. During pregnancy all women are screened for syphilis, as this can affect the developing foetus.

Immunisations and pregnancy

Before considering pregnancy, women should make certain that they are immune to rubella (German measles). Women infected by rubella during pregnancy, particularly during the first three months, are likely to give birth to a baby with some abnormality. Abnormalities considered to be associated with the rubella virus can be very severe – they include heart defects, cataracts and deafness. However, if a woman is immune to rubella there will be no risk to the foetus should she encounter the disease during pregnancy.

Many women over 30 years of age will be unsure whether they are immune. It is a simple matter to check. A blood sample is taken and analysed to see if antibodies to the rubella virus are present in the blood. If antibodies are not found the woman is not immune and will need to be immunised.

It was once thought that it was essential for women to avoid pregnancy during the three months following a rubella injection. There is no evidence to suggest that pregnancy during this period will result in foetal deformity. However, it is probably advisable for women to avoid pregnancy at this time.

Women who are considering travelling abroad during pregnancy should consult their doctor about any immunisations that may be necessary and whether they are considered safe in pregnancy. Some vaccines contain a live virus, others a killed virus. There is no danger to the foetus from a killed vaccine, and therefore these are safe to give during pregnancy. The killed vaccines are typhoid, cholera, influenza, rabies and hepatitis. Tetanus toxoid and oral polio vaccine are also entirely safe during pregnancy because they are not live.

The live vaccines which should be avoided in pregnancy and given as necessary prior to conception are rubella, yellow fever, measles and mumps. Women who have inadvertently had any of these vaccines in early pregnancy should seek medical advice as soon as they realise that they are pregnant.

Anxieties about pregnancy

Pregnancy and childbirth are part of women's psycho-sexual life, and will affect how they see themselves as women, as mothers and in their relationship with their own parents. Both pregnancy and childbirth are events of enormous psychological and social importance and because of this they can be sources of great anxiety.

For women seeking help and advice, the National Childbirth Trust holds classes and publishes literature about preparation for childbirth. Members of the medical and associated professions – doctors, midwives, nurses, psycho-therapists and social workers – can also be consulted about particular problems. Although it is likely that many women on a low income, and/or with little or no support from a partner, would benefit from more pre-conception care, unfortunately the onus is with the woman herself to seek advice and help while she is planning to have a baby – such a lot can be done to help her, and to give her baby the best possible start in life (see pp 146-149).

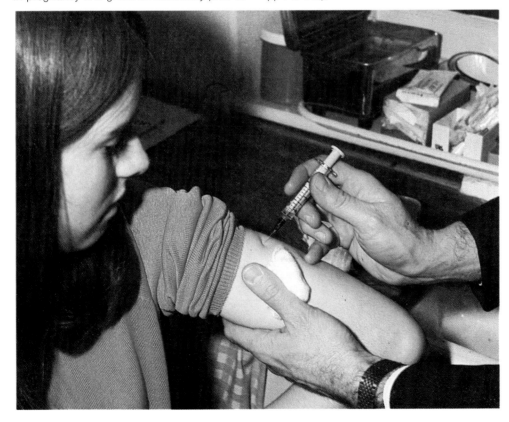

Vaccination of young girls against rubella is an efficient way to protect them and their babies later in life. A single dose is all that is necessary, and it is usually given between the ages of 11 and 14. Women who were not vaccinated during adolescence should have the injection prior to pregnancy

GENETICS AND GENETIC COUNSELLING

Muscular dystrophy is an inherited disease. The diagram illustrates the manner in which it may be passed on through the female line from one generation to another. When an abnormal X-linked chromosome combines with a Y chromosome, a male child will have the disease, but there is only a 50 per cent chance that the male child of a female carrier will be a sufferer. This is because only one of the X chromosomes carries the abnormality and only one is used every time a child is conceived

Couples who come late to parenthood are often concerned about the possibility of having a malformed or handicapped baby. While it is true that the woman has an increased risk of having a child with an extra chromosome (*see* p 30), apart from this the genetic risks are not seriously greater than those incurred by her younger counterpart. However, the life experiences of many older couples have made them more aware of the possibility and implications of handicap and therefore they may wish to ascertain whether they should undergo certain tests before starting a pregnancy.

Unfortunately, tests for couples without a family history of inherited disorders are currently almost non-existent, simply because the technology is not yet available. The main focus of genetic testing and counselling therefore remains with couples who may be at risk of passing on inherited diseases.

Family and ethnic background

The couples most at risk of passing on a serious disorder include those in which either partner has a family history of Huntington's chorea, neurofibromatosis or muscular dystrophy, and those who have a family member carrying a chromosome rearrangement predisposing to miscarriage or the birth of a handicapped child. Women who have a family member affected by the severe (Duchenne) form of muscular dystrophy, haemophilia or mental retardation may be carriers of the disorder, and couples who are cousins may also carry certain risks. All such couples should ask their GP to refer them to a genetic counsellor or a genetic centre.

Couples of certain ethnic origins should be tested prior to pregnancy to establish whether or not they are carriers of specific genes common to their particular group. They include: Ashkenazi Jews for Tay Sachs disease;

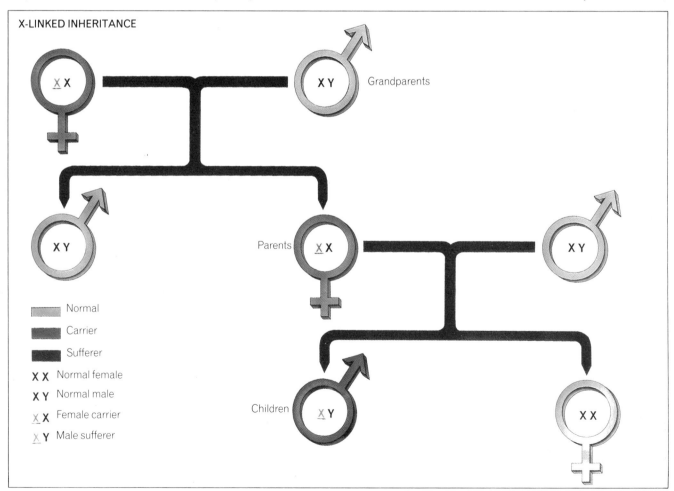

X-LINKED INHERITANCE

Grandparents
XX   XY

Parents
XY   XX   XY

Children
XY   XX

Normal
Carrier
Sufferer
X X Normal female
X Y Normal male
X X Female carrier
X Y Male sufferer

Couples of African origin could be carriers of sickle cell anaemia, although there is only a risk of their having an affected child if both parents are found to have the particular gene that produces the illness. Prospective parents can undergo tests to ascertain whether they are likely to have an affected baby

those of black African origin for sickle cell anaemia; and those from Mediterranean countries for thalassaemia. For each of these diseases the couple is *only* at risk of having an affected child if *both* partners are found to be carriers of the particular gene involved. Testing is done by analysis of a blood sample; this can be carried out only at certain laboratories, but the family doctor should have access to these facilities.

Investigation of inherited disorders
Before a couple meets with the genetic counsellor, it may be necessary for the counsellor to obtain information concerning affected members of their family. Details such as their name, date of birth and the hospital where they attend, if relevant, will be required; it may also be necessary for the genetic counsellor to obtain the permission of relevant family members to read their hospital and other records.

The amount of detail required will depend on the type of disorder, as will the importance of obtaining information about distant family relatives. With some disoders, such as Huntington's chorea or certain forms of visual handicap, particulars of distant relatives can be very helpful. However, the further back in a family's history a counsellor goes, the more it is likely that there will be an overlay of family folklore, so it may become exceedingly difficult for the counsellor to gain definite confirmation of the facts.

Therefore, unearthing family history can be difficult; some families are close and have easy access to one another, whereas many people have scant knowledge of one or the other side of their family. The usefulness and importance of the knowledge that is gained has to be balanced against the possibility of causing offence or distress to those approached.

When the necessary facts have been obtained the genetic counsellor will assess the need for physical examination or tests, such as chromosome analysis, DNA studies, X-rays or ultrasound scans. Sometimes, samples may be requested from other relevant family members, but again, the wisdom of approaching them will need to be assessed. Often tests are irrelevant and in such cases an evaluation of the risks depends on the pedigree analysis.

Once the genetic counsellor has completed the investigation, he or she will explain to the couple the conclusions drawn and how they have been reached. These aspects will vary enormously according to the disorder present in the family.

Where a couple are faced with a high risk of having an affected child, they will be given the facts about the possible degree of severity of the condition and the options available to avoid having an affected child. These may include various methods of prenatal diagnosis, or, for those couples where such tests cannot be carried out, the use of techniques such as artificial insemination by donor (AID) or in-vitro fertilization.

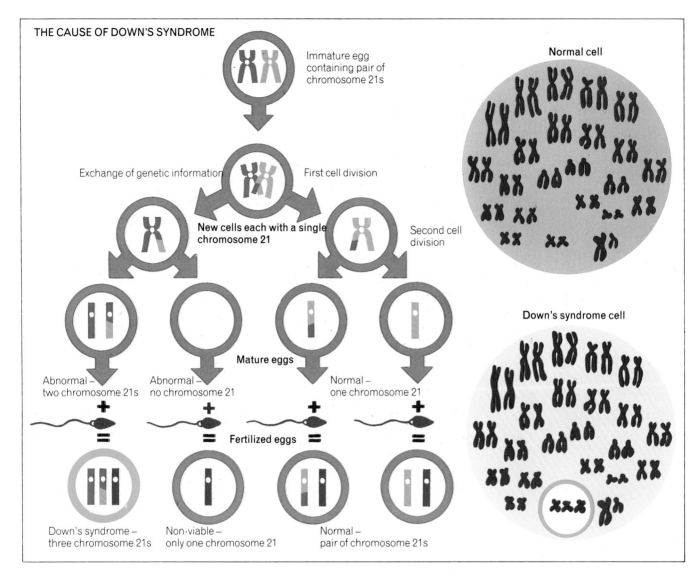

THE CAUSE OF DOWN'S SYNDROME

Immature egg containing pair of chromosome 21s

Exchange of genetic information

First cell division

New cells each with a single chromosome 21

Second cell division

Mature eggs

Abnormal – two chromosome 21s

Abnormal – no chromosome 21

Normal – one chromosome 21

Fertilized eggs

Down's syndrome – three chromosome 21s

Non-viable – only one chromosome 21

Normal – pair of chromosome 21s

Normal cell

Down's syndrome cell

In Down's syndrome there are three chromosome 21s (circled above). The sequence that produces this starts with an immature egg (or an immature sperm), containing a pair of chromosome 21s. In the first cell division this starts to exchange genetic information. If this is normal each cell has one chromosome 21. When this is fertilized by a normal sperm, with one chromosome 21, the resulting fertilized cell will carry a pair of chromosome 21s. In abnormal division one cell may carry two chromosome 21s and one may carry none. Although these are fertilized by normal cells, the result is either Down's syndrome or a non-viable cell with only one chromosome 21

Particular risks for older couples

As a man gets older, there is a slight risk that he will sire a child with some disorder, due to a mutation in his genetic make-up. Such disorders are rare, the overall risk is small, and no action can be taken to prevent them.

As a woman gets older, the risk of giving birth to a baby with an extra chromosome increases steadily. This has been known for years, and yet doctors and genetic counsellors are unable to advise women on how to diminish the risk. All that can be done is to test the foetus when the woman is pregnant (see amniocentesis, p65). Should it be found that the foetus is defective then the pregnancy can be terminated. (See pp 49-51). As views on abortion in such circumstances vary from one individual to another, a couple should consider the matter carefully before embarking on a pregnancy.

The commonest of chromosome disorders in older women is Down's syndrome (see chart above, and pp 20-21).

Another arises when there is an extra chromosome which produces a female with three X chromosomes, or a male with two X chromosomes and a Y chromosome (normal females are XX; normal males are XY). Both of these conditions are compatible with normal physical growth in childhood and adulthood, although XXY males are sterile. Yet both are associated with learning difficulties and an increased risk of mental retardation. A more common chromosome disorder is Turner's syndrome, where the child has only one sex chromosome (XO). Prior to puberty the child will have the external appearance of a girl, but in adulthood will lack the secondary sexual characteristics of a normal woman. In such a person the ovaries and uterus will also be absent. If either of these conditions are discovered, the parents – who might otherwise have no hesitation in opting for termination of pregnancy in the case of Down's syndrome – may be faced with a very difficult decision.

Although it is possible for many older women to avoid the birth of a child with a chromosome disorder and thus surmount a major risk associated with her age, it is important to remember the frustrating fact that whatever tests are done, whatever care is taken, the possibility of a child being born with some handicap or defect must remain. For all the advances in modern technology, there has been little progress in the prevention of birth defects; this possibility must be faced by all who embark on parenthood.

Counselling
Where any perplexing situation arises following investigation of inherited or other genetic disorders, skilled counselling should be available to help the parents make a decision. This should involve a detailed explanation of what has been found and how it can be expected to affect the child if pregnancy is undertaken or continued. Couples vary enormously in the type and degree of problems they are prepared to risk in their child, and also in the degree of handicap for which they would find late termination of pregnancy acceptable.

The role of the genetic counsellor or other professional is to help a couple reach a conclusion that is appropriate for them, and with which they will be able to live the rest of their lives without regret.

CONCEPTION

There are three essential prerequisites for natural conception: the delivery of adequate numbers of motile, healthy male sex cells (sperm) to the upper vagina; the presence of a healthy female sex cell (ovum) in the Fallopian tube; and a free passage between the vagina and the Fallopian tube, allowing sperm access to the ovum.

The male role
The testes of the adult male have two principal functions. They produce the male hormone testosterone which is responsible for the characteristic masculine shape of the adult male body, distribution of hair and sex drive. The testicles also produce small quantities of female sex hormones. The second function is formation of spermatozoa – miscroscopic structures capable of fertilizing the ovum. Each sperm consists of a head containing the male contribution of genetic material, a short neck, or middle piece, and a long tail. The tail enables the sperm to move under its own power through the female genital tract.

Both testicular functions are under the control of a second gland, the pituitary, found at the base of the brain. The pituitary is intimately connected with an adjoining area of the brain, the hypothalamus, which produces releasing factors. Pituitary hormones, follicle stimulating hormone (FSH) and luteinising hormone (LH) are stored in the pituitary and released into the circulating blood on the instruction of the hypothalamic releasing factors. The names given to the two hormones are related to their function in the female. Both male and female pituitaries produce identical hormones. In the male, FSH is chiefly concerned with the production of sperm; LH stimulates and maintains the production of the hormone testosterone. The testes are located in the scrotum, outside the pelvic cavity of the male. The temperature within the scrotum is about 4° Fahrenheit

The male genital organs consist of the testes and the penis, which are situated outside the body, and the prostate gland, seminal vesicles and various tubes linking the genital system, which are located inside the abdominal cavity

MALE GENITAL ORGANS

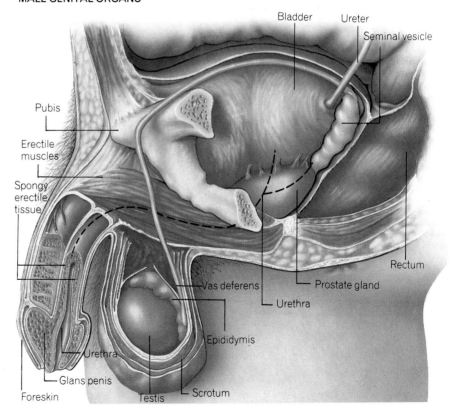

Bladder
Ureter
Seminal vesicle
Pubis
Erectile muscles
Spongy erectile tissue
Rectum
Vas deferens
Prostate gland
Urethra
Epididymis
Urethra
Glans penis
Testis
Scrotum
Foreskin

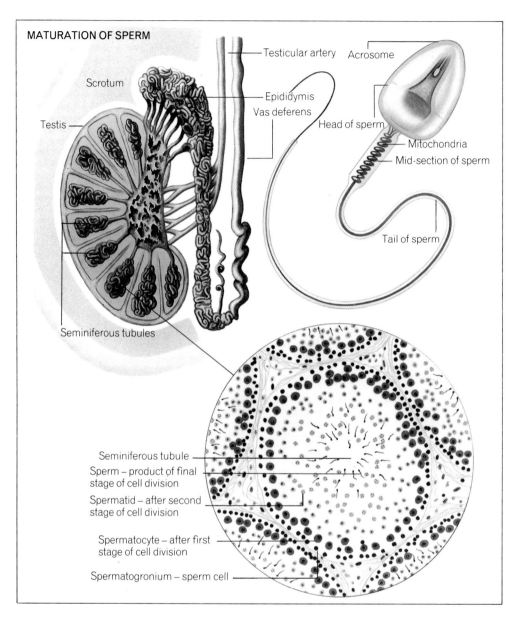

MATURATION OF SPERM

Scrotum

Testis

Seminiferous tubules

Testicular artery

Epididymis
Vas deferens

Acrosome

Head of sperm

Mitochondria
Mid-section of sperm

Tail of sperm

Seminiferous tubule
Sperm – product of final
stage of cell division
Spermatid – after second
stage of cell division

Spermatocyte – after first
stage of cell division

Spermatogronium – sperm cell

From puberty, sperm are constantly produced in the seminiferous tubules. To become mature, the basic sperm cells go through three stages of cell division (right) before passing through the tubules and into the epididymis, where they are stored (above left). A mature sperm has a head, mid-section and tail (above right)

lower than that inside the body; it is at this temperature that sperm production becomes optimal.

The internal structure of the testis consists of a series of coiled tubes in which sperm are produced. When nearing maturity, they enter the lumen of the tubule into a collecting system and eventually into the main duct of the gland, the vas deferens. Testosterone, produced by different cells, is not released into this collecting system but is discharged into the blood stream. An interruption of the collecting system (as in vasectomy) does not therefore interfere with distribution of the male hormone.

The production of sperm in the testicle takes about 100 days, the last two weeks of which are spent travelling through the collecting system; important changes occur in these tubes which make the sperm capable of fertilizing the ovum.

In the vas deferens, the sperm are joined by the secretions of two other structures, the seminal vesicles and the prostate gland. These secretions provide the fluid vehicle for the sperm and constitute the major part of the ejaculate. Ejaculation occurs through the urethra, the common drainage tube with the bladder. Interruption of the vas does not prevent ejaculation; in the vasectomised male the ejaculate is composed of fluid from the seminal vesicles and from the prostate, free of sperm.

For conception, large numbers of motile

INTERCOURSE

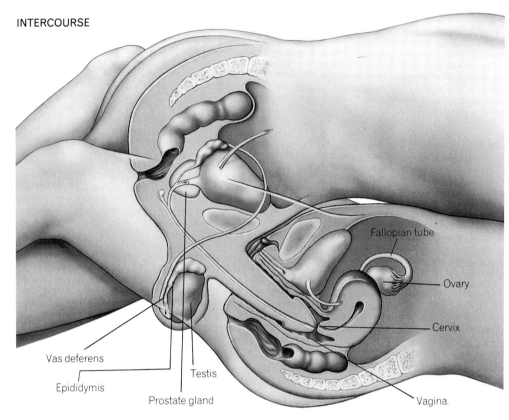

At the moment of ejaculation sperm are released into the vagina, and actively motile sperm pass through the cervix into the uterine cavity. Of the several million that entred the cervix, only a few hundred will continue into the Fallopian tube

sperm are essential. A normal ejaculate may contain 200 hundred million sperm, of which only a few hundred will progress to the Fallopian tube. Although only this small number reach their objective, the presence of many millions of sperm in the ejaculate seems to be essential if satisfactory conception is to take place.

Passage of sperm through the female body

The first obstacle the sperm has to negotiate in the female reproductive system is the cervix. At the moment of ejaculation, the female cervix is bathed in seminal fluid. The majority of the fluid remains in the vagina but the actively motile sperm enter the canal of the cervix. The high acidity of the vagina is hostile to sperm and any sperm remaining for more than an hour or so will be rapidly immobilized. The cervical canal, however, contains a fluid in which sperm can survive for much longer periods. This cervical mucus is of critical importance to fertility.

The mucus is secreted by glands in the cervical canal and its consistency varies throughout the menstrual cycle. Once ovulation occurs, the mucus rapidly becomes sticky and inpenetrable; it is at its most receptive in the few days before ovulation. As well as providing a suitable medium for the entry of sperm, the cervical mucus probably also

functions as a protective mechanism preventing infection of the uterus and the Fallopian tubes.

Once through the cervix, the sperm enter the uterine cavity and continue to move upwards; it is doubtful whether the uterus makes any significant contribution to their propulsion. One or two million sperm succeed in entering the cervical canal, probably only a few hundred reach the top of the uterus and the entry to the Fallopian tube. During this passage they undergo a change known as capacitation; this change is poorly understood but seems to be essential for successful fertilization. It was once thought that capacitation occurred only to sperm inside the uterus and cervix; now, however, it seems that the only necessity for capacitation to take place is the passage of time after ejaculation – time which is normally spent by sperm in the journey from the cervix to the Fallopian tube.

In the Fallopian tube the sperm must move against the tide. The muscle of the Fallopian tube tends to propel the contents *towards* the uterus; it is also lined by fine hair-like processes (cilia) whose wave-like motion is also towards the uterus. Nevertheless, the few sperm which survive the journey to this point continue their progress, and if unhindered, may leave the Fallopian tube and spill over into the peritoneal cavity.

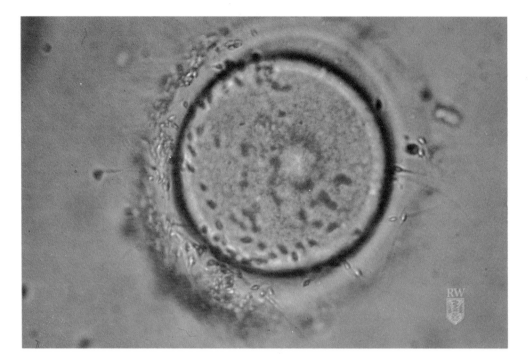

The moment of conception: chemicals in the tip of the sperm strip away the outer layer of the egg until one sperm can penetrate its smooth shell. Normally, chemical changes in the outer layer of the egg then ensure that no further sperm can enter

If there is partial obstruction of the Fallopian tube then some sperm may be able to pass through so that one can fertilize the ovum – however, the fertilized ovum may be too large to make its way through the narrowed tube, in which case it will embed in the wall of the tube, resulting in an ectopic pregnancy (below). The diagram (far right) illustrates how the hormones oestrogen, progesterone, LSH and FSH control the various stages of the menstrual cycle

Ovulation

Ova are not produced in the ovaries. All the ova a woman will ever have are present in her body, within the ovary, during foetal life. At birth up to half a million ova may be present, of which only a few hundred will reach maturity. During each normal menstrual cycle, one ovum reaches maturity and is expelled from the ovary. The obvious exception to this is multiple ovulation resulting in multiple birth.

Maturation of the ovum is under the control of FSH and LH. Whereas these hormones seem to be produced continuously in the male, their production in the female is inter-mittent and cyclical. The process begins at puberty and continues throughout menstrual life.

At the beginning of each menstrual cycle the hypothalamus releases FSH, distributed through the circulating blood, initiating development of an ovum. In each menstrual cycle, only one ovum matures, but the process of selection is totally mysterious.

A developing ovum is surrounded by a group of cells which, under the influence of FSH from the pituitary gland, begins to grow. This 'follicle' forms a tiny structure on the surface of the ovary. The follicle has two functions: it is responsible for nurturing the developing ovum; and it also produces the principal female hormone – oestrogen. Oestrogen production gradually increases over the first two weeks of the menstrual cycle and is distributed through the blood stream. Oestrogen has many effects on the female body, principally in the uterus where it begins to prepare the lining for implantation of the successfully fertilized ovum. Oestrogen also has widespread effects on the woman's body: it is responsible for the development of secondary sexual characteristics; and it also has an important function on the hypothalamus where it tends to damp down the production of FSH. When oestrogen secretion reaches its peak after about two weeks, it stimulates the release of the second pituitary hormone, LH. A rapid surge of LH, in response to the oestrogen stimulus, is responsible for ovulation – the release of the developing ovum from the follicle. The follicle rup-

ECTOPIC PREGNANCY

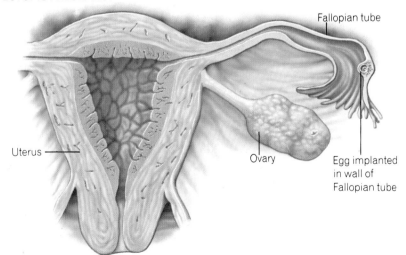

Fallopian tube

Uterus

Ovary

Egg implanted in wall of Fallopian tube

THE MENSTRUAL CYCLE

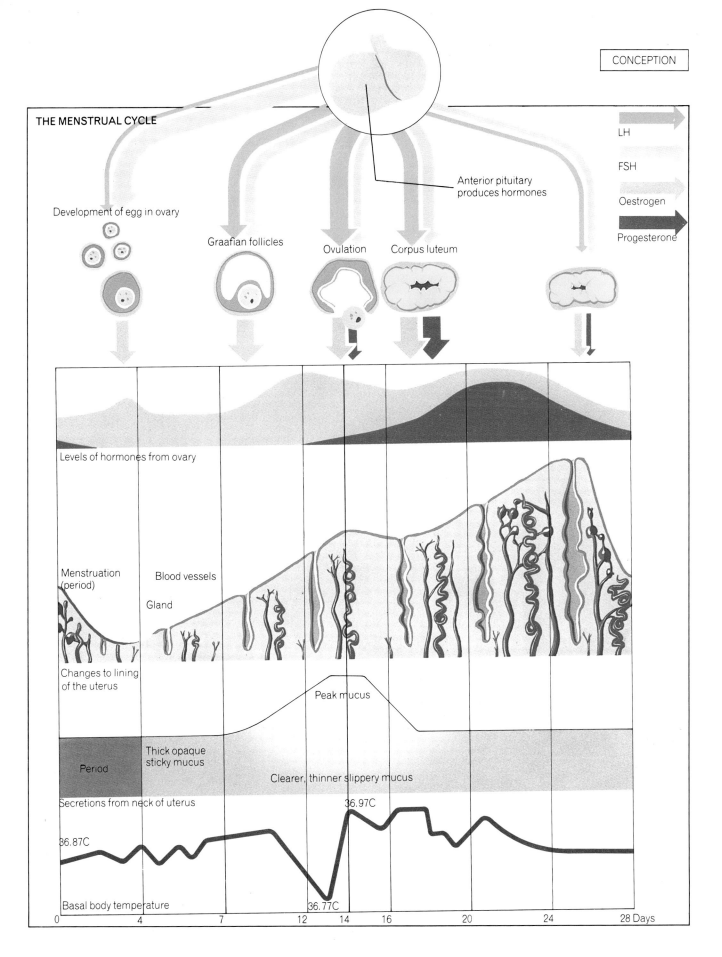

Anterior pituitary produces hormones

LH

FSH

Oestrogen

Progesterone

Development of egg in ovary

Graafian follicles

Ovulation

Corpus luteum

Levels of hormones from ovary

Menstruation (period)

Blood vessels

Gland

Changes to lining of the uterus

Peak mucus

Period

Thick opaque sticky mucus

Clearer, thinner slippery mucus

Secretions from neck of uterus

36.97C

36.87C

Basal body temperature

36.77C

0   4   7   12   14   16   20   24   28 Days

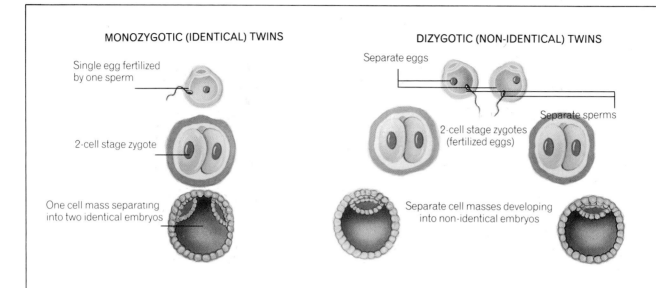

MONOZYGOTIC (IDENTICAL) TWINS

Single egg fertilized
by one sperm

2-cell stage zygote

One cell mass separating
into two identical embryos

DIZYGOTIC (NON-IDENTICAL) TWINS

Separate eggs

Separate sperms

2-cell stage zygotes
(fertilized eggs)

Separate cell masses developing
into non-identical embryos

TWINS IN THE WOMB

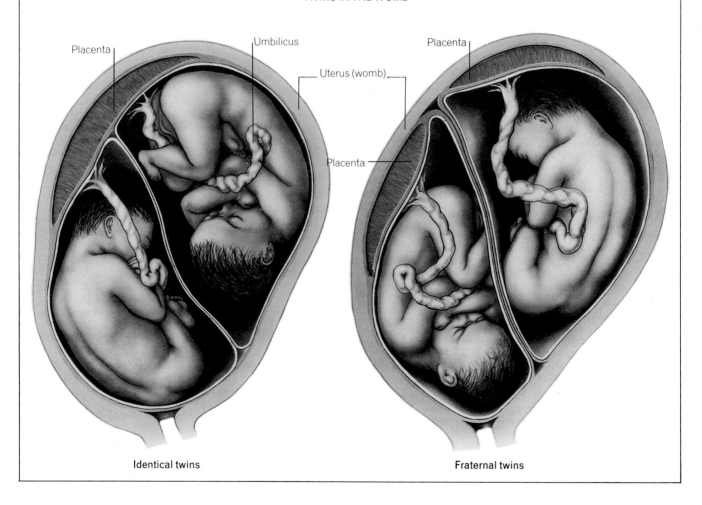

Placenta

Umbilicus

Uterus (womb)

Placenta

Placenta

Identical twins

Fraternal twins

tures, propelling the ovum into the peritoneal cavity; the follicle immediately seals off and takes on a new character.

The post-ovulation follicle has a yellow lining and is called a corpus luteum – hence luteinising hormone. Once released into the peritoneal cavity, the ovum has no means of propulsion and depends upon the Fallopian tube to pick it up. The Fallopian tube ends in a rosette of finger-like structures, the fimbria. The muscular Fallopian tube moves to envelope the ovum in its fimbria, moving it slowly towards the uterus. Movement is achieved partly by the muscular activity of the wall of the Fallopian tube and partly by the cilia. If sperm are present in the Fallopian tube fertilization will occur during this journey. Complete obstruction of the Fallopian tube prevents the sperm and the ovum meeting. Incomplete obstruction may allow the passage of the smaller sperm but prevent the larger fertilized ovum from gaining the uterine cavity. The fertilized ovum then embeds in the Fallopian tube and an ectopic pregnancy results.

Implantation

For the remainder of the menstrual cycle, oestrogen continues to be produced by the corpus luteum. In addition, this new structure has the ability to produce a second hormone, progesterone. Oestrogen and progesterone in combination prepare the lining of the uterus for the implantation of the fertilized ovum.

Passage of the fertilized ovum through the Fallopian tube takes three or four days, during which time it has begun to divide and develop. By the time it reaches the uterine cavity it has divided into eight cells, and this embryo is now ready to implant in the uterine lining (endometrium). If no fertilization has occurred, the unchanged ovum passes through the uterine cavity and is lost, quite unnoticed, in the normal vaginal discharge. At the end of 14 days the corpus luteum dies, shrivels and ceases to produce its horrnone. Without the influence of oestrogen and progesterone, the endometrium also shrivels and dies, bleeding as it does so. The resulting discharge of endometruim and blood is menstruation.

If implantation is successful, the developing embryo puts down roots into the endometruim, forming finger-like processes which will eventually form the basis of the placenta. These structures, or chrionic villi, have a central core of foetal cells, the trophoblast which develops a new hormone, human chorionic gonadotrophin (HCG) with precisely the same functions as LH. Under the influence of HCG, the corpus luteum survives and continues to make oestrogen and progesterone, which in turn continue to stimulate

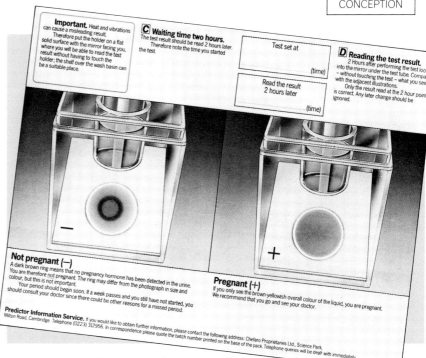

the endometrium to grow and so secure the pregnancy.

Recognition of pregnancy

The first sign of a pregnancy is the failure of menstruation. At the same time changes occur in the woman's body due to the increased and continuing levels of oestrogen and progesterone and of the new hormone HCG. Symptoms include breast tenderness, discomfort in the pelvic area (because of the enlarging uterus) and nausea. The nausea is probably due to relaxation of the involuntary muscles of the stomach and upper intestine.

By the time the menstrual period is two weeks late, these symptoms are often well developed. An experienced doctor can often detect uterine enlargement at this time, making a diagnosis of pregnancy virtually certain.

The pregnancy test

All pregnancy tests depend upon the recognition of the hormone HCG. The difficulty about pregnancy tests is the similarity of HCG, in almost every respect, to LH.

Until about 25 years ago, biological tests were employed to recognise HCG. Extract of the pregnant woman's urine was injected into a female rabbit or toad. If the animal ovulated, the test was positive. In the case of a frog, this could be recognised without sacrificing the animal but the rabbit test depended upon killing the rabbit and establishing ovulation by dissection of the ovary. Both of these tests are now no longer employed.

Modern pregnancy tests depend upon the recognition of HCG by immuniological means. HCG is injected into an experimental animal; as a foreign protein it engenders the

Predictor is one of the many home pregnancy tests on the market. A brown ring means the test is negative, no change in the colour of the liquid means a positive result

In the normal course of events, an ovary only releases a single ovum in every cycle. Exceptionally, two ova are released at the same time, and both may be fertilized by separate sperm. This occurance results in dizygotic, or non-identical twins (far left). Monozygotic, or identical twins result when a single ovum is released and fertilized but then divides completely to form two embryos. Monozygotic twins usually share the same placenta, unless the cells separate at a later stage of development. Each dizygotic twin has its own placenta

production of a specific antibody in the recipient animal. The animal's blood is then treated to separate the antibody. When confronted with the original antigen (HCG) the antibody combines with it; a suitable system can be devised in a test tube to demonstrate this combination of antigen and antibody. A sample of the pregnant woman's urine is examined in such a system; the positive result depends upon recognition of the reaction. The difficulty in distinguishing HCG arises because high levels of LH in the pregnant woman's urine will also combine with the antibody, LH and HCG being almost indistinguishable. Women who are accidentally producing high levels of LH may therefore give wrongly positive pregnancy tests. This is particularly important for the older woman. At the menopause, the ovary is no longer capable of responding to the brain stimulus and no longer produces oestrogen or progesterone. The result is ever increasing levels of FSH and LH, produced by the woman's brain in a forlorn attempt to stimulate the unresponsive ovary. The woman does not, of course, menstruate. Urine gives a positive pregnancy test, not because of the presence of HCG but because of the high levels of LH.

For this reason, the sensitivity of the pregnancy test had to be set high enough to exclude all but the very highest levels of LH, to avoid false positives. Even so, menopausal women often gave wrongly positive results. A recent new development has overcome this difficulty.

HCG differs from LH in one important chemical respect – it has a small variant of a chemical structure called the Beta sub-group. If, instead of producing an antibody to the whole HCG molecule, the manufacturers produce one to the Beta sub-group alone (a sub-group which is not represented at all in the LH molecule) a positive test means HCG and nothing else. Within the last few years pregnancy tests based on the Beta sub-group of HCG have become available and are much more reliable. They are capable of detecting pregnancy at very low levels of HCG, within ten days of conception. Thus pregnancy can now be diagnosed by the immuniological test *before* the period has been missed. However, no pregnancy test is infallible.

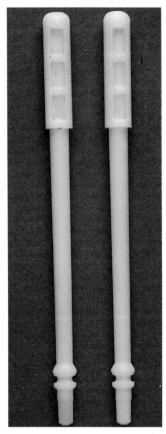

Clearblue is one of the easiest to use home pregnancy tests. Allegedly effective even on the day your period should have started, the special sampler (shown above) turns blue if you are pregnant, stays white if you are not, and gives you a result in thirty minutes

Discontinuing contraception is the first positive step towards pregnancy. Shown here (left to right) are a uterine sound used to check the uterus when inserting an IUD; Copper T; Lippes Loop; Copper 7 and Saf-T-Coil

ACHIEVING CONCEPTION

For most women who decide to embark upon pregnancy, the first positive step is to discontinue contraception. There are no difficulties in discontinuing barrier methods of birth control such as the condom, diaphragm, cap or sponge methods, but the contraceptive pill and the IUCD may occasionally present difficulties. Both have earned an undeserved reputation for causing long-term infertility and are discussed in the following pages.

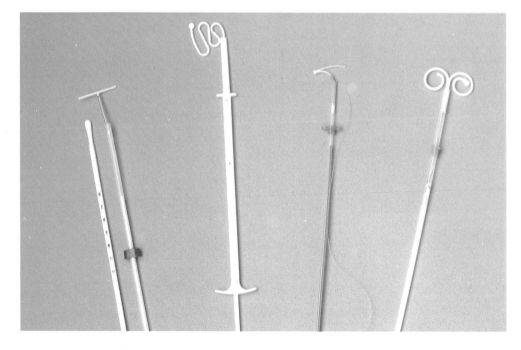

FERTILIZATION OF THE EGG

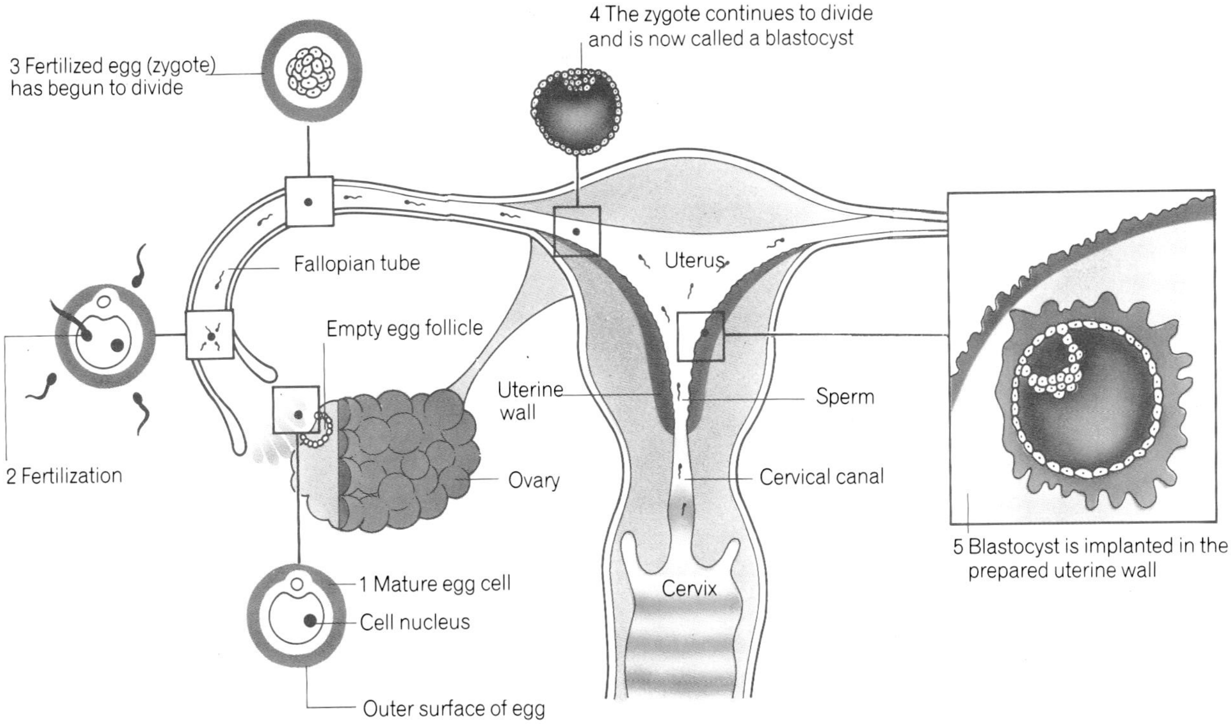

3 Fertilized egg (zygote) has begun to divide

4 The zygote continues to divide and is now called a blastocyst

Fallopian tube

Uterus

Empty egg follicle

2 Fertilization

Uterine wall

Sperm

Ovary

Cervical canal

1 Mature egg cell

Cell nucleus

Cervix

Outer surface of egg

5 Blastocyst is implanted in the prepared uterine wall

The diagram shows the process of conception and the journey of the zygote (fertilized ovum) into the uterus, where it embeds in the uterine wall

The IUCD

Relatively more women aged 30 and over use the IUCD for whom it is often an efficient and convenient method of birth control. However there is an association between the IUCD and pelvic infection. It is difficult to be precise about this relationship. Pelvic infection is very common but is notoriously difficult to diagnose with certainty – many more women are treated for pelvic infection than actually have it. There is, nevertheless, general agreement that women who wear IUCDs are more likely to have infection than women who do not. Serious and damaging infection is uncommon and it almost always causes symptoms. A woman who has worn an IUCD without apparent trouble is most unlikely to have suffered serious infection, but very occasionally, the infection may involve damage to the Fallopian tubes. Once established, such infection is not likely to cure itself and may need surgical treatment.

Discontinuing the pill

The combined contraceptive pill, taken for 21 days out of 28, remains a popular method of contraception up to the age of 35 – thereafter it is actively discouraged by doctors because the increased risk of death from thrombosis and embolism is five times as great as it is in younger women. The problem in discontinuing the pill is that menstruation may not resume immediately. Usually the delay is no more than a few months, but occasionally it may persist for a year. If it does, there is a serious risk of long-term infertility, and more than half of such women will remain infertile in spite of treatment.

Such infertility is very uncommon. Probably no more than two or three women in a thousand have a serious delay in resumption of menstruation. The cause of the delay is not altogether clear. Sometimes there is an obvious excess or deficiency of one of the hormones required for conception; more often there is not. In the majority of cases it would seem that the vital communications between the hypothalamus and the ovary which trigger ovulation have never been re-established. Treatment with drugs such as Clomiphene is often successful.

It is important to distinguish between delay in the resumption of menstruation and the absence of withdrawal bleeding while taking the oral contraceptive pill. The two phenomenon are not related; if a woman fails to bleed during the pill-free week while taking oral contraception, it should not be seen as an indication that she will fail to menstruate spontaneously when she finally stops taking the pill.

Because of the occasional delay in the

resumption of menstruation, it is wise to discontinue the pill a few months before pregnancy is desired. Some other method of birth control, such as a barrier method, should be used during this interval so that regular menstruation can be established in advance of attempts at conception.

Having discontinued contraception, it is usually unnecessary to take any positive steps to achieve conception. Couples who do not immediately achieve the desired pregnancy will normally be given advice by their doctor; most of it concerns the timing of intercourse in relation to menstruation.

Detecting ovulation

For those who want to, keeping a basal body temperature chart will usually establish whether ovulation is occurring and when. The woman takes her temperature on waking each morning. A typical biphasic pattern will emerge (see below); the change in temperature is due to the hormone progesterone.

Progesterone has a specific effect on the control of basal body temperature, raising it by about half a degree. In the early part of the menstrual cycle, before ovulation, there is no progesterone. Once ovulation has occurred, progesterone is released by the corpus luteum and the rise in temperature signals that ovulation has already occurred. It follows, therefore, that once the temperature is raised, the egg is well on the way and it is then probably too late for conception. The likely time for conception is the preceeding four days (the day of ovulation and the three days before). The temperature chart therefore can-

not be used as a traffic light, signalling the moment for intercourse to occur; rather it establishes a pattern over a number of months indicating when ovulation is likely to occur. However, some women do experience abdominal pain during ovulation, which might be taken as an indication that ovulation has occurred.

Timing of intercourse

In general, couples do not need to be told when to have intercourse. It is only very occasionally that such advice can be helpful; more often it is harmful. If there are four days of opportunity preceeding ovulation, it follows that any couple having intercourse twice a week must automatically include one of those days. For such couples, any advice about the timing of intercourse is gratuitous.

But what if intercourse is less frequent than twice a week? The pressures of professional and business life in the 30s and 40s is often associated with diminished sexual activity. From the point of view of fertility, it is clearly important in these circumstances that sexual activity should be timed to coincide with ovulation. For the woman, who is physically capable of intercourse at any time, this may not be a problem. For the man who is anxious about proving himself as a father and whose sex drive diminishes, instructions to have intercourse on a particular day (whether he feels like it or not) may be counter-productive. It is usually preferable for the couple to simply record intercourse after it has happened; if this recording is made on the same chart as the basal body temperature, it is easy for the

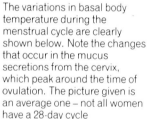

The variations in basal body temperature during the menstrual cycle are clearly shown below. Note the changes that occur in the mucus secretions from the cervix, which peak around the time of ovulation. The picture given is an average one – not all women have a 28-day cycle

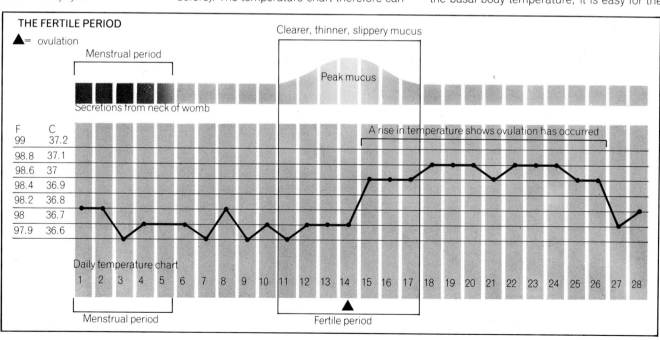

doctor to see whether opportunities for conception are being consistently missed. If they are, a word of advice may be necessary, but extreme caution must be exercised if impotence is not to be added to the problem of delayed conception.

For a few women, a change in the character of the cervical mucus at mid-cycle can be used as a predictor of ovulation. The clear, abundant fluid mucus of the pre-ovulation cervix can certainly be recognised by the doctor; its recognition by the patient is difficult. Basal body temperature charts are therefore preferable.

INFERTILITY

Pregnancy does not necessarily occur within the first few months of unprotected intercourse. Young couples, who subsequently prove to be normally fertile, often take several months to achieve pregnancy. The reasons for this are not entirely clear. Undoubtedly, the age of the woman is a powerful factor in increasing this unexplained delay. In the early twenties the probability of conception within a year is about 95 per cent. This is reduced to about 80 per cent in the late 20s and early 30s; by the late 30s it may be as low as 65 per cent. Put another way, for women in their early 20s the monthly probability of conception is between 20 and 25 per cent; by the early 30s the monthly probability is considerably lower, about 10-15 per cent. In the case of women who already have a history of infertility, the situation is exaggerated. A 20-year-old woman with one year's infertility has a 76 per cent chance of conceiving within the next 12 months. The chance of pregnancy decreases to 57 per cent for a 30 year-old-woman and further to 40 per cent over the age of 40.

The reasons for this falling off in fertility with the increasing age of a woman are unclear. It may be that older couples tend to be less sexually active, or, as older women tend to ovulate less frequently and less predictably, the quality of ova remaining in a woman's ovaries towards the end of her reproductive career may be significantly reduced. Gynaecological disease is commoner in the 30s than the 20s. The two diseases of most significance are pelvic infection and endometriosis.

Getting professional help
The right time for a couple to seek medical advice is when infertility is perceived as a problem. To some couples, a delay of a year or two will not be important; for others, a delay of only a few months will cause anxiety. Unfortunately the advice given is not always well-informed or sympathetic. Advances in the investigation and treatment of infertility have been very rapid in the last 20 years, therefore most general practitioners have limited knowledge of this field. In addition,

they may be reluctant to refer to a specialist infertility clinic until a statutory time has passed – perhaps one or even two years – or the option of a specialist infertility clinic may not be available. The woman may be referred to a gynaecologist; some gynaecologists deal with infertility as part of their routine gynaecological work; others have little interest in the subject. For a man the problems are even greater. He may be referred to a genitourinary surgeon, but only a minority of these have any real interest in infertility; or he may be more fortunate and be referred to a specialist in male fertility, but they are very few and far between.

It is impossible to lay down rules about the length of time which should pass before infertility is actively investigated. Some doctors require their patients to have had unprotected intercourse for two years before undertaking investigation; for a woman of 38 this is clearly inappropriate.

Some of the delay imposed upon infertile couples is due to lack of resources; some is

Couples who have difficulty in conceiving should seek medical advice as soon as they become anxious about their fertility. If they are not satisfied with their GP's response to their problem they should insist on a referral to a specialist infertility clinic

due to doctors' insensitivity. Without treatment many apparently infertile couples conceive. It is the experience of every clinic that during the evaluation period, when no treatment is being administered, some 10-20 per cent of infertile couples manage to get pregnant. Imposing a delay therefore decreases the workload. In the days when doctors knew almost nothing about the treatment of infertility, this saved a great deal of embarrassment; there is less excuse for it now.

The couple who are concerned about infertility should insist upon referral to a specialist infertility clinic – or to a gynaecologist with a fertility interest. The timing of referral is a decision for the individual patient and, particularly in the older woman, should not be subject to arbitrary rules.

Finding a cause

It is not always possible to establish the cause of infertility. Where doctors can find no cause they label the infertility idiopathic. Some 50 years ago the idiopathic group formed the majority. Now, with increasing knowledge, particularly of female reproductive function, only 10 per cent of infertile individuals deserve this label, and the figure is decreasing all the time.

Tests for infertility are becoming increasingly complicated. A little background information about the likely investigations is often helpful and takes much of the mystery out of infertility clinics.

History and examination

Most doctors will investigate infertility only in couples. The single woman trying to conceive is not normally regarded as a suitable subject for investigation. This is partly a matter of practicality and partly of morals. Most doctors would take the moral standpoint that a single woman is not a suitable person to be encouraged to have a baby; others might take the view that that was a matter for the woman rather than the doctor. The more practical consideration is that about 50 per cent of infertility is due to inadequacy in the male, and investigating only half of a relationship is often unproductive. If the woman has a variety of sexual partners, however, this argument evaporates into mere prejudice.

Most often, it is a couple who present for investigation and treatment. Their history may give a clue to the cause. The woman's history of previous contraception, previous pregnancies and previous surgery are particularly important. The relevance of a previous pregnancy may operate in two directions; clearly the woman who has been pregnant has proved herself capable at least to a certain point. Conversely, a complication of that pregnancy, such as infection (for instance after abortion) might explain her infertility. A history of many repeated miscarriages has a special significance, not least because the history is not always what it seems; proof of pregnancy is often lacking; what seems a miscarriage may be a menstrual disturbance.

During investigation there is a tendency to inquire into the woman's history in considerable detail; the history of the man seems less important. This is not chauvinism, merely practicality. If the man can produce a satisfactory semen specimen for analysis, it matters little what his history is. The male medical history therefore becomes important only when he is shown to be potentially defective. In that case, his social habits are as important as his medical history. Excess alcohol consumption and heavy smoking seriously impair fertility in some men.

A physical examination follows, where the same considerations apply. In many infertility clinics, the man is not examined unless he is shown to have a defective sperm count. The woman, however, is always examined. Physical examination seldom provides an explanation on its own.

Once the preliminaries are taken care of, a specific search is made into the likely areas of conception failure: a specimen of semen is analysed; ovulation is investigated; and finally, the woman's internal anatomy is checked to exclude obstruction to the passage of semen through her genital tract. This procedure often takes six months or a year in a busy

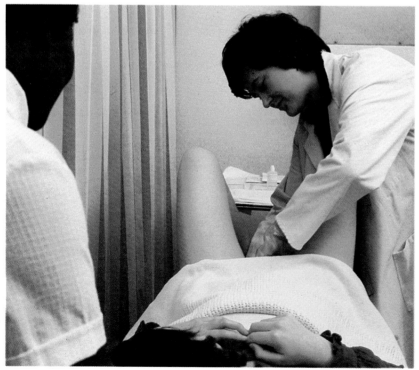

Preliminary investigation of possible infertility in a woman includes a routine internal examination. In most cases further tests will be necessary as the examination does not usually provide an explanation of the cause

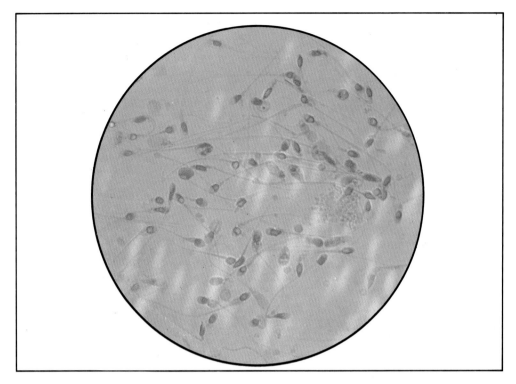

Mature sperm under the microscope. A great number of sperm in any ejaculate, however are immature and in many cases will not be able to swim properly

infertility clinic, in which the junior staff are constantly changing and the woman (it is often the woman who attends alone and repeatedly) is seen by a different junior doctor each time. Yet it need not take more than about three weeks, given motivation and organisation.

The post-coital test

As well as examining a sample of semen, some doctors begin the investigation by examining a sample of mucus taken from the cervix after intercourse. If a large number of healthy, motile sperm are found in the cervical mucus, this can be taken as a good sign. The difficulty about the test is that experts disagree about the details of its performance (the day of the test, the interval after intercourse before examination, the site of sampling from the cervix or uterus, the number of sperm necessary to constitute a satisfactory test and so on.)

A more serious objection is that there is virtually no effective treatment for the negative test. There is no doubt that the quality of cervical mucus and the passage of sperm through it are of the greatest importance for successful conception; unfortunately, it is not yet known how to influence the cervical mucus to make it more receptive – it is not even known with certainty how to recognise its quality. A number of treatments have been suggested for the poor post-coital test but none have yet been shown to have more than

the 10 or 20 per cent success rate which is known to occur in untreated couples.

While the post-coital test has little treatment value, it does have one potential danger. Not all men respond positively to a request to have intercourse at a particular time on a particular day, to suit the doctor.

Problems with semen

Semen analysis is somewhat imprecise. A man who produces less than 20 million sperm per millilitre of seminal fluid has a less than average chance of fathering a child. The count may vary according to the man's general health, and a repeat count some weeks later may be entirely within the normal range. Persistent low counts can often be corrected by simple measures such as weight loss and a reduction in alcohol intake and smoking. It is the successful man in his 40s and 50s particularly who may need such advice. Obesity probably contributes by raising the temperature of the scrotum; a similar effect may be achieved by the persistent wearing of tight underclothing or by varicose veins (varicocele) in the scrotum. A correction of the defect and a reduction in the temperature of the scrotum usually results in an improved semen count.

Persistent very low counts, below a million, are less likely to respond to treatment of any kind. Occasionally, serious hormone abnormalities can be corrected by medical treatment – but this is rare.

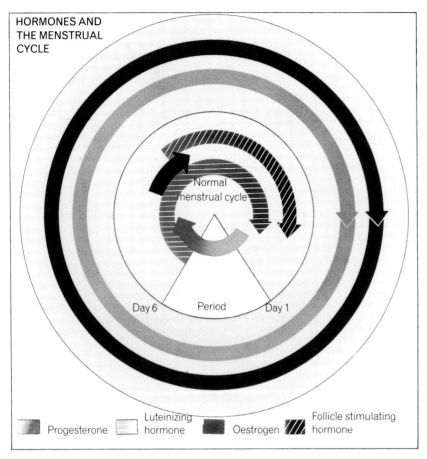

HORMONES AND THE MENSTRUAL CYCLE

Normal menstrual cycle

Day 6   Period   Day 1

Progesterone   Luteinizing hormone   Oestrogen   Follicle stimulating hormone

During normal menstrual cycles, follicle stimulating hormone (FSH) and luteinizing hormone [LH] activate the ovary's production of progesterone and oestrogen (top)

Definition of any ovulation defect depends greatly on accurate record keeping by the woman and her doctor

Ovulation problems

It is the area of ovulation, detection and induction which has seen most progress in the last few years, with much benefit to the older woman. The quality of ovulation is the likely determining factor as the menopause approaches. The precise identification of these problems becomes the single most important contribution in restoring fertility to women in this age group.

The release of the ovum from the mature follicle and its collection by the fimbria of the Fallopian tube has already been described (*see* p. 34). The process can be intensively investigated and errors corrected. The basal body temperature chart gives a guide to the production of progesterone, the peculiar feature of the corpus luteum. It will readily be appreciated however, that the temperature chart is a very crude test, since a woman's temperature depends on so many other factors. More precise information about the hormone progesterone can be obtained by sampling the blood four and eight days after the expected time of ovulation.

There is no absolute agreement on the levels of progesterone necessary for conception. Three states can be recognised – une-

quivocally normal progesterones, progesterones clearly incompatible with ovulation and progesterones which are border-line. This last condition, the inadequate luteal phase, commonly seems to occur in the last ten years of menstrual life. Paradoxically, it is more difficult to treat than anovulation.

Where an ovulation problem exists, a careful search should be made through the other hormonal systems since a defect in one of them (such as the thyroid) can upset the balance. The inappropriate production of the other hormones such as prolactin (the milk-producing hormone) and the male hormone also interfere with ovulation. Where one of these can be demonstrated as responsible, the results of treatment are excellent. It is the inadequate luteal phase, in the presence of otherwise normal endocrinology which proves most obstinate.

Treatment of ovulation problems

The principal of treatment is to boost the communication between the hypothalamus and the ovary. The hypothalamous depends on information from the ovary in the form of oestrogen production. Two approaches to treatment are possible. Drugs which interfere with the oestrogen 'message' may be used to increase the level of activity in the hypothalamus and pituitary. Drugs such as Cyclofenil and Clomiphene act in this way. They are sufficiently similar to oestrogen to occupy the special receptors in the hypothalamus which oestrogen normally activates. The drug occupies the receptor but fails to transmit the message. The net result is that the hypothalamus perceives the ovary to be inactive and increases its output of FSH.

In some women this is insufficient, because the basic defect is in the hypothalamus or the pituitary. In these circumstances, the injection of FSH provides a solution. Pergonal, produced from the urine of menopausal women (which contains high levels of FSH produced in a forlorn attempt to stimulate the unresponsive ovary) has been successfully employed; unfortunately it has a serious potential to over-stimulate the ovary and produce multiple ovulation. It also contains high levels of LH. More recently, FSH has been successfully separated from LH and pure FSH (Metrodin) has become available. This is particularly useful for women suffering from poly-cystic ovary syndrome, in which characteristically high levels of LH persist throughout the menstrual cycle; this is associated with high levels of male hormone produced by the ovary because of a biochemical fault.

Towards the middle of the menstrual cycle, the release of LH from the pituitary depends

PARTS OF THE BODY WHICH AFFECT MENSTRUATION

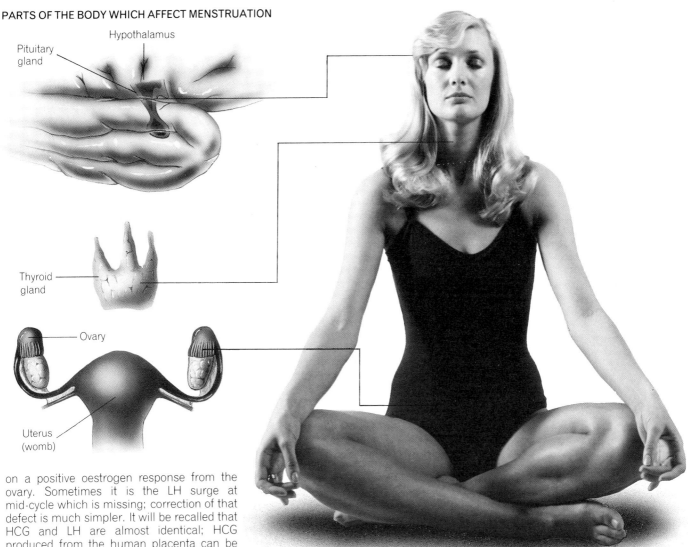

Hypothalamus

Pituitary
gland

Thyroid
gland

Ovary

Uterus
(womb)

on a positive oestrogen response from the ovary. Sometimes it is the LH surge at mid-cycle which is missing; correction of that defect is much simpler. It will be recalled that HCG and LH are almost identical; HCG produced from the human placenta can be injected as a substitute for LH.

Most ovulation defects can be corrected by a combination of such biochemical re-arrangements; the essential pre-requisite is the accurate definition of the defect. This is often laborious, expensive and time-consuming; it requires a degree of commit-ment on the part of the woman and the doctor if success is to be achieved. Record-keeping must be accurate and the drugs must be taken at precisely the right time on exactly the correct day. The busy professional or busi-ness woman in her late 30s may find this difficult. The infertility clinic which operates only five days a week is a serious obstacle to treatment.

Alternative treatment for problems

Recently it has become clear that the bioche-mistry may be correct but the ovum never released or never picked up successfully by the fimbria. These problems can now be investigated by ultrasound techniques which can visualise the release of the ovum from the follicle. Correction is more difficult; some-times the defect must be by-passed by the artificial collection of eggs and their subse-quent replacement (see p. 48).

The Fallopian tube

Damage to a Fallopian tube and an obstruc-tion to the passage of the egg is usually the result of previous pelvic infection. The single most important antecedent event is an in-fected pregnancy; sexually transmitted pelvic infection and previous surgery to the Fallopian tube or ovary are other important causes. Occasionally, disease elsewhere in the pelvis (such as a ruptured appendix) may be re-sponsible. Such conditions are uncommon in teenagers, but with the passage of time the

Many parts of a woman's body can affect menstruation: the hypothalamus in the brain controls the 'menstrual clock' and disorders of the pituitary or thyroid glands can cause problems in the uterus or ovaries

opportunity for such infections increases; the maximum incidence occurs in the late 30s. Investigation is by laparoscopy, a technique in which a telescope is passed through the umbilicus to allow the surgeon to visualise the pelvic organs. By passing a dye through the uterus and into the Fallopian tubes, the patency of the Fallopian tubes can be established; that is, it can be seen if there is an obstruction. The investigation is superior to older techniques since it also allows the examiner to investigate the ovary and the fimbria of the Fallopian tubes. The sticking together of adjacent pelvic organs (adhesions) may prevent the passage of the ovum into the tube, even when the tube is patent.

Surgery for the correction of obstruction is a possibility; relatively new surgical techniques, including microsurgery, are a great improvement on the cruder old-fashioned methods. They are all, nevertheless, subject to the criticism that surgery itself produces adhesions and results are often disappointing. It is particularly in this group of older women that fertilization outside the body (invitro fertilization) is most applicable.

Endometriosis

Endometriosis is found in 20 per cent of infertile women who are in their late 30s. It is a poorly understood disease; still more difficult to understand is how it causes infertility.

When endometrium is shed at menstruation, it normally travels downwards, through the cervix and vagina, with menstrual blood. Some of the menstrual flow travels upwards through the Fallopian tubes and spills back into the abdominal cavity. A portion of the endometrial tissue may be implanted into adjacent organs, where it begins to grow in the form of small cysts. At the end of each menstrual cycle, this endometrium is shed and bleeds, and the cysts become larger in the process. Many months of menstruation are necessary in order to create the favourable circumstances for this disease; it therefore reaches its zenith in the late 30s. Usually, the Fallopian tube remains unaffected; although the disease usually affects the ovaries, ovulation may be unimpaired. Quite why it causes infertility is unclear. Perhaps it does not; it may just be that endometriosis occurs more frequently in infertile women because while other women are becoming pregnant, the infertile woman menstruates every month. Perhaps because it diminishes menstruation, the contraceptive pill appears to reduce the incidence of endometriosis compared with other methods of birth control.

Whatever the explanation, endometriosis in association with infertility often proves a difficult obstacle. Treatment of the endometriosis by drugs or surgery sometimes results in the correction of infertility, but the results of treatment are disappointing. Paradoxically, the one condition which normally successfully treats endometriosis is pregnancy. Because endometriosis depends upon regular hormonal stimulus for its continuation, the condition always gets better at the menopause. The only certain way of diagnosing the condition is by laparoscopy.

Unexplained infertility

When all the investigations have been performed, for 10 per cent of couples, even with the most sophisticated methods, there appears to be no explanation for their infertility. Sometimes, the doctor will suggest that no treatment be undertaken and that the couple should await spontaneous pregnancy. Various empirical treatments have been attempted in the past, but the results of such treatments have produced success only in the same portion as appears to occur naturally.

During a laparoscopy, the abdomen is inflated with gas (below) and the laparoscope is inserted (bottom) to illuminate the reproductive organs. Note that the point of entry of the needle may vary from that shown – some doctors prefer to insert it closer to the pelvic bone

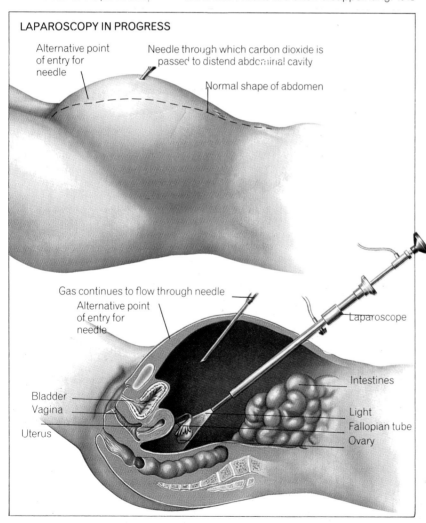

LAPAROSCOPY IN PROGRESS

Alternative point of entry for needle

Needle through which carbon dioxide is passed to distend abdominal cavity

Normal shape of abdomen

Gas continues to flow through needle

Alternative point of entry for needle

Laparoscope

Bladder
Vagina
Uterus

Intestines

Light
Fallopian tube
Ovary

NORMAL AND INFECTED FALLOPIAN TUBES

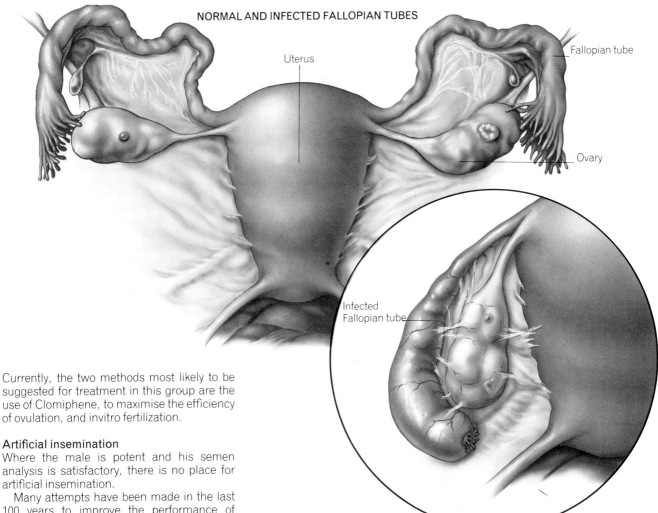

Uterus

Fallopian tube

Ovary

Infected
Fallopian tube

Currently, the two methods most likely to be suggested for treatment in this group are the use of Clomiphene, to maximise the efficiency of ovulation, and invitro fertilization.

Artificial insemination

Where the male is potent and his semen analysis is satisfactory, there is no place for artificial insemination.

Many attempts have been made in the last 100 years to improve the performance of sub-fertile semen. They have all proved disappointing and there seems to be very little, if any, place for artificial insemination using the semen of a sub-fertile partner. The doctor who abrogates the male partner's role in insemination must justify his interference; the result may be seriously to diminish the man's perception of his sexual identity.

The concentration of sperm throughout the ejaculate is uneven. The first millilitre contains many more sperm than the four or five millilitres that follow. This has lead to the suggestion that the freezing and pooling of split ejaculate might improve a sub-fertile male's chances of impregnation. It sounds a good idea, but unfortunately it does not work – at least it does not produce more pregnancies than the 10 or 20 per cent which would occur in any group of infertile patients without treatment. One of the reasons for this may be that the technique involves the deep-freezing of semen, which inevitably interferes with its quality; there may also be other factors in the seminal fluid not as yet understood, that interfere with the performance of sperm.

Where the man has no sperm, or such small numbers as to be irrelevant, artificial insemination by sperm from an anonymous donor (AID) may be the solution. This is a very delicate and personal decision for any couple to make; counselling is an essential prerequisite. Decision-making, however, is the most difficult part of the procedure. The actual insemination is simplicity itself and the only real justification for the doctor's involvement is to preserve the anonymity of the donor. Results of treatment are good but not quite as good as might be expected. There seems to be a higher incidence of infertility in the partners of infertile males – a phenomenomen which is as yet incompletely explained. The average time taken for successful conception is four inseminations (four menstrual cycles); if success has not been achieved after six, the woman's fertility should be intensively investigated immediately.

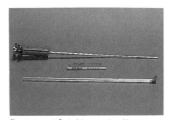

During artificial insemination a long, thin plastic tube is attached to a syringe to introduce sperm into the vagina

The illustration (top) shows normal female reproductive organs. A pelvic infection can produce large amounts of a clear, watery fluid that accumulates in the Fallopian tube, causing distension (inset); the distension may persist after the infection has cleared up, resulting in a blocked tube

In-vitro fertilization

Since July 1978 and the birth of Louise Brown, the practice of in-vitro fertilization (IVF) has spread throughout the developed world. For women whose Fallopian tubes have been irreparably damaged, or previously removed, it is the only solution. Other problems may also be overcome by this technique. Those women in whom the egg is successfully produced but not effectively released or collected by the Fallopian tube; those men in whom sperm are produced in adequate numbers but have poor motility; women with endometriosis; in all of these IVF offers some hope of success. Some centres are also prepared to take on couples with idiopathic infertility, since no other treatment is available for them.

The technique involves the induction of super ovulation by the use of drugs such as Pergonal, Metrodin and Clomiphene. Several eggs are then simultaneously produced and can be recovered, usually by laparoscopy. More recently, other techniques involving the insertion of a needle under ultrasound control have been introduced; these are particularly useful in women whose pelvic anatomy is so disorganised that even laparoscopy could not successfully reach the ovum.

Once recovered, the ovum is incubated in the laboratory and fertilized by the partner's (or if necessary a donor's) semen. The embryo is then replaced in the woman's uterus and pregnancy proceeds as normal.

As yet, the results of IVF have not exceeded the spontaneous cure rate of 10-20 per cent. It is, however, used only in circumstances where infertility has been subjected to rigorous investigation and previous treatment without success; results are improving all the time and there is every expectation that this trend will continue. Age is, however, a prob-

lem. Most centres will not accept women for this technique over the age of 40. The reason is the practical one that for these women the results are very poor. The problem is again that of achieving successful ovulation in a woman who has only a very few ova remaining in the ovaries.

General principles

To the infertile woman in her mid 30s, the situation often seems to be an urgent crisis. Not only is she all too conscious of time running out; her disappointment at failing to conceive may be tinged with regret about the postponement of pregnancy or perhaps earlier termination. The result is a rapidly increasing anxiety, perhaps even an obsessional neurosis about her infertility. The stress of

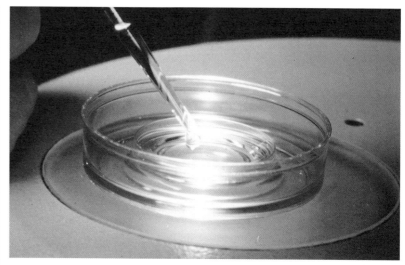

Below left: A phial of human sperm is removed from a flask of liquid nitrogen at the in-vitro fertilization unit in London's Cromwell Hospital, where it was labelled and frozen immediately after ejaculation. Below right, a technician examines a petri dish in which two or three ova (eggs) have been mixed with the sperm, to determine whether successful fertilization has occurred

Top right: Natalie Potter, one of many healthy babies born by process of in-vitro fertilization in recent years, with her proud parents

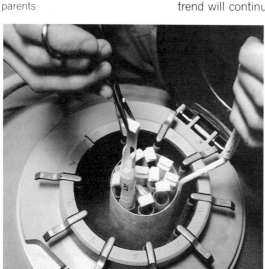

such a distracted state of mind probably makes its own contribution to infertility, disrupting hypothalamic function and interfering with ovulation. The only cure for the distress is pregnancy; continuing failure exacerbates the problem.

There is no denying this vicious circle; there is no easy solution to it. The anxious infertile woman in her middle 30s deserves speedy and thorough investigation. No time should be wasted in eliminating those causes which can readily be identified. If, as seems disproportionately common, the infertility is idiopathic, a short trial of Clomiphene and HCG is worthwhile to maximise ovulation. Thereafter, serious consideration by the doctor and couple should be given to the possibility of IVF before it is too late.

TERMINATION OF PREGNANCY

Some 160,000 pregnancies are terminated each year in England and Wales: of these some 45,000 are in women over the age of 30; two-thirds are married. (Abortion Statistics 1983 for England and Wales. HMSO).

Under the 1967 Abortion Act pregnancy may be terminated on the certification of two registered medical practitioners. There are two main grounds on which they may reach their opinion. The first concerns the life, physical or mental health of the pregnant woman or any of her existing children.

The risk of continuation must be 'greater than if the pregnancy were terminated'; since statistically termination in the first half of pregnancy is *always* safer than delivery at term, this clause is wide enough to allow abortion in any circumstances in which the woman wants it, particularly since the Act specifically allows the woman's 'actual or reasonable foreseeable environment' to be taken into account. Although the draughtsmen of the Act never intended abortion on demand to be legal, that is what they achieved.

The second justification for abortion is that there is 'a substantial risk that if the child were born it would suffer from such physical or mental abnormalities as to be seriously handicapped.' It is this which becomes particularly important for the over-30s.

Many foetal abnormalities are discovered late, and there is a gestation limit to abortion. As the Act does not specify a limit it implies that abortion up to 28 weeks is legal. In practice, since the Lane Committee reported to Parliament in 1974, responsible doctors have followed the Committee's recommendation that the limit should be 24 weeks. In any case, the occasional foetus survives at 24 weeks and a doctor terminating pregnancy after that time might be in danger from the Infant Life Preservation Act (1929).

Reasons for termination of pregnancy
The vast majority of pregnancies are terminated for reasons relating to the health of the mother. Health, in this context, is probably more concerned with the mother's social circumstances than with actual physical disease. Some 85 per cent of all terminations fall into this category. There are very few instances in which pregnancy must be terminated for medical reasons in a woman who would prefer to continue. Only two per cent of abortions are certified as indicated on the grounds of foetal handicap; most of this small group occur in the over-35 age group. The foetal abnormalities are not discovered until late in the pregnancy; therefore the pregnancy must often be terminated at 18 or even 20 weeks gestation. Newer techniques are now developing which will eventually facilitate earlier diagnosis for foetal abnormality – at perhaps eight or nine weeks. (*See* p 67.) At present, however, these are only in the developmental stage, and for the next few years late termination of pregnancy on the grounds of foetal handicap will continue.

Methods of termination
The chief determining factor in the choice of method is the size of the pregnancy. In order to empty the uterus, the cervix must be dilated sufficiently to allow the passage of the largest part of the foetus – the head. As a rough guide, the diameter of the foetal head may be regarded as equivalent in millimetres to the length of the pregnancy in weeks (from the last menstrual period). It is necessary to dilate the cervix to about 2 mm less than the diameter of the head to empty the uterus.

During the normal operation of dilation and curettage (D&C), the non-pregnant cervix can easily be dilated without injury to 10 mm. It follows, therefore, that a pregnancy in the first three months can be readily terminated by a similar process. In the second three months of pregnancy the situation becomes more complicated.

Termination in the first three months
In pregnancy, the cervix is rather softer than normal and can be dilated to 12 mm without

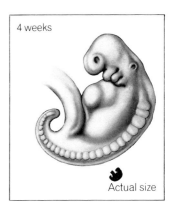

4 weeks

Actual size

The foetus at four weeks old

undue resistance. By the use of a flexible plastic cannula, which is similar to a drinking straw, the pregnancy can be evacuated by the application of suction. The operation is technically very easy, safe and almost painless. If the cannula employed is no larger than 6 or 8 mm, general anaesthesia is usually unnecessary, particularly in a woman who has previously born children. Even in women who have not, the procedure can usually be performed with no more discomfort than is experienced during a painful period – given proper explanation by the doctor and co-operation by the patient. Lack of skill or patience on the part of the doctor or unusual apprehension on the part of the patient may demand general anaesthesia. When larger cannula are employed, general anaesthesia is often necessary.

Termination in the second three months

Once the pregnancy has reached the fourteenth week, dilation of the cervix to allow evacuation of the uterus presents a problem. Because diagnosis of foetal abnormality is often delayed until the sixteenth week, these operations in particular present difficulties. There have always been a few doctors who have been prepared to extend the dilation and evacuation method into the second three months. The operation calls for great skill, and many doctors and theatre nurses find it aesthetically objectionable. For many years it was considered dangerous to dilate the cervix to the necessary 16-18 mm to achieve the result. Several recent developments have changed this view. Two techniques are now available which allow for easier (and therefore less damaging) dilation of the cervix: the application of a prostaglandin pessary into the vagina which makes the cervix soft and pliable; and the insertion of an expanding hygroscopic rod (lamicel) into the cervix before the operation, which often makes dilation unnecessary. With these techniques, more surgeons are prepared to terminate late pregnancies by the vaginal route, particularly since the results of the alternative method have proved disappointing.

The alternative approach in the second three months is to induce labour. Various drugs have been used to do this, some of which have proved dangerous. The most popular current method is to inject a mixture of two substances through the abdominal wall and into the uterine cavity. The first substance is a strong solution of urea (which kills the foetus) and a small quantity of the drug prostaglandin which produces intense uterine contractions. The labour which follows is extremely painful but very efficient; it achieves evacuation of the uterus within about eight

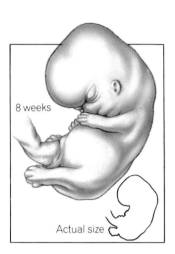

8 weeks

Actual size

The foetus at eight weeks

METHODS OF TERMINATION

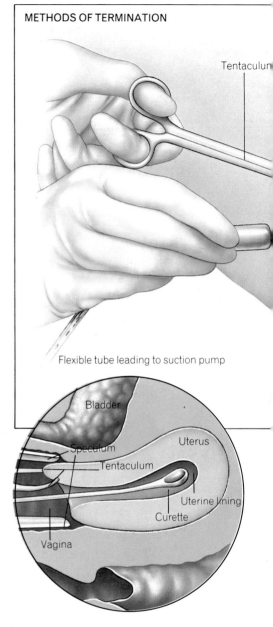

Tentaculum

Flexible tube leading to suction pump

Bladder

Uterus

Speculum

Tentaculum

Uterine lining

Curette

Vagina

hours. The procedure is distressing for the patient but can be made more acceptable by the provision of epidural analgesia. An alternative technique is to apply a prostaglandin solution through a catheter passed through the cervix. This produces uterine contractions and achieves evacuation, but it may result in the delivery of a live foetus.

The advantage of the prostaglandin method was thought to be the prevention of cervical injury and a reduction in the failure of any subsequent pregnancy. Recent surveys have been disappointing. Dilation and evacuation under general anaesthesia as a short procedure appears to be only a little worse in this

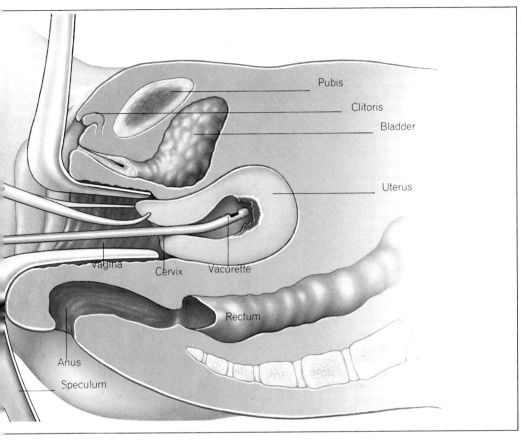

Pubis

Clitoris

Bladder

Uterus

Vagina

Cervix

Vacurette

Rectum

Anus

Speculum

Early abortions can be carried out by dilation and evacuation (left). The vagina is opened with a speculum and the exact depth of the uterus measured. The cervix is then gently opened. A cannula holds it open and the tip of a vacurette is inserted. This is attached to a suction pump which frees and draws out the foetal material, along with the after birth. Dilation and curretage (below left) is done in the same way except that a curette loosens the foetal material, which is removed from the uterus with forceps

respect than prolonged labour.

Surgical incision into the uterus (hysterotomy), as in Caesarean section, is possible at all stages of pregnancy. Except in very unusual circumstances it is never justified and always more dangerous. Quite apart from its increased risks and prolonged hospitalization, it leaves scars on the uterus.

Complications of abortion

In the first three months of pregnancy, complications are rare, particularly if general anaethesia can be avoided. The commonest problem is the necessity for a second evacuation. Estimates for this occurence vary, but between two and five per cent would be a reasonable guess. When the products of conception are left behind, there is an increased risk of infection; infection may occasionally occur even with complete evacuation. Haemorrhage is uncommon but it increases with the length of pregnancy. The most dramatic complication is perforation of the uterus, but this is very rare, and with an experienced doctor should occur no more than once or twice per thousand operations.

In the second three months, all of the complications listed above will tend to increase, particularly the risk of haemorrhage.

The main concern in this group, however, is the fate of subsequent pregnancies. If the cervix is stretched to the point where the deeper muscles are torn, it may be incapable of holding in a subsequent pregnancy. Figures are at present impossible to obtain because of the lack of follow up. The danger undoubtedly exists and probably increases with the length of the pregnancy; it certainly increases with the number of abortions.

Psychological effects

The psychological effects of abortion should not be underestimated. It is difficult always to distinguish the harmful effects of abortion from the harmful effects of the circumstances which lead to it; no abortion is undertaken lightly or for trivial reasons. Counselling in advance is the single most important preventive measure. Doctors make poor counsellors; a woman seeking termination of pregnancy should have the opportunity to discuss her decision with a counsellor who can be compassionate but detached, whose skills are directed towards helping the woman to assess all the factors concerned. There will usually be grief, recrimination and regret; if these can be dealt with in advance the psychological sequelae are minimised.

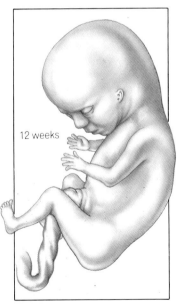

12 weeks

The foetus at 12 weeks

Chapter 3

PREGNANCY, LABOUR AND BIRTH

Confirmation of a planned and often long-awaited pregnancy is a joyful event – a time of celebration and much excitement. During the coming months the woman and her partner will be drawn closer together by their concern about and fascination with the developing foetus and the changes that take place in the woman's body. There will be endless discussions about life after the baby is born, what the baby will look like and so on. If the parents are wise they will also discuss together, and with the obstetric staff, worries and anxieties they have about pregnancy, labour and the health of the baby.

For the older couple, anxieties may be greater than those of their younger counterparts, as they will appreciate that there may be age-related problems both in pregnancy and labour. Yet they should gain confidence from the fact that doctors, with the aid of modern technology and science, will do all that is possible to minimise any risks and try to ensure the birth of a normal and healthy baby.

The following sections of this chapter discuss the potential problems that may arise in the older woman during pregnancy and birth, but always with the proviso that in the majority of cases the outlook for normal pregnancy and delivery is very satisfactory. Nevertheless, as elsewhere in this publication, it is stressed that women and their partners should be realistic about what pregnancy in the older primagravida entails, so that they can have as fulfilling a pregnancy and labour as possible.

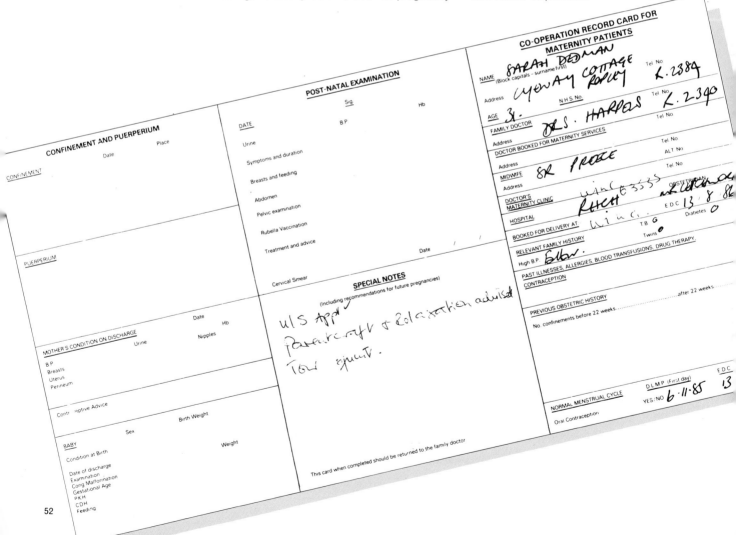

PREGNANCY AND ANTENATAL CARE

One hundred years ago, the maternal mortality rate (mothers dying during pregnancy and labour) was 650 per 100,000. Today the rate is 11 per 100,000 and this includes those women dying, from whatever cause, within one year of pregnancy. There are many factors to explain this great improvement, including the use of drugs such as antibiotics, blood transfusion, safer anaesthesia and a great number of other scientific and technical advances. However the advent of antenatal care has also made an important contribution.

In the 1890s, antenatal care as we know it did not exist, and most pregnant women presented themselves to a midwife or doctor only when labour was established. This obviously meant that complicating factors were often not discovered until a very late stage – possibly too late for mother or baby.

The whole essence of antenatal care, which had its beginnings in the early 1900s, is the prevention of pregnancy and labour problems, and early detection and treatment of those that arise.

The booking visit
Once a pregnancy has been confirmed by a pregnancy test or ultrasound examination, it is usual for the woman's GP to make arrangements for an initial consultation with the obstetric team at the local hospital. This is often referred to as the booking visit; it usually entails a visit to the hospital antenatal clinic, but in some areas community antenatal care is being developed where the consultation is carried out in the GP's surgery or health centre. The booking visit is probably the most important consultation during pregnancy, since it sets the pattern for pregnancy care. For women aged 30 or over it is particularly important that the consultation is carried out early in pregnancy (preferably prior to eight weeks gestation) to anticipate any tests which may be needed to ascertain foetal normality.

Continuity in antenatal care is achieved by way of the co-operation card. This is kept by pregnant woman and filled in by the doctor, midwife, and any specialists she might see during pregnancy. The card is helpful in that it gives an 'overview' of the pregnancy

The visit allows the woman and the medical staff to discuss and investigate all aspects of health in order to try to predict any possible complicating factors in pregnancy and labour. The woman is given a thorough physical examination, including a vaginal examination and various blood tests. A midwife, obstetrician or trainee in either field then takes the woman's medical history, during which the woman is asked about any serious, or potentially serious, conditions such as cardiac disease, diabetes, long-standing kidney disease, malignant disease or other chronic medical condition. The object of this is to gain knowledge of any facts that may be relevant to the forthcoming pregnancy. Many questions are asked of a personal nature that may at first appear unnecessary; they include details of the woman's age, country of origin, marital status and occupation if working. The woman is also asked about her intentions to continue work throughout pregnancy and whether or not she plans to return to work following the birth. Details about her partner's occupation and the medical history of her own and her partner's family are also taken. The doctor will want to know about any hereditary disease or disorder and conditions such as sickle cell anaemia, and about multiple pregnancies or any abnormality of pregnancy on either side of the family.

The doctor should also be made aware of any previous anaesthetics and operations, especially of any operations on the uterus – hysterotomy, myomectomy or Caesarean section – as these may directly influence the management of labour.

Once the history has been completed, it is then necessary to enquire about the present pregnancy. Is it a planned pregnancy? Is the mother well supported at home? Did it take some time to achieve conception? If this is a first pregnancy and the woman is in the older age groups, why was pregnancy delayed? All these factors must be taken into account in order to understand, or to go some way towards understanding, the woman's feelings about her pregnancy. If she is terribly anxious, for example, it is vital to know this at an early stage.

The doctor will want to know details of the last menstrual period in order to calculate the expected date of delivery (EDD). The doctor cannot give an expected date of delivery with certainty if the period was not on time, if it was not normal, if the woman's menstrual cycle is usually irregular or if there has been bleeding since the last menstrual period. In such cases the EDD will be confirmed by ultrasound scan.

If, however, the last period was normal and on time in a regular cycle, then the EDD will be estimated using Naegele's equation: LMP (last menstrual period) + 1 week – 3 months + 1 year = EDD. It must be stressed however that only five to ten percent of women actually deliver on the estimated date, but 80 per cent do so within two weeks either side of that

A vaginal examination is carried out during the first antenatal visit to confirm the pregnancy and check the health of the reproductive organs

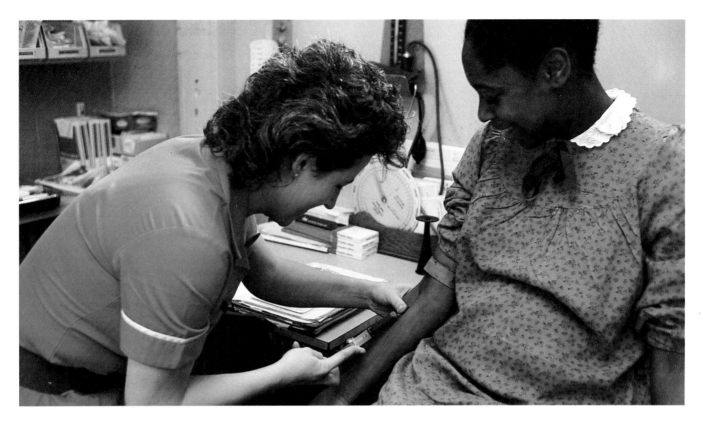

date. The pregnancy is therefore calculated to last 40 weeks from the last period – that is, usually 38 weeks from conception. Many women prefer to think in terms of months, and a pregnancy is therefore ten lunar months (40 weeks) but nine calendar months.

Even with accurate dating, it is advisable to confirm the gestational age and the normality of the pregnancy with an ultrasound scan at approximately 16-18 weeks. (See pp 63-65.)

The physical examination
A thorough physical examination is carried out to confirm good general health; particular attention is paid to taking the woman's blood pressure, examining the breasts and giving a vaginal examination.

A vaginal examination should be performed for the following reasons: to confirm the pregnancy and its gestational age; to exclude cysts or other pelvic swelling; to estimate pelvic size; to detect any vaginal infection; to inspect the cervix; and to take a cervical smear.

Some women are reluctant to be examined vaginally for various reasons, but a gentle vaginal examination can elucidate all the necessary information without putting the pregnancy at risk.

Attention will also be paid to weight, height and the testing of urine. The urine test is done to exclude urinary infection, and, later in

pregnancy, to give an early indication of toxaemia or the development of diabetes.

Blood tests
Following the physical examination, some blood will be taken for testing. The woman's blood group can then be determined – A, B, O, AB, and the Rh type, Rh positive or Rh negative. The sample will also be tested to determine whether there are any antibodies present in the maternal blood that might affect the foetus. If antibodies are present then further blood samples will be required as pregnancy continues; however, problems arising from antibodies are uncommon and usually only occur if their level rises during the pregnancy.

An Rh negative blood group is not abnormal – it is found in 15 per cent of women – and will only be potentially harmful in future pregnancies if the partner and the foetus are Rhesus positive.

As well as determining the blood group, the blood sample will also be used to determine haemoglobin levels. This will indicate whether the woman is anaemic and whether iron therapy is required. Not all pregnant women need iron supplements during their pregnancy, but it is almost impossible to predict those who will become anaemic; some doctors therefore feel that it is much safer to prescribe iron tablets after the first trimester rather than

During the booking visit a blood sample is taken to test for antibodies in the mother's blood that may affect the foetus; to determine the level of haemoglobin; and to detect disease. The sample will also be used to determine the woman's blood group and RH type

treat an established anaemia later. However, those women who wish to avoid taking iron supplements unless absolutely necessary can take preventive measures by ensuring that their diet includes iron-rich foods. (*See* pp 70-71.)

A more detailed examination of the haemoglobin (electrophoresis) will also be done. This will determine whether the haemoglobin is normal or abnormal, as for example in sickle cell anaemia or thalassaemia. It is important to detect the presence of abnormal haemoglobin early in pregnancy as it will then be possible to investigate the pregnancy and check on the haematological normality of the foetus. In such cases it is also essential to check the father's blood as well to accurately predict the extent of the problem.

Blood will also be tested for various other diseases such as syphilis, hepatitis and rubella. Rubella can be prevented by immunisation and ideally every woman should have her rubella status checked prior to pregnancy and have immunisation if necessary. (*See* p 26.)

In most clinics, a blood test for alphafetoprotein is also performed at 16 weeks gestation to screen for spina bifida and other foetal abnormalities. For this test it is necessary to have ultrasound confirmation of foetal age in order to interpret the alphafetoprotein result correctly, and both the scan and the blood test can be done at the same time. It is important to realise that a higher than normal level of alphafetoprotein does *not* indicate foetal abnormality; it merely indicates that further investigation is necessary to clarify the situation. This will take the form of a detailed scan, perhaps combined with amniocentesis. Only approximately five per cent of cases in which there are high levels of alphafetoprotein will eventually show foetal abnormality; in such cases termination of pregnancy may be offered if appropriate.

It has recently been found that there is a correlation with abnormally low alphafetoprotein levels and Down's syndrome, but low levels do not necessarily mean that Down's syndrome is present; it only indicates that further investigations are required to exclude the possibility.

Screening tests for Down's syndrome – amniocentesis or chorionic villus sampling (*see* pp 65-68) – are performed at varying maternal ages in this country, depending on the regional policy. (It is a saluatory thought that most Down's syndrome babies are born to women under 35 because of the vastly greater numbers of these women giving birth compared to older women, although older women are still more at risk statistically.) It is possible that the addition of alphafetoprotein screening may give valuable assistance in the antenatal diagnosis of such abnormalities.

Following the initial consultation and the appropriate tests, it will become reasonably clear whether the woman is likely to have problems with the pregnancy and/or the delivery. Appropriate arrangements for the

Women should be weighed at each visit and a record kept of any excessive gain or loss in weight. The normal overall weight gain during pregnancy is about 11 kg (24 lb). The contribution to this made by the growing foetus, placenta and so on is shown in the chart (right), together with the average amount of weight gained week by week

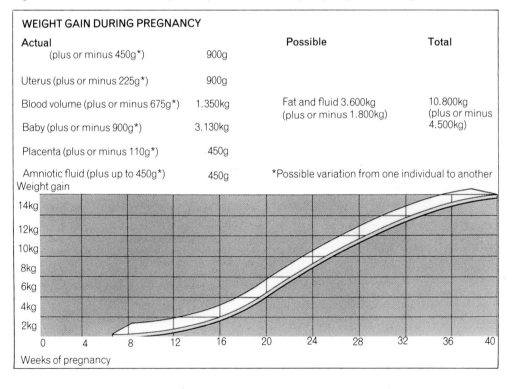

WEIGHT GAIN DURING PREGNANCY

Actual		Possible	Total
(plus or minus 450g*)	900g		
Uterus (plus or minus 225g*)	900g		
Blood volume (plus or minus 675g*)	1.350kg	Fat and fluid 3.600kg (plus or minus 1.800kg)	10.800kg (plus or minus 4.500kg)
Baby (plus or minus 900g*)	3.130kg		
Placenta (plus or minus 110g*)	.450g		
Amniotic fluid (plus up to 450g*)	450g	*Possible variation from one individual to another	

Weight gain

14kg
12kg
10kg
8kg
6kg
4kg
2kg

0 4 8 12 16 20 24 28 32 36 40
Weeks of pregnancy

best type of antenatal care and the place of delivery can then be arranged. It should be obvious, for example, that a woman with diabetes or cardiac disease needs careful antenatal care from an appropriate specialist as well as her obstetrician. Any other risk factors demand perhaps a more diligent approach to antenatal care. These other risk factors may include short stature, maternal age over 35 (especially over 40), previous relevant operations and so on.

Antenatal care

The decision concerning the type of antenatal care should be made by the woman and obstetrician together, combining the medical reasoning of the doctor and the wishes of the woman. Antenatal care may be undertaken by an obstetric team in a hospital clinic, by the GP or a combination of both. Delivery may be under the guidance of the obstetric team or under the supervision of the GP in hospital – occasionally it may take place in the woman's home.

Some doctors believe all deliveries should be conducted in hospital rather than at home, on the basis that even the most normal pregnancy and delivery can give rise to an emergency at the last moment, for example by the lack of suitable support for the resuscitation of a newborn infant in distress. There is, however, a great deal of conflicting opinion concerning the merits of hospital versus home confinement, so every woman should discuss the matter fully with her medical attendants.

As far as the woman over 30 having her first child is concerned, there is little doubt that it is better for her to have antenatal care under the hospital team, with the involvement of her GP where appropriate. Confinement should also be in hospital and be overseen by the hospital obstetric team. The course of a first pregnancy and labour is unpredictable and there should be expert antenatal supervision in order to anticipate any problems that may arise. For example it is vital to pick up the early signs of toxaemia, and it is important to predict the long and difficult labour or the foetus that is not growing as well as it should at an early stage.

At each subsequent antenatal visit various examinations are made to ensure that the pregnancy is progressing normally. In most clinics women are weighed at each consultation – an overall weight gain of around 11 kg (24 lb) is normal for pregnancy, although there is considerable variation within the normal range. For example it is quite possible (especially if a woman is overweight at the commencement of pregnancy) to actually lose weight during a pregnancy and still be obstet-

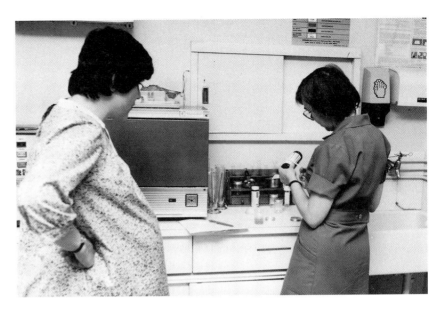

rically healthy. Yet some women find it impossible not to gain an excessive amount of weight, usually due to fat or fluid retention. Normally however, with sensible dietary advice, weight gain should not be excessive.

By weighing the pregnant woman at each visit it may be possible to be forewarned about an obstetric complication – excessive weight gain may herald impending pre-eclamptic toxaemia, or weight loss may indicate poor foetal growth. Ideally a woman should always be weighed on the same scales with the same weight of clothing on, but this is not always possible.

It will also be necessary to provide a urine specimen at each consultation. The specimen taken at the booking visit is sent to the laboratory to screen for urinary tract infection, but at subsequent consultations a dip stick test is all that is necessary. This is done to test for the presence of sugar or protein which should normally be absent from the urine. The presence of sugar may indicate the necessity to arrange further tests to exclude the development of a tendency to diabetes during pregnancy (gestational diabetes). This is commoner in overweight women, those with a family history of diabetes, those with previous large babies and those with gestational diabetes in previous pregnancies.

The presence of protein may indicate a urinary infection. These are relatively common in pregnancy and it is important to treat them promptly. Protein may also be a contaminant from a vaginal discharge, and if this is due to a specific cause (most usually a yeast infection) then this must also be treated. The most important reason for testing urine for protein however is to try to detect pre-eclamptic toxaemia in its early stages.

A sample of the woman's urine is tested at each antenatal visit to determine whether sugar and protein are present. If sugar is found in the urine it may indicate the development of gestational diabetes; protein in urine may be symptomatic of a urinary infection or pre-eclamptic toxaemia

As well as being weighed and having a urine sample tested it is usual to have blood pressure measured. Normally there is a physiological fall in blood pressure in the second trimester but blood pressure should still remain normal throughout the early and later pregnancy. A rise in blood pressure may indicate impending toxaemia and should always be taken seriously. There are obviously other causes of raised blood pressure in pregnancy and these should be excluded. Blood pressure is more likely to be raised in the older primigravid patient and if continuously or excessively raised constitutes a real risk to both maternal and foetal well being.

An abdominal examination is performed to estimate the size of the growing uterus. There is obviously considerable normal variation in abdominal findings at a given stage of pregnancy due to variation in the woman's height, weight and so on, but it is important to know that the foetus is growing at the correct rate. An alteration in the rate of growth early in pregnancy may indicate at either extreme that the pregnancy is not viable or that there may be a multiple pregnancy. At a later stage, lack of growth of the uterus may indicate a growth-retarded foetus from placental insufficiency (*see* p 82); excessive growth may indicate a large foetus or an excess of amniotic fluid.

Movements of the foetus may be felt from around 18 weeks gestation (sometimes earlier, sometimes not until 22 weeks) and the examining hand can actually distinguish the parts of the foetal anatomy from approximately 24 weeks onwards. The foetal heart beat can be heard using a conventional foetal stethoscope from around 25-26 weeks gestation, but it may be detected earlier, at around 10 weeks, by use of sonic aid. This is obviously very useful and reassuring for the mother, particularly in cases of previous miscarriage due to failure of foetal development.

Ultrasound examination of the pregnancy is usually routinely performed at 16-18 weeks gestation to establish normality of the pregnancy and to confirm gestational age. It is the practice in some centres to repeat this at 32 weeks or so to confirm normal foetal growth and to accurately localise the final placental position in utero. There is no evidence that ultrasound is harmful to a developing pregnancy but obviously the number and timing of obstetric ultrasound examinations will be at the discretion of the obstetrician, based on sound clinical reasons for each examination that is performed.

A blood count will be checked at intervals during the pregnancy (usually four to five times) and other blood tests will be carried out as and when necessary throughout the antenatal period.

Occasionally it may be necessary to perform a vaginal examination at the antenatal visit. This is usually only done at the initial consultation for the reasons mentioned previously, and again after 36 weeks gestation when indicated, for example to confirm the presentation of the baby (head or breech), to assess the size of the pelvic bones or to examine the cervix.

As well as the procedures outlined above, the antenatal visit should be an opportunity for the woman and medical staff to communicate freely and to discuss any problems that may arise during the pregnancy. It is also terribly important that, during the pregnancy, each woman prepares for her labour in a realistic way. Most antenatal visits will be every month until 32 weeks gestation, then every two weeks, then every week after 36 weeks. Combined with these there will be antenatal, relaxation and fitness classes, all of which ensure that the woman has the best possible preparation for labour. The aim of such classes is not only to prepare the mother for a normal delivery but also to make her aware that delivery may deviate from the normal, and that when unfavourable factors prevail she will hopefully have confidence in and take advice from the obstetrician in

Technical advances in the last 20 years or so have made it possible for doctors to examine the foetus *in utero*. One of the most recent of these developments is the fetoscope (right), a telescope that can be inserted through the abdominal and uterine walls to enable the doctor to view the foetus

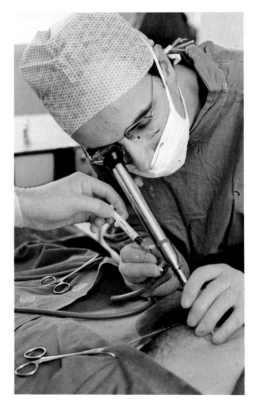

charge. Obstetricians do not interfere with labour without a good reason and women in labour must be prepared to take advice on changes in management where they are indicated for sound medical reasons and are in the best interests of herself or her baby. Therefore, an essential quality of antenatal care is that it prepares the woman for all eventualities and keeps things in their proper perspective.

The high risk pregnancy

The high risk pregnancy is a relatively recent concept. During pregnancy women are assessed according to various risk factors, and depending on the score achieved, are either allocated to high or low risk categories. If a woman is allocated to the high risk category it is because there is a likelihood that she will have a complication of pregnancy that may adversely affect her well being or the well being of the foetus. Women who are at high risk therefore need more regular antenatal consultations with specialists in obstetrics and, if relevant, other disciplines, in order to anticipate and detect problems and treat them as early as possible.

Foetal health and development can be determined in several ways. Perhaps the most important of these is by ultrasound examination. If indicated, further measures may be taken to ensure foetal normality. These may include chromosome analysis, either from a chrionic villus biopsy or by cytogenetic analysis following amniocentesis at 16-18 weeks gestation or from foetal blood supplied by fetoscopy.

Fetoscopy is the direct visualisation of the foetus by use of a small telescope inserted through the abdominal wall into the uterus. It enables foetal blood or skin samples to be taken and is extremely useful in the antenatal diagnosis of hereditary or congenital abnormalities. Obviously the above mentioned procedures are not without their complications and the reasons for their use should always be discussed in detail with the woman concerned.

Drugs in pregnancy

The use of drugs in pregnancy is a complicated subject, and one on which it is difficult to obtain accurate information due to the difficulty of investigating the effect of drugs on a woman and the foetus. When considering the effects of drugs in pregnancy the problem relates to drugs that may cause foetal abnormalities. However it must be realised that in the absence of any drug therapy, many abnormal pregnancies result. Thankfully the majority of these end in early miscarriage, but nevertheless approximately 1 in 50 neonates

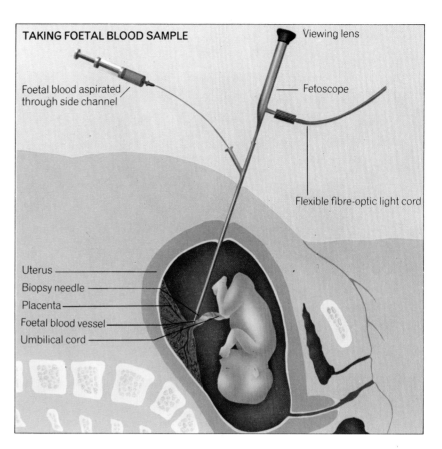

TAKING FOETAL BLOOD SAMPLE
Viewing lens
Foetal blood aspirated through side channel
Fetoscope
Flexible fibre-optic light cord
Uterus
Biopsy needle
Placenta
Foetal blood vessel
Umbilical cord

The fetoscope is introduced into the amniotic cavity to visually check foetal growth. If abnormalities are suspected, a sample of foetal blood can be aspirated through the side channel

have some major abnormality and 1 in 20 will have some degree of minor abnormality that is recognisable at birth.

Anything that may increase this overall risk should be avoided and it therefore makes sense to regard all drugs as potentially harmful in pregnancy. The most vulnerable time for the foetus is during the first ten weeks of development, and although there are few drugs that are known to cause foetal abnormalities the use of any preparations at this time should be questioned.

Vomiting may be troublesome in early, mid or late pregnancy but usually occurs in the first trimester; occasionally it is necessary to prescribe antiemetics for this, but the situation has been complicated by the implication of Debandox as a teratogenic influence. Although there is no real evidence to support this, most women assume that antiemetics are harmful. While it is preferable to avoid medicines if possible, if vomiting is severe or if maternal health is at risk then one of the commonly used antiemetics, Maxolon or Avomine, may be prescribed.

The majority of pregnant women have no need of other medications during their pregnancies. If it is necessary to take any medicine it should be prescribed after full consultation with the doctor who will naturally exhibit caution. For women with pre-existing medical conditions such as diabetes or chronic chest disease it will be necessary to take other preparations, but these are obviously required for maternal health (and thus indirectly foetal health). Well-tried preparations are safer than relatively new drugs. Any woman who is on any treatment prior to pregnancy should really consult her doctor and inform him pregnancy is intended. Current treatment would then be reviewed with pregnancy in mind.

In general terms women should avoid drugs in pregnancy unless there is good medical reason for their use and then only use preparations on medical advice.

Working women in pregnancy

Today a large proportion of women work during and after pregnancy. There are many reasons for this: it may well be financially necessary for a woman to work in order to maintain a reasonable standard of living for the family unit; it may be that she feels that there is no reason to stop working because of a pregnancy or, in some cases, the woman may be the main breadwinner and her partner may wish to stop work after the pregnancy to look after the baby.

Some employers make provision for a woman to work until a reasonable stage of pregnancy (normally 11 weeks before the birth) and return to work some time after childbirth without financial penalty. This maternity leave is obviously very useful for women who wish to pursue their careers after childbirth as it ensures their job is secure during their absence.

It is usual for a woman to work until 28 weeks of gestation and return to work some three to six months after childbirth, although there is obviously great variation in this. Many women prefer to work as long as possible during their pregnancy, feeling that, quite rightly, pregnancy is a normal sequence of physiological events and not an illness. Most doctors applaud this philosophy and could not agree more. However, it must be realised that each pregnancy is unique. No two women have identical pregnancies, either physically or emotionally, and certainly for first pregnancies it is impossible to predict in advance what the individual woman's reaction to her pregnancy will be. Pregnancy is a period of great physical and emotional change occurring over a relatively short period of time. Most women adjust to this change remarkably quickly and are able to continue their normal routine without much difficulty, but some women do experience problems that may affect their working life.

These may be major or minor disturbances and may commence early in pregnancy. A woman may have all the symptoms of early pregnancy or relatively few. Breast tenderness and frequency of micturition are common and rarely a major problem, but the nausea that accompanies early pregnancy may be a difficult problem to cope with. Of course some women do not experience nausea at all, most will have a small amount with which they can cope very well, but some women may experience an excessive amount and may vomit in the mornings or even during the entire day. It is clear that this may present problems in getting up and getting to work on time each day, and for such women it is important to have an understanding employer. In some cases vomiting is repetitive throughout the day and very difficult to deal with; this is obviously incompatible with working. Such excessive vomiting (hyperemesis gravidarum) is uncommon but when it occurs often requires treatment in hospital.

In addition to nausea and vomiting most women will feel tired during their pregnancy. This may be only in the early or later stages or during the entire pregnancy. Provided anaemia and other physical conditions have been excluded the degree of tiredness and therefore the amount of sleep and rest required will vary tremendously from individual to individual. It must be said that more women aged 35 and over will often find it physically more difficult to continue work during their pregnancy. Tiredness usually increases as the pregnancy advances and is obviously greater in certain conditions, such as a twin pregnancy.

Heartburn is another physical symptom

Pregnant women who work will need to rest during the time spent at home, so their partners (if any) should be willing to take on more than an equal share of the domestic chores

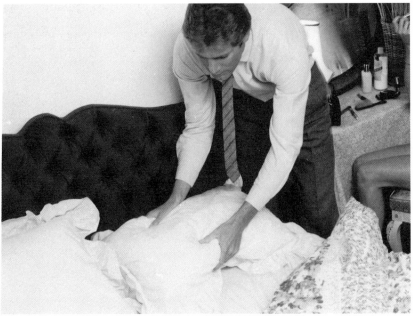

which may make life somewhat difficult, especially towards the end of pregnancy. In addition, women may suffer from backache, constipation, varicose veins, vaginal discharge and many other minor complaints which may well make life more difficult for the working woman, not forgetting, of course, her gradual change in shape.

Life would be much easier for pregnant women who work if they could continue to work as usual and rest during the time spent at home. Unfortunately most women have work to do in the house so any help from their partner with the domestic chores will be much appreciated. For some women, trying to fulfill their role at work and at home, as well as coping with pregnancy, can give rise to feelings of guilt or emotional conflict. For example they may feel that they have neither the time nor the energy to give enough attention to their relationship with their partner. The solution may be to let standards of cleanliness and so on slip a little so that the couple can spend some quiet time together.

Pregnancy can affect work, and work pregnancy, in other ways as well, and various occupations are potentially hazardous in pregnancy. Any work involving exposure to X-rays or toxic substances should be avoided; although the actual risk is minimal it is best to completely remove it. In such situations and those of physically strenuous work it may well be necessary for the employer to alter the nature of work until after the birth. In some instances this will necessitate a letter from the doctor to the employer.

It is vital that working women are diligent in their attendance at antenatal clinics to ensure that the pregnancy is progressing smoothly, although this is not always easy. Some clinics run evening clinics and this, of course, is one benefit of attending the GP's surgery rather than the hospital antenatal clinic.

Obstetric problems may alter the pattern of working so ideally there should be flexibility about the intention to work full time throughout pregnancy. For example, bleeding may occur during early pregnancy (threatened miscarriage) and the time-honoured treatment for this is bed rest. It is very difficult to say whether this is essential and whether it makes a significant difference to the outcome of the pregnancy, but to continue working and to subsequently miscarry may cause feelings of guilt. It is best therefore to cease work in the event of any bleeding early in pregnancy and to return once things have settled down. Any bleeding later in pregnancy (antepartum haemorrhage) must be taken seriously; it will almost certainly involve ceasing work. For the older woman having her first child the pregnancy may be very unpredictable and com-

plications such as toxaemia of pregnancy, intrauterine growth retardation and other problems will be more common, perhaps necessitating stopping work earlier than originally intended. Multiple pregnancy is also commoner with increasing age and this, of course, will have implications for continuing work until the birth.

Returning to work after the baby has been born can be difficult (especially if breast feeding) and many women find it physically and emotionally exhausting. Help will be needed either from a nanny, child minder, creche facilities or a relative or partner who can look after the baby while the mother works. It is impossible to predict during pregnancy what the mother's attitude will be to her baby and to returning to work afterwards, and many women who originally intended to continue work do not do so after the baby is born.

Many mothers who return to work after their baby is born rely on a registered childminder to care for their children during the day

Women's attitudes to pregnancy vary greatly, as does the level of their anxiety about labour. Although it is perfectly normal to be worried about the outcome of labour, learning about the process and about what to expect goes a long way towards alleviating fear. Any woman who is excessively anxious should discuss this with her medical attendants prior to birth

Parental anxieties

Pregnancy, however normal, is a potentially worrying time for both parents, and naturally the older the mother in a first pregnancy, the greater the worry. It would not be realistic to tell all anxious parents not to worry and that everything will be perfectly alright. Doctors are only too aware that pregnancy does not always continue without complications. It is terribly important for the whole pregnancy and delivery to be looked at realistically and in its proper perspective. The majority will be uncomplicated, but complications do occur and it is only by good antenatal care that these can be detected and minimised.

Most women who are pregnant for the first time do have anxieties about their pregnancies. The two main ones are whether the baby will be normal and whether pregnancy and delivery will be without complications. Every woman who is pregnant wants a perfect baby and is anxious about its normality. Unfortunately some babies are not born normal, but with the advent of screening tests such as amniocentesis it is becoming possible to pick up many abnormalities antenatally. Although the prospect of a termination of pregnancy is not pleasant, for some couples it is a far less traumatic event physically and emotionally than either losing a new baby or having the problems of abnormality to deal with. The answer to anxiety about the baby is that with screening tests and ultrasound examination it is uncommon for any significantly serious abnormality to be missed and that in the case of early diagnosis of foetal abnormality the possibility of termination may be discussed.

Anxieties about the pregnancy and delivery are best dealt with by diligent antenatal care and by maintaining good communication with the obstetric attendants. In this way problems of pregnancy will be minimised and anxiety about labour and birth should be alleviated by discussion and help in antenatal classes. Once again, to say glibly that all with be well is not enough. The preparation for childbirth should mean that a woman enters labour, with her partner, fully aware that she is in good hands and trusting in her attendants to look after her labour correctly. The couple should realise that although a straightforward labour and delivery is the normal course of events, in the event of any problems (which may not become apparent until well into labour) it may be necessary to deliver the baby either with forceps or by Caesarean section, and that procedures such as these or the administration of epidural anaesthesia if indicted should be seen as necessary help in the appropriate situation and not feared or considered as interference.

Worries or anxieties about pregnancy and the unborn baby are natural feelings and should be understood by the woman and her partner, and by her obstetric attendants. Pregnancy is obviously a very personal experience, but one where emotions of joy or anxiety are often much easier to manage if they are discussed openly rather than being constantly dismissed. Pregnancy is not an illness: it is probably the most important sequence of events ever to happen to a woman, especially if it occurs later in life. It is usually uncomplicated but never uneventful, and by good antenatal education and preparation combined with good obstetric care, doctors can minimise the complications and treat them when they arise. There will also be the maximum likelihood of a good healthy baby delivered in the safest possible way.

ULTRASOUND IN OBSTETRICS

Ultrasound is a method for antenatal diagnosis which was first introduced in Glasgow in the late 1950s by Professor Ian Donald. Early equipment was crude and only scant detail of the foetus could be identified, but estimates of the size of the foetus, the position of the placenta and some complications of pregnancy could be assessed. Advances in medical knowledge, and perhaps more particularly in equipment technology, have meant that ultrasound is currently widely used in antenatal care.

The nature of ultrasound

Diagnostic ultrasound uses high frequency sound waves (which vibrate beyond the audible range of human hearing) to gain information about structures within the body. There are several different types of ultrasound equipment, but those used in antenatal care fall into two main groups: pulse echo equipment, which is used to produce images of the foetus and uterine contents – often called ultrasound scanning; and Doppler equipment, which is used to obtain continuous tracings of the foetal heart rate. Doppler ultrasound is sensitive only to moving structures and may therefore detect changes in heart rate and rhythm.

Most of the equipment used for ultrasound scanning allows dynamic examination of the foetus – real time scanning. Rapidly repeated short pulses of ultrasound allow the observation of foetal movement as well as simplifying the various measurements that are performed in an antenatal scan. Some of the more sophisticated ultrasound scanning machines also allow the recognition of the more subtle parts of the foetal anatomy.

Techniques of ultrasound scanning

Preparation for an ultrasound scan varies according to the stage of pregnancy and the reasons for the scan and also from one hospital to another. Usually, all patients are asked to attend with a full bladder. This is essential early in pregnancy when much of the uterus lies within the pelvis and may be obscured by overlying intestine unless the bladder is filled. Later in pregnancy a filled bladder is not always as essential, although if the position of the placenta needs to be established a full bladder is required to assess the relationship of the placenta to the internal os, or mouth, of the cervix. Maintaining a full bladder is difficult, particularly during pregnancy when frequency of micturition is a common symptom, but unfortunately it is necessary for the proper performance of the scan.

Ultrasound scanning is usually performed with the mother in a supine position. Acoustic gel or oil is applied to the abdomen to allow the transmission of sound into the maternal abdomen and thence into the uterus. A small probe, or transducer, which generates pulses of ultrasound, is then moved over the abdominal surface. With modern real time equipment image production may be instantaneous; with others, it may be gradual. Because the images produced are tomographic (in the form of slices) they can be difficult to interpret, particularly later in pregnancy when only part of the foetus is imaged at any time. However, a sympathetic and knowledgable sonographer can explain many of the salient features. The duration of the examination is usually of the order of ten minutes or so, although a longer examination

Below left: In this picture of an ultrasound scan, the embryo can be seen as a distinct patch in the uterine cavity
Below right: Measuring the diameter of the baby's head from the scan

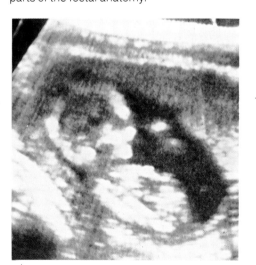

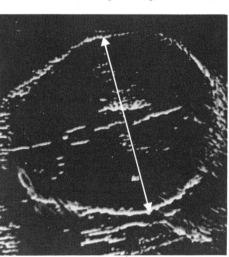

does not necessarily suggest that a foetal abnormality is suspected. It may simply indicate that the lie of the foetus is making accurate measurement difficult.

Scanning in antenatal care

During a routine scan certain specific features of the pregnancy are evaluated by the sonographer. This includes an assessment of the number of foetuses present, the lie of the foetus, the position of the placenta and the volume of amniotic fluid. In addition, certain measurements are made which correlate foetal size with foetal age – the measurements of the foetus are compared to a table of average measurements for normal foetal growth at each stage of pregnancy. This allows the sonographer to make an accurate calculation of the age of the foetus. In the first trimester of pregnancy the measurement taken is usually the crown-rump length; in the

second and third trimesters measurements are made of the biparietal diameter (the transverse diameter of the foetal skull) and the diameter or circumference of the foetal abdomen. Other measurements may also be made: for instance, of the length of a long bone (usually the femur); the total volume of the uterus; the distance between the eyes; or even the size of individual organs such as the kidneys.

These last measurements however are usually part of a more detailed scan, performed in patients with a high risk of foetal abnormality. This may be as a result of family history, an abnormal child resulting from a previous pregnancy or other tests suggesting possible foetal abnormality.

Although ultrasound allows visualisation of the foetus, the images produced are representative slices through the foetus and not a picture of the whole. Careful examination of the foetal structures is therefore time consuming and requires technical expertise. While much of the routine scanning will be performed either by a radiographer or a midwife, such highly specialized scans are usually performed by a doctor, most frequently an obstetrician or a radiologist. With a scan of this nature it is possible to detect significant structural abnormalities of the foetus, including hydrocephalus, spina bifida, congenital heart abnormalities, abnormalities of the kidneys and intestines and certain abnormalities of the limbs and locomotor systems. Early diagnosis (usually before 18 weeks of gestation) allows the parents the opportunity to consider termination in severe or lethal abnormalities and allows their medical advisors to consider the best perinatal care of a baby with a minor defect. Scans later in pregnancy (from about 28 weeks onwards) are usually performed in an attempt to diagnose retardation of growth.

Measurement of foetal abdominal girth appears to be a sensitive indicator of poor foetal nutrition resulting from premature placental failure. Poor growth of the foetal abdomen therefore suggests intrauterine growth retardation.

A more recent advance in the assessment of foetal well-being is the use of Doppler ultrasound to assess blood flow within foetal vessels. Research suggests that this may make it possible to predict those babies who are at risk if they remain in-utero, and allow doctors to plan a pre-term delivery for them.

Doppler ultrasound is also used to monitor foetal heart rate in late pregnancy and labour. This technique may indicate foetal distress (*see* p 75), either in severe intrauterine growth retardation or during labour. The Doppler transducer is strapped to the maternal abdo-

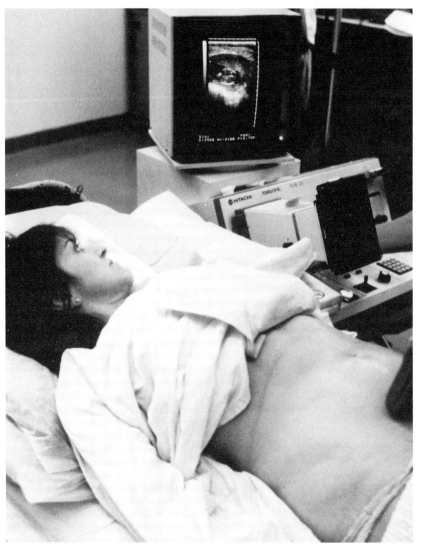

An ultrasound examination of the foetus usually takes place at 18 weeks gestation. For many mothers, particularly those who have not yet felt any foetal movement, seeing the ultrasound picture of their baby is a very reassuring experience

men to produce a constant recording of foetal heart rate. Sudden changes in heart rate can be detected and the baby delivered early or by Caesarean section if necessary.

Ultrasound scanning practice

Although by 1973 ultrasound had been used in obstetrics in the United Kingdom for 15 years, probably only 15 per cent of pregnant women throughout the United Kingdom had had an ultrasound scan during pregnancy. Ultrasound is now much more widely available; a recent survey by the Royal College of Obstetricians and Gynaecologists indicates that 66 per cent of hospitals perform at least one routine scan during the course of a pregnancy. This practice is very similar to other European countries, although in Germany virtually 100 per cent of pregnant women have two routine scans antenatally, whereas in the United States the practice is very much more variable. Depending on locality, the percentage of pregnant women receiving antenatal ultrasound ranges from 15 per cent to over 60 per cent.

Why routine ultrasound?

If ultrasound scans used to detect foetal abnormalities in high-risk pregnancies cannot be offered to all pregnant women, why perform ultrasound at all in a pregnancy that does not carry a high risk? Unfortunately, the clinical definition of a high-risk pregnancy will not detect all those in whom complications develop. Indeed, 10 per cent of patients who are not at risk on the basis of prenatal evaluation will develop significant problems during pregnancy or labour, and 50 per cent

of growth-retarded babies will go undetected using clinical methods alone. Further, accurate gestational dating by ultrasound scanning allows confident prediction of the delivery date, avoids inappropriate early induction of labour and at the same time allows the sensible planning of labour induction when the pregnancy has exceeded term.

In addition to the clinical role of ultrasound it is clear that in the right setting, with a confident operator, the early view of the foetus by the parents can be a most rewarding, exciting and pleasurable experience, and it has been suggested that early ultrasound scanning may improve parent-child bonding.

Risks of ultrasound

It seems unlikely that there is a significant harmful effect of ultrasound during use in antenatal diagnosis. In spite of widespread and increasing use during pregnancy over the last 20 years, no substantiated evidence has emerged that ultrasound is harmful. (In one estimate, the figures given were that over 50 million people throughout the world had diagnostic ultrasound when they were in utero.) It is reassuring however, that professional groups have not become complacent; specialist professional watchdog groups have been established in the United Kingdom, Europe and the United States to monitor all studies of the bioeffects of ultrasound.

Ultrasound represents an important diagnostic aid in the management of pregnancy. While its routine use is not advocated by all, most obstetricians would agree that in many pregnancies it provides invaluable information not otherwise available.

AMNIOCENTESIS

In spite of the improved accuracy of ultrasound as a diagnostic technique for structural foetal abnormality, this technique does depend on the recognition of anatomical abnormalities in the foetus. Clearly, not all foetuses which are abnormal have structural abnormalities that can be recognised by ultrasound. Many such abnormalities are due to chromosome deficiencies and may be evident only after birth. For instance, the infant with Down's syndrome has clearly recognisable facial features, although these are frequently difficult to identify in the neonatal period and are certainly too subtle to be recognised by current ultrasound techniques. There are, however, methods for detecting chromosome abnormalities if foetal cells can be obtained for examination.

Uses of amniocentesis

The amniotic fluid surrounding the foetus contains cells shed from the foetal skin, respiratory, gastrointestinal and urinary tracts. Therefore, samples of amniotic fluid can be used to provide a culture of foetal cells (cytogenetic amniocentesis) which can then be examined for chromosomal abnormalities. The same technique can be used also in Rhesus iso-immunisation, to assess the likelihood of foetal compromise (anaemia and subsequent heart failure), to evaluate foetal lung maturity in pregnancies in which preterm delivery is being considered and to decompress polyhydramnios (excess amniotic fluid) when this is causing significant maternal discomfort.

Although amniocentesis is not offered to all

PREGNANT WOMAN AT 16 WEEKS

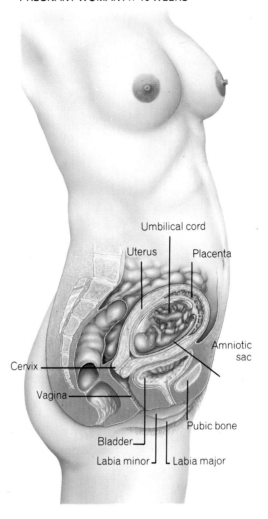

Umbilical cord

Uterus

Placenta

Amniotic sac

Cervix

Vagina

Pubic bone

Bladder

Labia minor ⌐ ⌐ Labia major

A sample of fluid from the amniotic sac is not taken until pregnancy has advanced to 16 weeks at the very earliest. At this stage of gestation the uterus is large enough to provide a significant pool of fluid

the placenta, the foetus and a suitable pool of amniotic fluid; it also allows exclusion of major foetal abnormalities which would obviate the need for cytogenetic amniocentesis.

The mother's abdomen is cleaned with antiseptic, and amniotic fluid is then withdrawn through a fine needle which is passed first through the maternal abdominal wall and then through the uterine wall and into the amniotic cavity. A local anaesthetic may be used, but this requires an additional needle puncture, and may cause uterine contraction if it is injected close to the uterine wall. Although this does not put the pregnancy at risk it makes the procedure more difficult and many doctors prefer not to use local anaesthetic. While it cannot be claimed that the procedure is pain free, the discomfort is similar to that experienced during puncture of a vein. A small amount of amniotic fluid is withdrawn and discarded, since this may be contaminated by a small amount of maternal blood following the needle path through the maternal tissues. A second sample is withdrawn into a syringe and this is sent to the laboratory for cytogenetic examination. The needle is removed from the abdomen and ultrasound is either resumed or continued to demonstrate the continued well-being of the foetus by the demonstration of foetal movement and a normal foetal heartbeat. The puncture site is sealed with a plastic skin (aerosol) or a piece of Elastoplast. The mother is usually advised to rest for the remainder of the day, although this may reflect superstition rather than sound scientifically-based clinical practice.

Because the cells from the sample have to be cultured to provide a sufficient number for cytogenetic analysis, the results of amniocentesis are not usually known for three to four weeks following sampling. After this time however, it is possible to provide a complete chromosomal profile of the foetal cells, as well as the sex of the foetus.

Amniocentesis in twin pregnancies is somewhat more complicated, since both amniotic cavities have to be entered. Ultrasound guidance is again used, but in addition after the first aspiration a small amount of an inert dye is injected into the amniotic cavity of the first twin to ensure that this is not punctured on the subsequent occasion and that fluid from both gestations is achieved.

Risks of amniocentesis

The risks of amniocentesis are a little difficult to define. Several scientific studies have been performed which attempted to compare foetal loss after amniocentesis with the foetal loss-rate for the general population. Comparisons of this type are not necessarily valid, since the

pregnant women, there is an increase in the incidence of Down's syndrome particularly in women over 35. Amniocentesis may be offered to mothers over the age of 37 and at the mother's request after counselling at ages younger than this. Occasionally, there are other indications for cytogenetic amniocentesis; these include delivery of a previous abnormal child and a family history of congenital abnormality.

Techniques

Genetic amniocentesis is usually performed at about 16 weeks gestation, although it may be done somewhat later for other indications. At 16 weeks the uterus is large enough to allow access to a significant pool of amniotic fluid and there are sufficient live cells in the amniotic fluid to allow cell culture.

In the United Kingdom, amniocentesis is usually performed with ultrasound guidance. This allows the identification of the position of

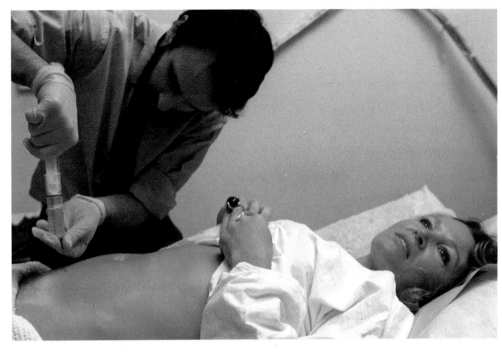

During amniocentesis a fine needle is passed through the abdominal and uterine walls. The procedure does not usually involve any more discomfort than when a vein is punctured

group of women who have amniocentesis performed are usually in a high-risk category as a result of maternal age, previous foetal abnormality and so on. While a study in the United Kingdom suggested that the increase in spontaneous abortion after amniocentesis was as high as 1.5 per cent, a study in the United States showed no difference in foetal loss from a control group not undergoing amniocentesis. None of the studies have shown any significant damage or abnormality to infants born to mothers who have had amniocentesis during their pregnancy. If there is a risk associated with amniocentesis this risk is slight and of the order of 1 per cent. The careful selection of women for amniocentesis means that the possible benefits of the examination in terms of identification of foetal abnormality far outweigh the risks involved.

Limitations
The technique of amniocentesis is limited by the ability of the cytogeneticist to identify the particular chromosome abnormality. Many chromosome abnormalities have now been identified, but there are several which defy diagnosis. For example, it is difficult to identify the genetic abnormality responsible for cystic fibrosis, and although several research units offer a diagnostic service for this, the results to date are not uniformly accurate. Similarly, other abnormalities have complicated hereditary patterns. There is a genetic element, for example, in diabetes, but this is ill-understood and certainly cannot be detected antenatally given current techniques

and medical knowledge.

Perhaps another major limitation of the technique is its timing. Amniocentesis is performed at approximately 16 weeks of gestation and cell culture takes a further three to four weeks. By the time the diagnosis of a foetal abnormality is known the mother feels and looks pregnant, has usually felt foetal movement and is beginning to become emotionally prepared for the pregnancy. Termination at this stage is more emotionally charged and the method of termination is not as simple as that which can be performed before 12 weeks of gestation.

Alternatives to amniocentesis
A method which provides genetic information about the foetus safely and reliably earlier in pregnancy is desirable. Work in this country and abroad has demonstrated that chorionic villus biopsy appears to provide this alternative. The technique involves inserting an aspiration (suction) catheter through the vagina and cervix into the uterine cavity. Under direct vision with simultaneous ultrasound control, the catheter is advanced to the site of implantation of the gestational sac, and a few chorionic villi (these contain foetal cells from the placenta) are aspirated into the catheter.

The advantages of this technique are that it can be performed as early as nine weeks of gestation and has a similar rate of foetal loss as does amniocentesis. It also provides immediate information about the chromosome make-up of the embryo, since the villi contain sufficient cells to obviate the need for cell culture. Any necessary termination can be easily performed before twelve weeks of gestation.

Although this technique appears to provide the ideal alternative to amniocentesis, experience is still limited and is largely restricted to research institutions in which the early experimental work was carried out. It should become more widely available in the future.

Benefits of antenatal diagnosis

Much can now be learnt about the foetus prior to delivery: accurate foetal age assessment can be made; foetal growth can be monitored; and early work on Doppler suggests that foetal well-being can be assessed. Also, many foetal abnormalities can now be recognised. With improvement in technology and training of personnel it ought to be possible to screen for foetal abnormality with ultrasound. However, several abnormalities will still require obtaining foetal cells. Chorionic villus

biopsy may well replace amniocentesis in this role.

Much has been said of early foetal diagnosis allowing termination of abnormal pregnancies but early antenatal diagnosis not only allows planned terminations but also allows parental counselling and hopefully better preparartion for coping with a handicapped child, and better management in the early perinatal period. If the diagnosis of a cardiac abnormality or renal abnormality can be made in the antenatal period, the mother can be delivered in (or early transport of the infant arranged to) a centre specialising in such problems. Earlier diagnosis allows earlier treatment from which better results are usually obtained.

Finally, improved antenatal diagnosis raises the possibility of treatment in-utero. Although any such treatment remains experimental in most instances the foetus with a birth defect may in the future be able to receive curative treatment prior to delivery.

PREPARATION FOR BIRTH

Fathers are encouraged to attend antenatal classes with their partners, not only to learn about pregnancy and labour, but also to learn about the physical care of the infant (above) Antenatal exercises include learning about positions, movements and techniques of breathing that will help the baby to be born with the minimum of difficulty

This section is designed to highlight the importance of preparation for childbirth and some of the ways in which women can cope with the stress of labour. Much of the available information on this subject raises women's hopes for a romantic experience in labour; here the emphasis is on encouraging women to familiarise themselves with all aspects of pregnancy, including the un-

romantic ones. Such preparation is particularly important for women over 30 years of age having their first baby, since they have a slightly increased risk of complications during childbirth.

Before 1939 the majority of women in Great Britain gave birth at home, with little or no medical care. Such deliveries were associated with a high rate of maternal and infant

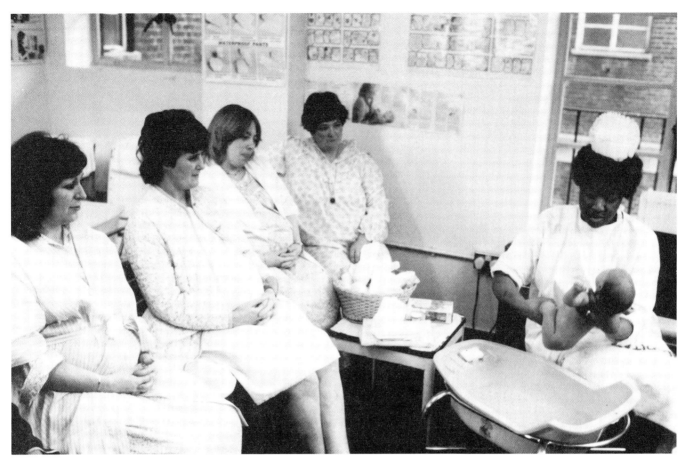

deaths. Following World War 2 there was increasing emphasis on the problems of childbirth; antenatal clinics were established and hospital confinements became the norm, resulting in an improvement in infant and maternal health. However, planning and decision-making for delivery were largely in the hands of the medical staff; the women were rarely consulted and generally their opinions were felt to be unimportant. Although most delivered safely, the pleasure and personal experience of childbirth were lost and a large number of mothers felt unable to cope satisfactorily with the stress of labour.

Today women are better informed, and they not only want the benefits of modern technology, but also the right to choose and make their decisions with the guidance of professionals. Combined with this is the desire to have their individual needs taken into consideration. All of these needs are now recognised by most medical staff.

Antenatal classes

As knowledge of pregnancy can eliminate much of the anxiety and fear about childbirth, mothers and their partners should be aware of the anatomy and physiology of pregnancy,

and any complications that may arise and how the latter can be prevented or treated. Much of this information is available through childbirth classes held at local antenatal clinics or maternity units, and through groups such as the National Childbirth Trust and yoga and active births groups.

Introductory classes are usually held where women are advised about diet and the minor ailments of pregnancy as well as what to expect at the antenatal clinic. At 28-30 weeks of pregnancy, classes are held for both women and their partners to help them prepare for labour and teach them how to cope with the newborn baby. These classes are usually held weekly for six to eight weeks during the day or in the evening. Open discussions are encouraged and exercises and relaxation techniques are taught by the midwife or obstetric physiotherapist.

In addition, many hospitals have instituted the use of a birth plan, based on the woman's and her partner's views and expectations about delivery. Although the aim is to follow the birth plan it is sometimes necessary to alter it because of unforeseen circumstances.

Where the hospital attended does not have a birth plan, women are advised to approach

Child care does not necessarily come naturally to women, and many prospective mothers benefit from instruction given at antenatal classes on how to bathe, feed and generally care for the baby

the consultant obstetrician and express any specific views about the delivery.

During the antenatal period women should also consider how they will feed their newborn infant. Breastfeeding depends on the mother's understanding about the functions of the breasts and the positioning of the baby to achieve successful sucking. In addition to the numerous books and pamphlets explaining this, there are groups of women who support breastfeeding mothers, including the La Leche League, National Childbirth Trust and the Association of Breastfeeding Mothers. (*See* Help and Advice on p 146 for relevant names and addresses).

Women who intend to bottle-feed should discuss this with the midwife well in advance so that preparations can be made. (*See* also p 90.)

In the antenatal period, women should learn about the techniques of breastfeeding and the structure, care and function of the lactating breast. This will enable them to make an informed decision about whether to breast or bottle-feed and in most cases will result in successful breastfeeding if this is chosen

Nutrition

During pregnancy, appetites and nutritional needs change, and anything a mother eats or drinks can affect her well-being and that of the foetus. An average weight gain during pregnancy is 11 kg (24 lb). This might be made up from a gain of 115 g (4 oz) a week for the first ten weeks of pregnancy and 300 g (10 ½ oz) for the remaining 30 weeks.

Good nutrition is therefore important not only for maternal and foetal health but also for weight control. The nutritional chart opposite indicates the foods that should be eaten for a well-balanced diet.

Vegetarians should observe their diet carefully, especially for the protein and iron content. Vegans need to seek diatetic advice as their diet may be lacking in vitamin B_{12} which aids the development of the foetal brain.

Prescriptions for iron and vitamin supplements may be given by the doctor, depending on the results of blood tests taken at the antenatal clinic. If iron tablets are prescribed, they should be taken either with a drink rich in vitamin C, such as unsweetened orange juice, or with the foods rich in vitamin C such as fresh vegetables, salads, citrus or berry fruit, as vitamin C facilities the absorption of iron in the body.

Iron tablets can cause side-effects such as constipation and nausea, and if these occur another type of iron supplement should be taken with the doctor's advice.

Exercise and relaxation

Pregnant women should lead an active normal life unless otherwise advised by their doctor. Most forms of exercise are acceptable in pregnancy; swimming is of particular value as it exercises all the muscles in the body including perineal muscles – the muscles at the bottom of the pelvis including those of the vulva and anus. Regular swimming is advisable in pregnancy but it should not be done too strenuously.

Pregnant women should be conscious of their posture, adopting an upright position when walking and standing, with the shoulders straight. When bending or lifting it is important to bend using the knee joints and not to bend the back and risk straining the muscles and vertebral ligaments.

Exercises to support the pelvic floor are essential in pregnancy. A simple exercise to be done when passing urine is to tighten up the muscles in the pelvic floor and stop the flow of urine for a few seconds each time.

One of the most commonly used relaxation techniques is the Mitchell method, based on the physiological laws governing muscle work. Its aim is to relieve muscle tension.

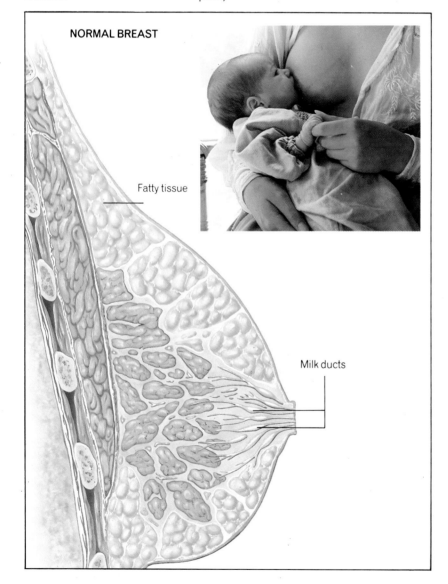

NORMAL BREAST

Fatty tissue

Milk ducts

NUTRITION IN PREGNANCY

For the pregnant woman, a well-balanced diet should include the following nutrients in the amounts given:

☐ *Protein* provided by two helpings a day of protein-rich foods such as red meat, offal, poultry, fish, eggs, nuts, seeds and pulses.

☐ *Calcium* provided by 600 ml (1 pint) of milk or an equivalent substitute: 28 g (1 oz) of cheese, or a small carton of yoghurt are equivalent to 200 ml (⅓ pint) of milk

☐ *Iron* provided by red meat, liver, kidneys, eggs, spinach and wholewheat bread. Red meat, liver or kidney should be eaten at least twice a week

☐ *Other minerals and vitamins* provided by green leafy vegetables, cooked as little as possible. The daily intake should be at least two helpings a day, with two helpings of citrus fruit for vitamin C

Vitamins, protein, energy-giving foods and fibre – which helps control constipation – are found in cereals. The pregnant woman should have at least four helpings of cereals a day in the form of wholewheat bread, brown rice, oats and other whole grain cereals

Fats and sweet foods should be avoided as they lead to excessive weight gain

Indigestion, if experienced, might be alleviated by eating meals without a beverage and only drinking at least half an hour after the meal is finished. Make certain that enough fluid is drunk between meals: water, unsweetened fruit juices, herb teas and tea are ideal

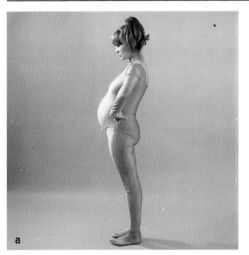

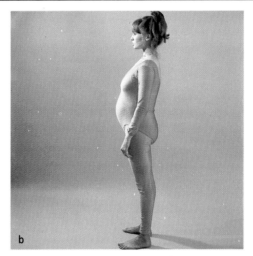

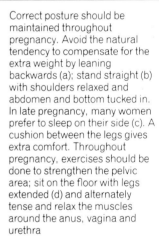

Correct posture should be maintained throughout pregnancy. Avoid the natural tendency to compensate for the extra weight by leaning backwards (a); stand straight (b) with shoulders relaxed and abdomen and bottom tucked in. In late pregnancy, many women prefer to sleep on their side (c). A cushion between the legs gives extra comfort. Throughout pregnancy, exercises should be done to strengthen the pelvic area; sit on the floor with legs extended (d) and alternately tense and relax the muscles around the anus, vagina and urethra

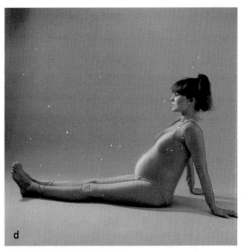

Posture and exercises during pregnancy

Correct posture while sitting is just as important as when standing. Sit comfortably in a relaxed position, with the back straight and supported by the back of a hard chair (a). When lifting objects, keep back straight and bend from the knees (b). Avoid bending over, which strains muscles. For abdominal muscle tone, lie on the floor as shown (c), tighten the abdomen, pulling the baby towards the backbone. Assuming the delivery position (d) tense and relax pelvic floor and thigh muscles. Back massage (e) will help during labour, relieving backache and any contractions that are felt in the back. In the all-fours postion (f) start by sitting on the heels; bend forward on to the knees; keep back straight, as relaxed as possible. Stand upright, legs apart, then squat. This helps prevent backache and constipation. Sit upright (g), on the front of the buttocks. Gently push knees down with elbows; lift thighs (h) then lower them

On page 73 are some of the breathing techniques taught in antenatal classes. These will help synchronise breathing with contractions, and to some extent help the mother to control the actions of the body. Deep, level A breathing comes from the diaphragm: breathe in deeply with mouth open. Hold and blow out through mouth. Level B breaths rise from the lower rib cage. Mouth open, emphasise out-breath slightly. Shallower than level A. Level C breaths rise from the area of the breastbone. Almost allow air to flow into lungs of its own accord. Say 'out' on out breath. Shallower still than level B. Level D breathing is almost in the throat, so there is practically no effort involved. It is shallow, natural breathing. Choose a song and mime it as you tap the rhythm against your lips with your finger

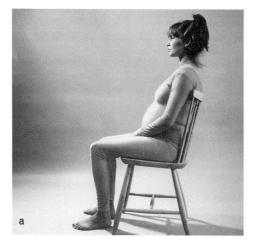

a

b

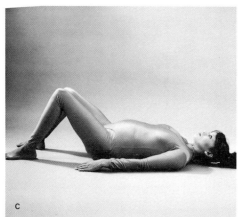

c

d

e

f

g

h

BREATHING TECHNIQUES FOR CHILDBIRTH

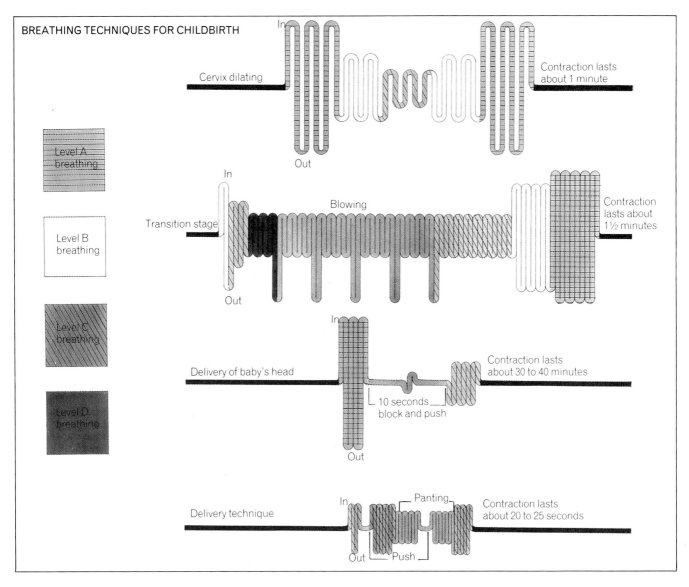

Level A breathing

Level B breathing

Level C breathing

Level D breathing

In
Cervix dilating
Out
Contraction lasts about 1 minute

In
Transition stage
Blowing
Out
Contraction lasts about 1½ minutes

In
Delivery of baby's head
10 seconds block and push
Contraction lasts about 30 to 40 minutes
Out

In
Delivery technique
Panting
Out — Push
Contraction lasts about 20 to 25 seconds

During stress the body develops a pattern of reflexes which is activated by recognition of the stress; this is followed by the adoption of a defensive position. The Mitchell method attempts to reverse this response by developing a position of ease and consciously registering the new position.

Adopt a comfortable sitting position with the head fully supported. Follow the instructions below to learn the position of ease. After every action, stop and think about the new position of the body and let the mind register that position.

Drag the shoulders down towards the floor. Move the elbows away from the body. Stretch the fingers long and hard and rest them on the support. Push the feet away from the face. Press the body into the support. Drag the jaw down. Let the tongue hang loosely in the mouth, teeth apart, lips together. Close the eyes and enjoy the darkness. Feel the tension ease away through the scalp.

This is the position adopted in labour at the beginning of a contraction or before an internal examination.

Breathing

The normal response to pain is to shut the eyes, hold the breath and concentrate on the pain. This enhances the perception and aggravates the sensation. Breathing techniques help to minimise the sensation. There are various types of breathing techniques adopted in labour. One of the simplest is to begin a long slow exhalation at the beginning of the contraction or vaginal examination, until all the air in the lungs is expelled. This is followed by a normal inspiration; the process

In the last few months of pregnancy serious consideration should be given to the items which will be needed for the baby, thereby avoiding unnecessary expense on clothing and equipment that are not really necessary.

should be repeated as long as the pain is experienced.

For some of the stronger contractions this may not be sufficient, and a different technique is required. This consists of two short fast inspirations followed by a rapid blowing out through the mouth.

It is advisable that both relaxation and breathing are practised with a partner, so that if the woman experiences difficulties in labour the partner will be able to give support and remind her of the technique.

Post-natal depression
Some women experience an anti-climax after the birth of their child and suffer varying degrees of depression. Recent research shows that this may be associated with changes in hormones such as endorphins which help us to cope with stress.

It is therefore important for the woman's partner, family and friends, to be aware of the possibility of post-natal depression in order to deal with the situation should it arise.

Mild depression is usually self-limiting and the symptoms will be overcome. However, severe depression or psychosis may occasionally require hospitalization.

Baby clothes and equipment
There are numerous factors to be taken into consideration when purchasing baby clothes and equipment, including the mother's lifestyle, the type of transport she uses, and the

availability and type of washing and drying facilities.

A layette should include the following: 2 dozen pairs of towelling nappies, or a supply of disposable nappies if preferred; 3 pairs of plastic pants; 3 nighties or babygros; 3 cardigans; 3 vests; 2 hats; 2 pairs of mittens (1 pair scratch mittens); 3 pairs of bootees; and a shawl. Obviously the amount of warm clothing needed will depend on the season.

Fitted sheets are most successful for the baby's cot. If choosing a quilt, make certain it is washable and carries the British safety symbol (a kite). Unless a carry cot is needed for transporting the baby, it is not always necessary. When buying a baby buggy, it is important to consider the weight, height and ease with which it can be opened and closed.

Anything purchased for the baby should be entirely safe. When buying or receiving second-hand equipment it is a good idea to have it thoroughly checked and serviced if necessary – especially the wheels and brakes of prams and buggies. Second-hand cots and high-chairs may be brightened up with a fresh coat of lead-free paint.

Summary
This has been only a brief account of the important aspects of preparing for childbirth, but it does provide some ideas of what all pregnant women should be considering. For sources of further information *see* Help and Advice, p 146.

PREPARING FOR HOSPITAL

Before delivery women should familiarise themselves with the maternity unit they will be using. Wherever possible, a visit should be arranged to see the labour ward, special care baby unit and other wards. During the visit the following information should be gained:
□ When to come into hospital and the admission procedure, such as the policy for shaving and enemas
□ The policy in the unit for inducing labour and how induction is performed
□ The type of pain relief available
□ The policy for foetal monitoring during labour and delivery
□ How the unit staff feels about active birth – that is,

does it encourage women to adopt different postures for delivery if both they and the baby are well
□ What the policy and management is for rupturing membranes and whether this is performed during labour
□ The policy for episiotomy
□ How involved the woman's partner can be and whether he will be allowed to be present for a forceps delivery
□ If a Caesarean section is necessary will it be possible with the partner present
□ The unit's visiting hours, and whether there is a time for partners only
□ What is provided for the baby while in hospital
□ What the mother needs to bring with her

LABOUR AND BIRTH

Although there is an increased risk to the baby during labour and birth with rising maternal age, many factors affect the outcome of labour, including the general health and nutritional status of the mother. The unwell and poorly nourished 20-year-old will be more likely to have a small or premature baby than the fit and active 35-year-old who has always had a balanced diet. The same bias occurs in the risk to the mother – the healthy 35-year-old is less at risk than the unhealthy 25-year-old.

As a group, women over 30 years of age have a slightly increased chance, and those over 35 a much greater chance, of labour complications, and as a result they have more forceps deliveries and more Caesarean sections. Even so, 60-70 per cent of women in these groups deliver normally and without complications.

Forceps delivery and Caesarean section are usually associated with problems such as foetal distress, a situation which occurs when the foetus is not getting a sufficient supply of oxygen. This is more common as maternal age rises and is normally a result of deterioration of the placenta, so that an insufficiency of nutrients reaches the foetus. Placental deterioration therefore results in slow or retarded foetal growth. Antenatal investigations may identify a small foetus with falling placental function, but many babies are born small-for-dates (born at term with a lower

than average birthweight) that have not been suspected in the antenatal period.

It is generally accepted that women over 40 are more likely to have an abnormal child, and that abnormality contributes to a higher perinatal mortality rate (the total number of stillbirths and neonatal deaths) in this age group. What is not accepted is the contribution placental failure makes to the perinatal mortality of normal babies. While the debate continues over the appropriate place of confinement for women generally, women who fall into the higher age groups should be

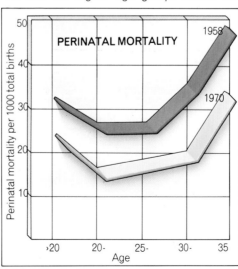

The graph illustrates the decline in the perinatal mortality rate in England and Wales since 1958

A woman will normally be admitted to hospital when the first stage of labour is well established. Women who are not certain about when to go in should ring their midwife

Facing page (left) shows a normal foetal heart tracing: the heart rate is in the normal range (120-160 beats per minute). The heart rate is slightly variable (normal beat-to-beat variation) and accelerates in time with the contractions. An abnormal trace is shown on the right: the rate is slow and the variation is small suggesting lack of oxygen, and deep decelerations are present. Such decelerations are the result of an inability of the heart muscle to respond to the fall of oxygen during a contraction. Small decelerations of the heart are common, but deep decelarations, especially with delayed recovery, as shown, indicate foetal distress requiring urgent intervention.

confined in units equipped for emergency delivery. The majority of these women have healthy babies in good condition, born without problems, but as a higher proportion of them have some difficulties in labour close supervision is essential.

Labour
Women over thirty are likely to be more anxious about the outcome of labour than younger women. Hopefully, many of their fears will have been allayed during antenatal preparation, but the reassurance of a sympathetic attitude and patient explanations are extremely valuable. So too is company. The presence of the woman's partner during labour can be of more help than reassuring words, especially if he has attended the antenatal classes. Where there is no partner, or the partner is not available, a suitable friend may be of considerable help to pass the time early on and to support and encourage the mother in established labour.

Onset of labour
Labour may start in a variety of ways. It is frequently preceded by a 'show' – the passage

of a sticky, usually blood-stained plug of mucus (the operculum). This mucus fills the canal of the cervix and is released as the upper part of the cervix begins to expand, either at the onset of labour or even some hours before onset. It is not to be confused with the loss, however small, of bright blood; such bleeding (antepartum haemorrhage) must be reported immediately as it may be the result of partial separation of the placenta. This is slightly more common with advancing maternal age.

Another symptom of labour may be intermittent backache or low abdominal discomfort with hardening of the uterus. Strong contractions may not occur for some hours, but some women have a rapid and short labour. The woman should be admitted to hospital when the contractions are uncomfortable, or are occurring every 20-30 minutes. If there is any doubt about whether or not to go to hospital the woman or her partner should seek the advice of the midwife.

The membranes may rupture in labour or before the onset of labour, with anything from a small trickle of liquor to a sudden flood. If the baby's head is engaged and pushed firmly against the cervix a small amount of liquor will drain away. If the head is not well down, a flood may occur. This occurs in women who have had a previous child and in cases where the head is in a poor position, such as the occipito-posterior position where the baby faces forwards instead of backwards. A flood may also occur when the baby presents abnormally to the mother's pelvis – face first, breech first or when lying transversely, across the uterus.

If the membranes rupture early, the mother should be admitted to hospital without delay. A check can then be made that all is well, especially that the baby is presenting normally to the pelvis and that the umbilical cord has not been brought below the head by the rush of escaping liquor.

The liquor should be as clear as water. If it is stained greenish with meconium (the first matter passed by the baby) it suggests that the baby has been relatively short of oxygen at some time. A light green tinge requires observation to make sure that foetal distress does not occur in labour. Heavy meconium staining reflects a high risk of distress, and if labour is not well advanced with a satisfactory foetal heart rate, immediate delivery may be advised.

The first stage
The total length of labour is variable, with a tendency to be shorter in the multigravidae (women who have had a previous child) than in the primigravidae (women expecting their

first baby). The latent phase of irregular uterine contractions may last some hours, but if the woman has had a baby before, this phase may be so short as to be unidentifiable. There is some evidence that labour in women in the older age group is slightly longer than in younger women, although statistical evidence is lacking, as earlier intervention occurs in women over 35 if labour is at all prolonged.

The active phase of labour involves strong uterine contractions lasting over 40 seconds, and occurring every 2-3 minutes. This is the phase of rapid dilation of the cervix. With an average-sized full-term baby, and with the foetal head well flexed – tucked up to present the smallest diameter to the pelvic tissues for the most efficient labour – the cervix must dilate up to 9.5-10 centimetres (3¾-4 inches) before it slips back past the foetal head. As the time of full dilation of the cervix approaches, the transition phase is entered. Here the last part of the cervix is stretched and will slip past the foetal head as the woman enters the second stage of labour.

Prolonged labour is associated with maternal exhaustion and a higher chance of foetal distress.

The second stage

The second stage is the phase of action – pushing and birth. At the beginning of the second stage the cervix has slipped past the baby's head and the feeling of pressure makes the mother want to bear down as each contraction occurs. This stage of labour lasts from 30 minutes to one hour in the primigravid woman, and is a time when the partner can be of great help. More and more women are adopting non-traditional but more natural positions for this active phase. Many will not

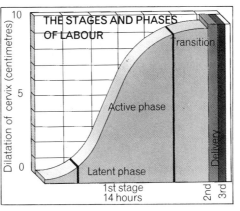

The normal progress of the first stage of labour (left)

wish to take to bed, although others will find the bed less uncomfortable than standing. Some labour wards provide mattresses on the floor and bean-bags for lumbar support but some women will want to push while on all fours or squatting. Various types of birthing chairs, stools and rings may be available for supporting the woman in a more upright position, to take advantage of the help that gravity can give. Although many hospital midwives encourage women to use a variety of different positions for labour and delivery, few units have an adequate variety of birthing equipment.

With the 30-34 age group there seems to be no reason not to go ahead with natural postures if all seems to be well with mother and baby. In the 35 plus age group, or where there is any suggestion of a problem, these natural postures must take second place to adequate observation of the baby's heart rate. The heart should be listened to at the end of every contraction in the second stage of labour, if not continuously. It must be said

Many women prefer to adopt a more natural position for labour and delivery

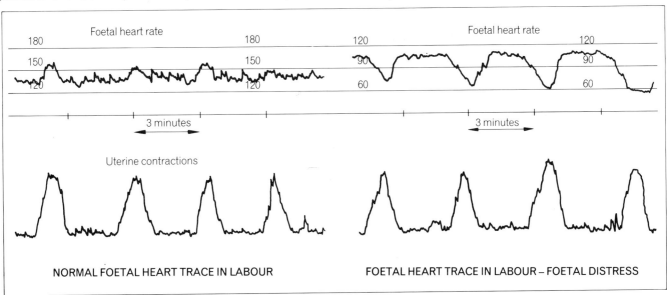

NORMAL FOETAL HEART TRACE IN LABOUR

FOETAL HEART TRACE IN LABOUR – FOETAL DISTRESS

As long as labour is proceeding normally and mother and baby are doing well, the mother may give birth in any suitable position which she finds most comfortable

Foetal monitoring during labour does not always necessitate sophisticated equipment. In its simplest forms it includes listening to the foetal heartbeat through a stethoscope

that every year babies die when extreme views over natural childbirth push aside advice based on safety. Such extremism cannot be justified.

The views and teaching of Leboyer and Odent should be respected. The delivery of a baby in quiet, calm surroundings with dim lights is to be encouraged, but will need to be modified for safety where there are problems or where higher risks are present. As the baby's head is born it is most important that the doctor can see that the baby's airway is clear and that the infant is in good condition.

To facilitate the birth of the baby an episiotomy is sometimes necessary. Episiotomy is a perineal incision made to enlarge the vaginal entrance and is performed after the administration of local anaesthetic. This practice has received a great deal of publicity in recent years – routine episiotomy has been abandoned in most units, but it has a greater place in the older primigravida. Foetal distress is more common in this age group, and if suspected, an episiotomy may shorten the second stage of labour by ten minutes – an extremely valuable ten minutes to the life and health of the baby who is suffering from oxygen deficiency. If the baby's heart rate stays normal throughout the second stage an episiotomy will probably not be required.

The third stage
There are various methods of delivery of the placenta: the most common is controlled cord traction. When the uterus is felt to contract firmly after delivery it is supported by the

midwife who places her hand on the mother's abdomen just above the pubic bone and maintains steady traction on the umbilical cord with the other hand. This method is usually associated with the administration of a drug such as syntometrine to aid uterine contraction. Syntometrine is given intramuscularly as the baby is being born: it contains a mixture of synthetic oxytocin (syntocinon) and ergometrine to contract the uterus and maintain the contraction over the following two hours. Over the last three decades this active management of labour has been associated with a dramatic reduction in the rate of haemorrhage.

A more natural way to deliver the placenta is to wait for natural uterine contraction and watch for the signs of placental separation – a slight blood loss from the vagina and lengthening of the visible part of the cord. The mother may then bear down to deliver the placenta. There are differing views about these methods: those who do not favour active management say that syntometrine may be given if bleeding starts – that is too late. If haemorrhage starts it can be dramatic. It must be remembered that the maternal death rate from post-partum (post delivery) haemorrhage had risen between the last two triennial Reports of the Confidential Enquiries into Maternal Deaths in England and Wales (published in 1978 and 1981 respectively). Post-partum haemorrhage is more common in the older women with less efficient uterine action, especially if the uterus is distorted by fibroids. These innocent uterine muscle tumours are found more in women who postpone their childbearing. They distort the uterine muscle giving poorer contraction and placental separation.

Monitoring labour
The term monitoring has received bad press unjustifiably. It seems to represent interference when it really reflects reassurance. Monitoring labour is carried out by examinations of the abdomen to feel how well the baby's head is descending, and by vaginal examinations to feel how well the cervix is opening. These two findings may be charted on a partogram – a graphic record of labour progress – which clearly shows if a slow labour is occurring. While a slightly prolonged labour may be accepted in the 30 to 35 year old group, those above 35 with a higher risk of placental failure should not have a prolonged labour. Early help is essential.

Monitoring of the baby *per se* is more complex. The foetal heart rate is audible through a Pinard's stethoscope and this is the simplest method of checking on the baby's well-being. However, during a uterine con-

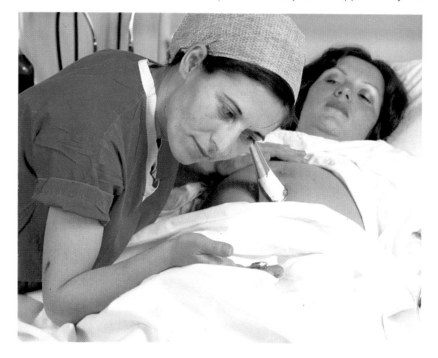

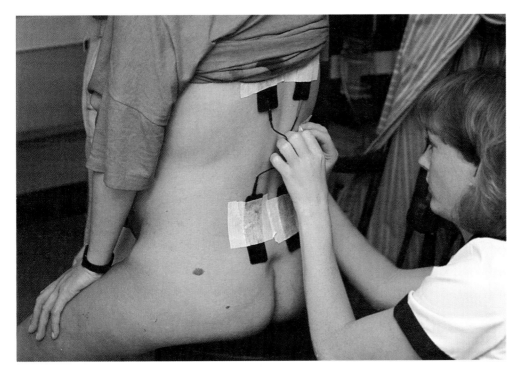

Transcutaneous Nerve Stimulation (TNS) could be the pain relief of the future. Electrodes taped to the woman's back are thought to ease the pain either by increasing the endorphin level or by distorting the nerve paths so that the pain does not register in the brain

traction, and as the contraction wears off, the heart sounds are muffled and difficult to hear. It is at this time, when the heart sounds are least audible, that the baby is under maximum stress; during the contraction the uterine muscle fibres reduce the flow of maternal blood to the uterine site of placental attachment, which in turn reduces dramatically the oxygen supply to the placenta and therefore to the baby. A healthy baby in good condition copes with this contraction time well and the heart rate will stay steady or slightly accelerate in compensation. The baby with poor placental function who is doing well enough before labour may be tipped into a distressed state by the oxygen reduction of active labour. Distress will first occur during contractions.

Electronic monitoring of the heart rate allows a constant watch to be kept on the heart during contractions – this may be by an external device on the mother's abdomen or by a small clip applied to the baby's scalp skin during a vaginal examination. Routine electronic monitoring of all labours is not normally recommended. A fifteen minute external recording at the onset of labour, perhaps repeated later in labour, can be reassuring. Such a policy would be reasonable in the 30-34 age group, but with increasing risks of foetal distress in the 35 plus group, and especially over the age of 40, continuous monitoring will be wise. Any suggestion of a small baby, a tendency towards prolonged labour or meconium staining of the liquor makes continuous recording essential.

Pain relief in labour

Uterine contractions are strong and many women will require some form of pain relief. The antenatal preparation and reassurance, combined with a calm atmosphere, significantly reduce the requirement for analgesia. The practice of relaxation and breathing pattern control will help, and here the partner or friend can be of great support. In some labours the contractions are very strong and those that are associated with the posterior position are especially painful. The posterior position is more a feature of first labours generally rather than one that is age-related.

Entonox is an oxygen/nitrous oxide mixture which takes the edge off pain. The high oxygen content results in an excellent supply to the baby so that inhalation is safe. Self administration by a mouth-piece or mask is also a safety feature. However, the use of Entonox should be limited to very rapid labours of multigravid women or, in the primigravidae, to the transition phase at the end of the first stage of labour. Here the last part of the dilation of the cervix is slow and painful, but labour is at a point when the administration of long-acting drugs is unwise because of the effects on the baby. The prolonged use of Entonox will produce nausea, disorientation and dehydration.

Pethidine is an intramuscular injection and is a common form of pain relief in labour. Its effects last three to four hours, after which the injection may be repeated. Pethidine reduces

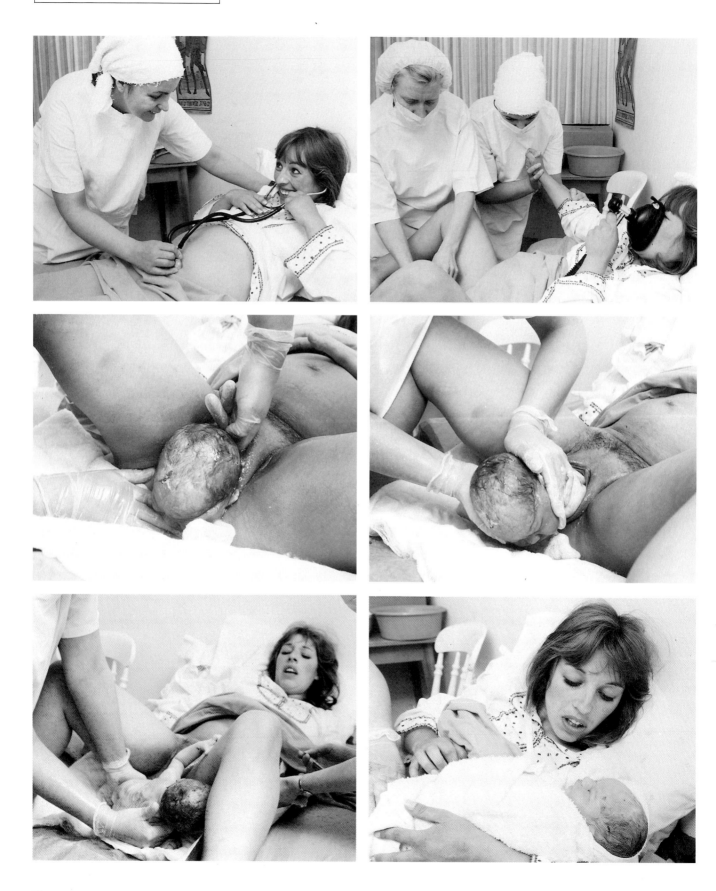

labour pain and allows the woman to rest, but it may cause nausea and confusion. It should not be given if delivery is imminent. If delivery does occur within two hours of a Pethidine injection some babies, but by no means all, will have delayed establishment of breathing and will require an antidote injection of naloxone.

Some doctors now use a new drug, Meptazinol, in place of Pethidine. This appears to have less of a depressing effect on infant respiration.

Epidural anaesthetic is an injection of local anaesthetic into the epidural space within the spinal column. A local anaesthetic is put into the skin and superficial tissues over the lumbar spine, and a needle is passed through this numb area into the epidural space. A very fine cannula is threaded down the needle which is then withdrawn. The cannula stays in place for the duration of labour and local anaesthetic can be administered as required to numb the pain nerves from the uterus and pelvic tissues. This procedure should not be confused with spinal anaesthesia used in emergency situations – the spinal anaesthetic is a deeper injection, into the cerebrospinal fluid which surrounds the spinal cord. An epidural does not reach this depth and does not carry the problems of the spinal injection.

Epidural anaesthesia is commonly used for pain relief in labour and can be used for forceps deliveries and Caesarean sections. The main disadvantage of epidural anaesthesia in the past was the reported increase in forceps deliveries associated with its use. Now that midwives are used to epidural administration they allow the epidural effect to wear off as the woman approaches the second stage of labour. As sensation returns,

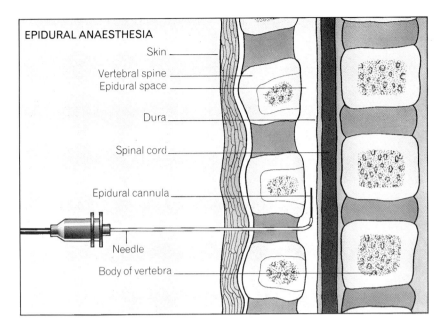

EPIDURAL ANAESTHESIA

Skin

Vertebral spine

Epidural space

Dura

Spinal cord

Epidural cannula

Needle

Body of vertebra

so does the urge to bear down and normal delivery is the rule.

The major advantages of epidural anaesthetic over pethidine are that the mother is totally aware of what is going on throughout the birth and not drugged, and the baby is similarly unaffected.

There is no reason for a woman in older age groups not to see how she gets on and try the form of pain relief that she wishes. However, any signs of a small baby, a premature infant or a child with early distress should lead to advice in favour of epidural anaesthetic. A baby in one of these categories has a higher chance of being born in poor condition, and will do better if unaffected by depressant drugs. An epidural may also be used if an assisted delivery is required.

In an epidural, a needle is passed between the spinal vertebrae and a fine cannula is threaded down the needle which is then withdrawn. Anaesthesia is administered through the cannula when necessary. This has the effect of numbing the nerves in the spinal cord which lead into the uterine and pelvic tissue

LABOUR COMPLICATIONS

Labour that occurs before the 37th completed week of pregnancy is preterm and it increases in incidence with advancing maternal age until, in the 35-40 age group, it is 50 per cent more common than in the 20-30 one. Preterm labour is partly associated with the increased risk of abnormality and partly due to placental failure reflected in an increased stillbirth rate in this group.

Where the membranes rupture prematurely, the woman will be admitted to hospital. If the pregnancy is at the 34th week or less, bed rest and observation will be advised; delivery of a baby less mature than this carries a high chance of respiratory problems which can be

harmful. If the membranes have ruptured but labour does not occur, the risk of respiratory problems may be less than the risk of infection within the uterus; in this situation labour may be induced with an oxytocin intravenous drip.

Preterm labour may start without ruptured membranes and in some circumstances it can be suppressed by intravenous drugs, but the increased risk of placental failure as a cause of preterm labour in the older age group makes the use of such drugs less advisable.

If labour continues, is delivery normal? If the baby is very small and presenting by the

Although a greater proportion of women over 30 have some complications during labour than their younger counterparts, most enjoy a normal delivery when they can participate fully in the birth of their child (far left)

head, a forceps delivery may be recommended to cradle the head and deliver the baby slowly and gently. Rapid delivery of a preterm baby may cause damage to, or death of the child from cerebral haemorrhage, and a gentle forceps delivery will help to prevent this. Epidural anaesthesia during such a labour will relieve pain without depressing the baby's respiration, so that the newborn baby's lungs get as good a start as possible. The epidural will also allow the protective forceps delivery to be carried out without pain. If the preterm baby presents by the breech there is an added risk of cerebral haemorrhage during delivery. Especially in the older age group, it is likely that preterm breech labour will be interrupted by Caesarean delivery for the safety and health of the baby.

Induction of labour

There are many reasons for induction of labour; where the pregnancy is straightforward and the age group is 30-34 the usual management will apply – induction for some complications and where the pregnancy continues to 10-12 days after the due date. The risk of placental failure in the 35 plus age group makes the continuation of pregnancy past term slightly more hazardous. Induction of labour may be advocated at about the expected date of confinement, but only if there are no other complicating factors. It is likely that a combination of being overdue with high blood pressure or a history of haemorrhage will result in the recommendation for Caesarean section, but if there are no other problems induction will be carried out.

There are several methods of induction; the least unpleasant is the use of a hormone (prostaglandin) vaginal pessary which is slowly absorbed and often results in the onset of labour. If the cervix, on vaginal examination, is already starting to open, a prostaglandin pessary may result in labour which is too strong, and in this case labour may be induced by rupturing the membranes. A vaginal examination is carried out, using a sterile technique, and a small plastic probe is used through the cervix to scrape the membranes and release liquor. This method has the great advantage in the 35 plus age group of showing the colour of the liquor – if the liquor is stained with meconium a much closer watch is kept on the baby's heart rate in labour. Such artificial rupture of the membranes may be linked with an intravenous syntocinon drip to get labour established.

Prolonged labour

Prolonged labour may occur as a result of disproportion – that is, the baby is too big for the pelvis or the pelvis is unusually small or

misshapen. Hopefully, such problems will have been identified antenatally. If there is a possibility that labour will be successful, where there is only a slightly reduced space, a 'trial labour' may be conducted. The labour is watched closely and the baby's heart rate continuously recorded. If progress is satisfactory the labour continues, but if too slow a Caesarean section is performed. A trial labour may be carried out in the 30-35 age group, but increasing risks in women who are older make it more likely that even minor degrees of disproportion will be managed by planned (elective) Caesarean section.

Prolonged labour may be due to a poor head position: the occipito-posterior position in which the baby faces forwards instead of backwards leads the head to tilt back from its usual tucked-up position (flexion). This deflexion results in the presentation of wider diameters of the skull with a slower labour. In young women the management will include epidural anaesthesia and the stimulation of the usually inefficient labour by a syntocinon intravenous infusion. This management will also apply to the 30-35 age group, but in the older age groups, or where there are other complicating factors, the delivery will be by Caesarean.

Foetal distress

As mentioned earlier, this is a major problem in the older age group of mothers. It is usually the result of poor placental function, although other factors, such as umbilical cord compression, may be the cause. Poor placental health may also give rise to a small baby and foetal distress is then common. Distress is more likely to be indicated when there is meconium staining of the liquor, but evidence can also come from decelerations of the baby's heart rate, especially if the rate recovers slowly after a contraction has ended. In some units, foetal distress may be confirmed by taking a tiny sample of blood from the

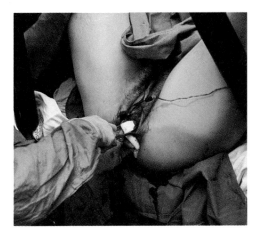
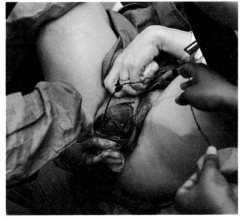

A modern forceps delivery will deliver the baby in a gentle and sympathetic way. Forceps are used when it is necessary to speed up a prolonged labour, but when a Caesarian delivery is not indicated, and are only applied when the baby's head is already low in the pelvis

baby's scalp (foetal blood sampling) through a special instrument inserted into the mother's vagina. If continuous heart monitoring shows a dramatic picture of distress, blood sampling would seem to be wasting time.

Distress in the first stage of labour requires Caesarean section. In the early second stage of labour forceps may be used, but in the later part of the second stage an episiotomy will speed up delivery of the baby and save valuable time.

Breech presentation
Three per cent of babies present by the breech, or bottom, in late pregnancy. In the young patient antenatal assessment of the baby's size and health and of the capacity and shape of the maternal pelvis will often lead to a decision in favour of labour and vaginal breech delivery. With the increased risk of placental failure to the baby of the older mother, a much more willing resort to Caesarean is the rule. With a breech, any delay in the second stage of labour leads to foetal asphyxia, as the baby is already born with the umbilical cord compressed, but the head is still inside and the baby cannot breathe. This risk, on top of the higher risk that exists of placental failure, is not justified in women in the older age group.

Forceps delivery
Forceps are used in the second stage of labour if the mother is exhausted and cannot push the baby out. They are also used if there are signs of foetal distress and if the second stage of labour is becoming prolonged and the baby's head is no longer descending. High forceps deliveries are no longer carried out; if the baby's head is not low in the pelvis, Caesarean section is still safer for the mother and baby. If the baby's head is low in the pelvis, forceps delivery may safely take place, and if the head is in a normal, anterior position (facing the mother's spine), ordinary forceps are used. There are various types of such forceps: Wrigley's, Rhodes', Simpson's, Neville-Barnes', and so on. If the baby is in the posterior position (facing forwards) the rotation forceps, known as Kjelland's forceps, may be required.

Non-rotation forceps deliveries are usually carried out in conjunction with a local (pudendal) nerve block within the pelvis. If a rotation forceps delivery is required, an epidural, spinal or even general anaesthetic is necessary.

Forceps deliveries are more common in the older age group. One contributing factor is that maternal exhaustion occurs more frequently, although this depends rather more on individual fitness than just on age. Another is that, in the age groups 30-35 and over 35, foetal distress is more common in the second stage of labour than in the first; in stage two, part of the baby is outside the uterus, in the vagina, and the uterus is therefore smaller than in the first stage. This means that the site of placental attachment is smaller, and consequently the amount of oxygen that crosses the placenta is lowered. A baby who has just sufficient oxygen in the first stage has insufficient in the second stage, and distress is apparent. Of course, the threshold for interference is low; obstetricians are more conscious of the risks in the 35-39 age group and especially over 40, and are more inclined to shorten the second stage by delivering the baby with forceps.

In most units, the fact that a forceps delivery is to be carried out is no reason for the partner to leave the room should he wish to stay. There will be great apprehension over the delivery on the part of the woman and the presence of the partner can be of enormous benefit. If the forceps delivery is carried out in a pain-free, gentle and sympathetic way, it can still be an exciting and rewarding time for the mother and she will still be able to play a major part in the delivery.

Caesarean section

Caesarean section is performed slightly more often in the 30-34 year age group of first-time mothers than in younger women. The rate of Caesarean rises more rapidly over the age of 35, and may be of the order of 20-25 per cent of births for women over the age of 40. Some of these Caesareans are for problems identified in the antenatal period that are more common in the older age group, such as raised blood pressure or small-for-dates babies. Others are for a combination of risk factors such as maternal age plus breech presentation, or age plus a history of bleeding in late pregnancy. All these are planned, or elective, Caesareans. Other operations are emergencies, and are undertaken for problems discussed earlier which are more common in the older age group, such as prolonged labour or foetal distress.

Caesarean section has the risks of a major operation, but it has become a much safer procedure over the past few decades with the advances in surgery and anaesthesia and the availability of blood transfusion. In addition, doctors are now dealing with a healthier population of women who recover quickly from surgery.

Anaesthesia for emergency Caesareans may need to be rapid, and the woman will be given a general anaesthetic. Where the operation is elective, or even in labour if there is

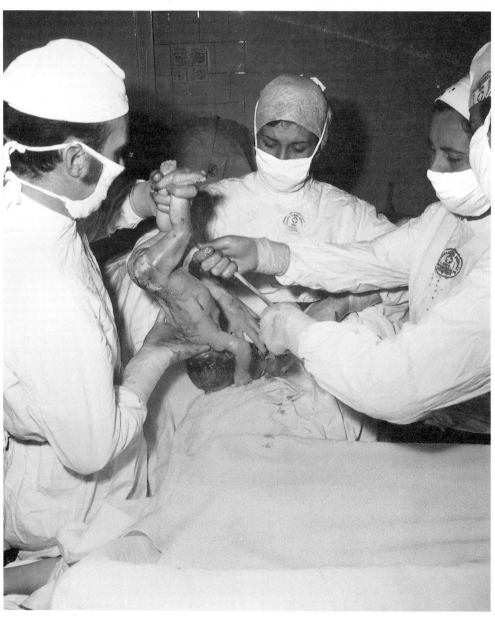

Ceasarean section need not be a horrific experience. It has become a far safer procedure of late, with the advances in surgery and anaesthesia

not too much of a rush, an epidural anaesthetic may be used. Most large maternity hospitals now have anaesthetists available all the time for maternity work and they are skilled in epidural use. Where epidural expertise is not available, general anaesthesia will be required. It will also be used where the mother does not like the idea of being awake. If the woman has an epidural for a Caesarean she cannot feel the operation, and the use of a small screen across her chest means that she will not be able to see the procedure. She will not be sedated and can see her baby immediately and hold him or her within seconds. The majority of obstetricians are happy to have the partner in theatre as well –

he will sit by his partner's head, giving moral support and also enjoying the moment of birth. The epidural cannula is left in place for 24 hours or so to provide initial pain relief. The post-operative recovery after epidural Caesarean section is usually rapid.

Having dealt with the complications that can occur in labour and with delivery, let it be said again that, in general, the 30-34 year age group of first time mothers can expect to have a fairly normal delivery. Thereafter, there is a slow increase in the complication and operative delivery rates. However, even in the 40 plus age group, the majority of labours start on their own and delivery of normal-sized healthy babies result.

THE NEWBORN BABY

The division of the umbilical cord following delivery confirms the final physical separation of infant from mother. This is the moment when the paediatrician usually takes over the care of the newborn infant.

It is the paediatrician's responsibility to examine the newborn immediately after delivery, during the early neonatal period and again prior to discharge from the maternity unit. Following delivery, the paediatrician will asses the infant to see whether he or she is suffering any immediate problem that will require urgent action. The most common assessment of neonatal adjustment or

adaptation is by use of the Apgar Score system to determine infant heart rate, respiratory effort, muscle tone, response to stimuli and the colour of the skin.

Respiration should be established within 60 seconds of birth, and is often heralded by a cry. The infant's mouth and pharynx are gently cleared using a sterile mucous extractor, and a catheter is then passed into the stomach to empty swallowed liquid. The rythmic respiratory pattern is not always established in the first few minutes of life, but this does not cause any problem if a rate of 30-50 breaths per minute then take place. The

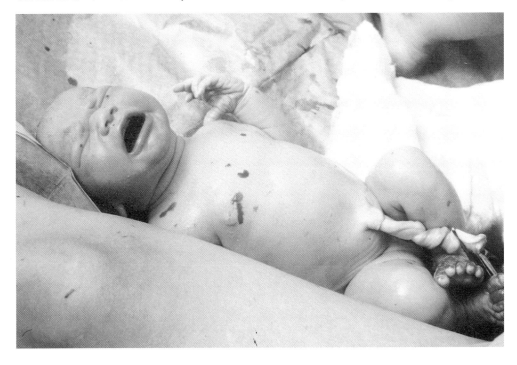

The cutting of the umbilical cord marks the beginning of the newborn's physical independence from the mother

heart rate drops after birth from about 160 beats per minute to about 120 within a short space of time and remains relatively steady.

Determination of Apgar score

The Apgar score provides a practical and quantifiable way of assessment of the state of the newborn infant, and should be determined at one and five minutes after birth.

Ideally, the score should be between 7 and 10; scores below that require supportive or remedial measures. Scores obtained for each factor can range from 0 to 2.

Scores above 7 require minimal support, whereas a score below 4 demands immediate passing of a tube into the trachea and ventilation of the baby's lungs. The tube can usually be removed within 2-3 minutes.

It is now accepted practice for the mother to hold her baby as soon as possible after delivery, so that both parents have the opportunity to share in the joy of birth (right)

APGAR SCORE			
Factors observed	0	1	2
Heart rate	absent	less than 100	greater than 100
Respiratory effort	absent	slow/irregular	regular/crying
Muscle tone	limp	some flexion	active movements
Response to stimuli	nil	grimace	cough, sneeze
Colour	blue	pink body, blue extremeties	pink

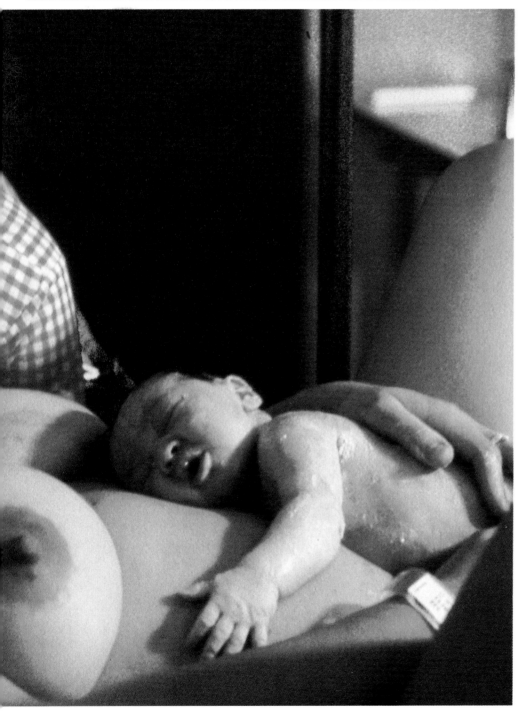

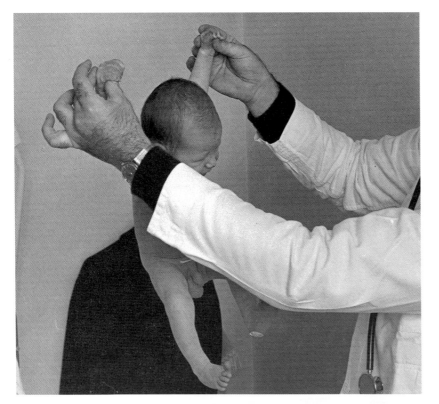

Scores between 4 and 7 necessitate warmth and stimulation and then reassessment within 60 seconds, applying the same criteria as above.

The aim of this system is to assess the situation in the first minute of life and then to correct any depressed (hypoxic) baby in 3-5 minutes. The five minute score is probably more important as there is some evidence that low Apgar scores at this time are related to delayed neurological performance at one year of age. Newborn babies can tolerate lack of oxygen far better than older children and adults; nevertheless, inadequate or delayed resuscitation can lead to brain damage.

Early neonatal examination
The neonatal examination usually takes place within hours following birth. It is normally carried out in conjunction with a knowledge of the antenatal and natal history. Symptoms such as vomiting, reluctance to feed, choking spells and diarrhoea are carefully evaluated and any respiratory difficulties are assessed. The infant's general appearance will be noted and his or her weight, length and maximum head circumference will be recorded if this has not been done immediately after delivery.

In order to examine all the essential areas,

Holding the newborn by the hands (above) the doctor will note the infant's response to danger. In a normal reaction the baby curls up his toes. During the routine early neonatal examination (right) the baby is checked from head to foot for factors such as hip dislocation and muscle tone

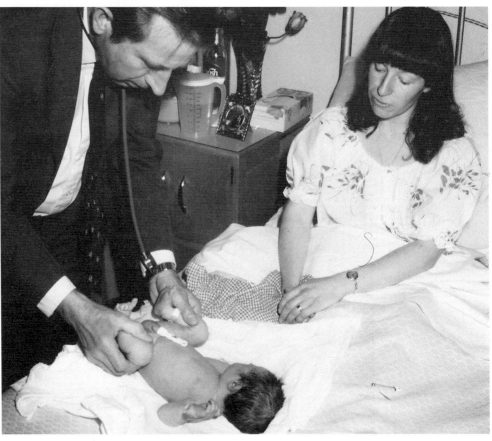

it is most convenient to start with the head and progress towards the feet. The shape of the head at birth depends on the nature of the labour, and unusual shapes are not uncommon in the first 24 hours of life, such as swelling over the back of the head and globular-shaped heads which occur after Caesarean section or breech delivery. A check on the facial characteristics may indicate some specific disorder, such as Down's syndrome.

During the examination the paediatrician will use a stethoscope to examine the heart and will then examine the nervous system. The hip joints will be looked at for signs of dislocation, a not uncommon problem that is relatively easy to treat if diagnosed early enough.

Abnormalities of the feet are frequently positional, reflecting the position that the foetus adopted in the uterus. Most of these postural deformities are transient and correct spontaneously over a period of weeks.

Examination prior to discharge
If the infant develops any problems after the early neonatal examination he or she will be examined again. Normally, however, the next examination is carried out on the day before the mother and baby leave hospital. This examination has at least four important functions: to assess the baby's progress from birth; to exclude any congenital malformations or trauma which were not present at birth or might have escaped notice; to exclude signs of skin infection; and to reassure the mother about specific conditions such as skin spots, which, although not of any clinical importance, may alarm her.

The mother's presence during examination is a decided advantage, as she can observe for herself and ask questions as they arise. If anything abnormal is found the situation can be explained at once and fears and anxieties can be alleviated.

The Guthrie test, a routine blood test performed on every baby for early detection of the condition known as phenylketonuria, is usually done between the seventh and fourteenth day of life. It may be carried out in hospital or at home by the health visitor. Phenylketonuria – or PKU – is a rare inherited disease. It is caused by the absence of an enzyme for dealing with the amino acid phenylalanine and leads to brain damage in the young child. Screening at birth and the starting of a special diet have meant that the affected child's brain will develop normally.

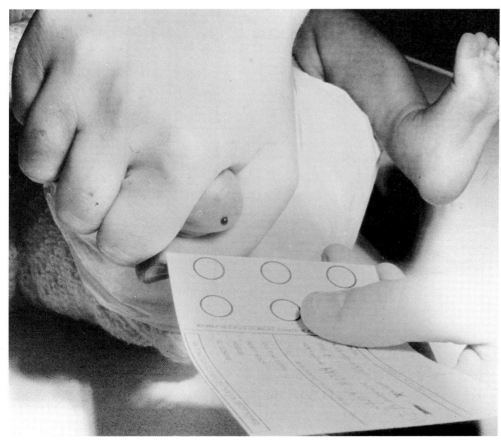

At 7-14 days a Guthrie test is performed to detect any signs of phenylketonuria. A small needle prick is made in the baby's heel from which samples of blood are taken

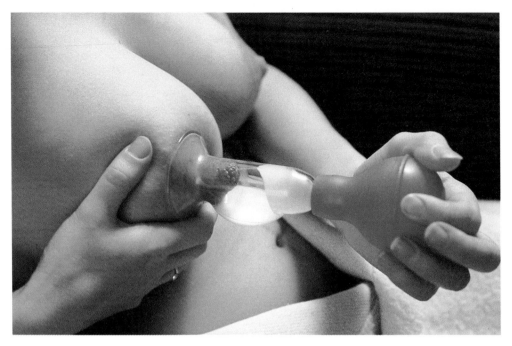

Breast milk can be expressed either by pump or by hand (above and below); it can then be used for bottle-feeds when the mother is at work or otherwise absent. However, for many mothers there is really no satisfactory alternative to the intimacy that is an intrinsic part of breastfeeding (far right)

Following the mother's and baby's discharge any problems or anxieties that arise about the baby should be discussed with the GP. Many new mothers need the reassurance of their doctor that all is well, and they should not be afraid to seek it.

Infant feeding

Paediatricians and other experts looking after the newborn baby should reinforce and restate certain basic principles of infant feeding

which in recent years may have been obscured by the dictates of fashion and the food manufacturers.

For most babies, the milk produced by most mothers is better adapted to the infant's nutritional needs than the milk of any animal or artificial formula. Breastfeeding, when it works well, provides a more enriching experience to mother and child than does bottle-feeding.

If breastfeeding fails, and artificial feeding has to be relied upon, the most convenient and suitable cow's milk preparation are the dried milks. Doorstep undiluted, unboiled cow's milk is not suitable for the baby in the first year.

The calorific requirement for growth for the average baby using milk feeds are met by at least 75 ml per kg (2 ½ oz per lb) body weight per day. Some newborn babies may need more and some will grow well on less. This requirement should be reached by the end of 7-10 days of life, when the baby's birthweight should have been regained. There is an initial weight loss of approximately 10 per cent in the first few days of life, usually correcting to birthweight when the full 75 ml per kg is being taken by the baby.

Milk alone is usually satisfactory for adequate growth at least until three months of age, when the average intake reaches 198-227 ml (7-8 oz) per feed and the baby has reached 5 kg (12 lb) in weight. Mixed feeding, or weaning, can then commence and in most babies is not required much before this time.

The decision whether to breastfeed or bottle-feed should be made well before the third trimester of pregnancy. Mothers who choose to breastfeed should obtain adequate information about breastfeeding and the management of lactation as well as where to seek support for achieving breastfeeding goals. (*See* p 146.) Other feeding choices should also be discussed in case of problems.

Breastfeeding by working mothers is a common and worldwide experience, but in most developed countries maternal employment usually mandates a prolonged daily separation, leading to the assumption that breastfeeding and working are mutually exclusive. With an increased interest in breastfeeding and the growing percentage of mothers that work, women have creatively sought options to combine employment with completing the full course of lactation.

Data indicates that as many as 20 per cent of women in the United States return to work within six weeks of delivery, and that maternal employment has a deleterious effect on the rates of initiation and duration of breastfeeding. Delaying the return to work for about 16 weeks and working part-time instead of full-time has been associated with longer duration of breastfeeding among working mothers.

Bowel movements

One of the first tasks of the bowel in the newborn is to get rid of all the matter which has been formed there during pregnancy. This substance, called meconium, is dark green, sticky and adhesive, and unusual if you are not expecting it. The baby usually gets rid of this by the second or third day of life. During the first few weeks bowel movements may be very frequent, as often as six times a day or more, or infrequent, once every few days – no two babies are the same. The only predictable difference in bowel movements is between bottle-fed and breastfed babies.

A breastfed baby passes soft mustard coloured stools. Initially these are passed frequently, for example 4-6 times daily, then a day or more may pass without any motions at all. Both patterns are completely normal. Cow's milk formula-based feeds have certain ingredients which the baby cannot wholly digest; this results in more frequent stools which are a darker brown colour, are more smelly and of a firmer consistency. Green stools imply that the bile acids, which should normally be absorbed, are being passed directly into the lower bowel and excreted unchanged. This is often temporary and does not always signify diarrhoea. Treatment is not usually required. Constipation may need attention if it persists; usually what passes for constipation is merely infrequent but perfectly normal bowel movements. Much variability may be noted from one infant to another.

Chapter 4

PARENTING·

The arrival of the first baby calls for considerable adjustment under any circumstances, but for the woman over 30 and her partner the birth of the baby brings additional complications. Both partners, who may previously have established a relatively independant lifestyle at work and in their private lives, will now face a certain degree of restraint on their activities and movements. Not only will their individual lives change but their life as a couple will take on a new dimension. The

freedom that they have previously enjoyed is bound to be somewhat curtailed.

All of this may sound daunting and even alarming, and certainly parenting does involve problems that demand solutions. Yet it also brings its own special kind of joy, excitement and reward that are the exclusive property of the family, whether that family is the more conventional one of mother, father and child or the single mother and child on their own.

THE NEW MOTHER

Despite the initial difficulties of settling into a new routine, the birth of the first baby can bring real joy and contentment

The new mother is something of a celebrity. The anxieties of pregnancy behind her, she feels, quite rightly, a tremendous sense of achievement in the hours following birth. Added to this, there are the visitors, congratulations, flowers and gifts for the baby. It is an intoxicating experience.

Amid the excitement, the fact that life has changed irrevocably may be overlooked. During the stay in hospital experienced staff will ease the new mother into her role and be on hand to give expert advice. It is often not until mother and baby are discharged from hospital that the immensity of the undertaking becomes apparent.

After the efficient bustle of the hospital, the home can seem strangely quiet and the mother may suddenly feel very much on her own. The baby appears so fragile, so very new, and the responsibility so total. And then the infant cries. Is he wet, hungry, too cold or too hot? Does he have wind? Should she change him, feed him, cuddle him or ignore him?

Naturally, mother and baby have not been abandoned to their own devices, and the newborn's hold on life is in fact a remarkably lusty one – he or she would not have been discharged if that were not the case. In most situations the father will be there at least part of the time to help care for the baby and give the mother support. The midwife will visit daily until the baby is ten days old and the GP will certainly call and examine both mother and baby. The health visitor will make contact to provide details about local baby clinics,

postnatal support groups, immunisation routines and so on. There will also be a flood of information in the form of leaflets, pamphlets, samples and advice from family and friends.

There is something about a mother with her newborn which attracts comment – people seem to have an irresistible urge to voice an opinion, usually with great conviction. The opinions often conflict, varying according to the age, sex and particular preoccupations of the individual. When the mother turns to baby care books for some signposts in this fog of conflicting advice, she may not fare any better than when listening to those close to her – most books also vary in their theories and opinions. All of this may leave the new mother feeling even more alone and confused. For the older mother, who has possibly held a fairly responsible job and has been used to being in command of a situation, the feeling of being a novice can be very unsettling.

Emotional changes
There is no doubt that the new mother, however competent and organised an individual, is in a vulnerable state. With the trend towards early discharge from hospital becoming increasingly widespread, the first week or so at home can often coincide with postnatal depression, and there may be days when the euphoria the mother felt immediately after delivery seems years away.

The mother may feel weepy, her stitches may hurt and her breasts may seem to be living a life of their own; her pre-maternity

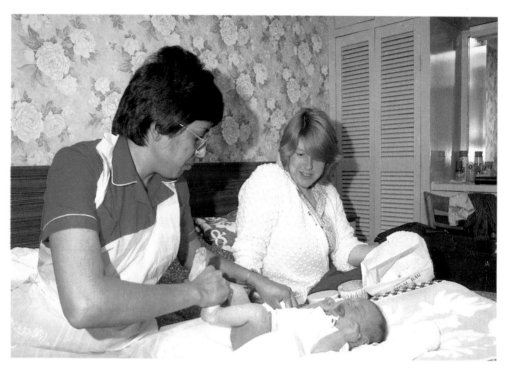

The new mother will appreciate the support of the midwife, who will make daily visits until the baby is ten days old

clothes will probably still not fit and she may be tired from a succession of broken nights. As a result, she may suddenly find herself bursting into tears and declaring that she never wanted a baby in the first place.

Reactions such as this are entirely normal, and generally very short-lived. It is only when depression is prolonged, or so severe that the mother cannot relate to her baby, or fears she might harm him, that a more serious underlying problem is indicated. In such cases, medical advice should be sought immediately, probably by her partner or a close friend, as the mother is usually in no condition to make an objective assessment of her emotional state.

In the vast majority of cases, however, professional help is not necessary. In fact, the best source of support may be a woman who has had her baby sufficiently recently to remember precisely what the feeling of being a new mother is like. She will be in a better position than most to appreciate the sense of unreality that comes from the sudden change in lifestyle entailed by becoming a mother. She will also be able to illustrate by example that the peculiarly sensitive emotional climate of the puerperium soon gives way to a more normal state of affairs as the baby settles into life and the mother into her new role.

Physical changes

The puerperium is also a time of great physical change, as all the changes which took place during the nine months of pregnancy are reversed. With the delivery of the placenta, oestrogen and progesterone levels drop dramatically. Immediately after the birth, the uterus can be felt just below the level of the umbilicus, but after ten days to a fortnight it has sunk back into the pelvis, and by six weeks, the time of the postnatal checkup, it has returned to its non-pregnant size – about 76 mm (3 in) long and 56 g (2 oz) in weight. The uterus contracts regularly in order to encourage this involution, or decrease in size, and these 'echoes' of labour are felt as afterpains, particularly at feed times if the mother is breastfeeding. A simple analgesic can relieve the pains if they are troublesome.

The length of time it takes for menstruation to start again after childbirth is very variable. As the milk hormone prolactin interferes with the menstrual cycle, the onset can be delayed for months while breastfeeding continues, during which time the mother will be less fertile than normal. Contraception should still be used, however, if another pregnancy is not wanted immediately, as ovulation usually occurs two weeks *before* the first period.

During the puerperium the breasts also undergo considerable change. Milk production is established by about the third day and in some cases this can lead to engorgement, when the breasts become swollen and hard – to the extent that the baby might have difficulty in grasping the nipple. Expressing a little milk before the feed begins may help, and bathing the breasts with alternate hot and cold flannels can be soothing. The supply of milk soon settles down and adjusts to the appetite of the baby. However, the mother may notice that a little milk leaks from the breasts when she hears her baby's hunger cry and picks him up for a feed.

For the bottle-feeding mother, some discomfort in the breasts has to be expected until her milk supply dries up through lack of stimulation. Restricting her intake of fluids and supporting the breasts should help. Injections to prevent the milk coming in the first place used to be given but were found to have unwelcome side effects.

The other most noticeable physical symptom of the puerperium is lochia, or loss of blood and debris from the uterus. It can last from two to eight weeks and gradually changes in colour from bright red to reddish brown and finally to yellow. The passing of clots, or sudden very heavy loss, should be reported to the doctor or midwife.

Mother-infant bonding

So far the discussion has been concerned with the profound effect the birth of the first baby will have. The experience is common to most women in western society. When that birth is postponed until after the woman has reached the age of 30, other considerations play a part. For example, most women over 30 have become accustomed to a certain degree of independence, of being their own person, whatever their personal circumstances – single, married, in or out of a stable emotional relationship.

In the period of adjustment following the birth, it is that sense of personal identity which probably suffers most, at least for a time. Until very recently the baby was physically part of the mother. Suddenly there is a new individual to contend with. A separate being, certainly, but one who depends for his or her very survival on a symbiotic bond – mother and baby are interdependent. It is the very intensity of the relationship which singles it out. Whatever the prevailing emotion, it is felt very keenly. The baby's fingers and toes are not just observed but marvelled at; his cries are not merely heard, but felt like a physical pain.

Many people assume that all mothers love their babies from the beginning, and therefore

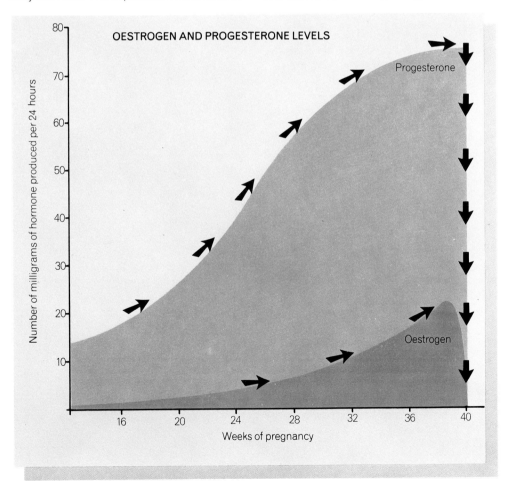

OESTROGEN AND PROGESTERONE LEVELS

Number of milligrams of hormone produced per 24 hours

Progesterone

Oestrogen

80
70
60
50
40
30
20
10

16   20   24   28   32   36   40

Weeks of pregnancy

The graph shows the startling drop in hormone levels that occurs after the birth of a child – it has been suggested that this contributes to post-natal depression

Some mothers respond well to the baby – and the baby to the mother – from the beginning, and both are intensely interested in each other (top). For other women there may be an initial period of difficulty when the mother cannot relate to the baby at all. This may be the result of post-natal depression, for which the mother will need help and support from her partner, relatives and friends, and, in some cases, from her doctor or other specialists

that they instinctively behave in a maternal manner. Yet it can take time to learn to love a baby. Much depends on what happened during pregnancy, the mother's relationship with her partner, how much medical intervention was required during labour and delivery and whether or not the mother and baby were fit and alert enough following the birth to be allowed some time together immediately. It is not so long ago that the baby was handed to the mother only after he had been bathed, weighed and wrapped like a parcel. However, the importance of the early bonding process is now recognised and, unless there are strong medical indications to the contrary, the mother will be given her baby to hold before, or as soon as, the umbilical cord has been clamped and cut. Many babies respond to their mother's attention with a frank and intently curious gaze and if put to the breast will suckle immediately - indeed the rooting reflex is at its strongest immediately after the birth.

Yet however smoothly the first moments go, there is no doubt that some babies, like some adults, are easier to get on with than others. If, on the one hand, the mother finds herself dealing with a baby whose personality blends

well with hers, then once the anxious first few weeks are over she is likely to relax and feel confident in her mothering role. She is energetic: the baby very active. They both enjoy outings and other physical activities. She is chatty, the baby friendly and outgoing – they spend time in 'conversation' and mutual admiration. The baby's response confirms that the mother is handling him well. If, on the other hand, the mother finds it difficult to understand her baby, her self-image as a mother may suffer because she will tend to blame herself. Some babies, for example, seem ill at ease with life outside the womb. They are nervous, or seem generally inclined to the miseries; handling such an infant until he has adapted to his separateness takes imagination and intelligence, and can seem a somewhat thankless task at first. But eventually even the grumpiest infant will settle down and begin to reward his mother with smiles and other signs of growing attachment.

At last the complicated feelings of love and affection which exist between a mother and child are showing signs of existence, and any mother is bound to feel gratified. A rapport between them builds as the days pass.

THE COUPLE'S RELATIONSHIP

And what of the father at this time? His position initially may be difficult. He has to allow his partner time to develop her relationship with the baby but be on hand to offer support, especially if the mother feels the infant is draining her of her individuality. The days are gone when fathers were largely ignored during pregnancy and regarded as an unhygenic menace during labour. Fathers are no longer content to remain on the sidelines – they recognise that they have a role in child care and a right to form their own special relationship with the baby from the moment of birth. Their partners and children can only benefit as a result.

Yet, however planned and eagerly awaited the birth, however involved the father indicated he was by helping with antenatal exercises and being present at the delivery, both partners should realise that once the baby has arrived their relationship is bound to change.

It is the arrival of the first child that turns a couple into a family, and the process is not always a comfortable one. If the mother appears to be totally involved with the baby the father may feel excluded, even resentful. It may seem to him that he will never have his partner to himself again; she may be tired from the exertions of labour and broken sleep and possibly irritable as a result. Her interest in matters unrelated to the baby may be minimal and yet she may complain at times that the baby is eating her alive. Her partner may therefore begin to wonder what happened to the bright, confident, organised woman he fell in love with. The home may be untidy and meals late, when they appear at all; the entire household may seem to revolve around the incessant demands of the new arrival. What the mother may need most of all at such a time may be what her partner might find hardest to give – tolerance. He may feel inclined to grumble that he is neglected, yet adding to the emotional demands on the new mother will not help at all. Order will, in a surprisingly short time, emerge out of the apparent chaos as the baby's behaviour settles into a more predictable pattern. Planning then becomes possible and a routine can be established.

Birth brings parents face to face with the very basics of human existence – issues of life and death, joy and pain. Many mothers have remarked that giving birth is the closest they have come to what might be termed a spiritual experience, and sharing that experience can certainly add a new dimension to

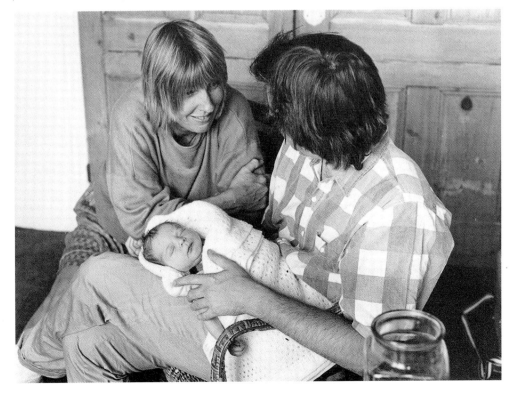

The birth of a first child creates a family unit; the man and woman are now responsible for another individual's life – at least until their child is ready to leave home and begin a totally independent life of his or her own

her relationship with her partner. Their love-making has borne fruit and they are often drawn much closer as a result.

The sexual relationship

Sexual expression of that closeness may have to wait a little while; some doctors recommend refraining from full intercourse until after the mother's postnatal check-up at six weeks, or until the lochia has ceased.

Both partners may feel a little apprehensive about having intercourse for the first time after the birth. The mother might be tense, fearing that intercourse could be painful, particularly if she has had an episiotomy; her partner may be equally nervous and reluctant to hurt her. In such cases, the couple may wish to express their sexuality and affection by finding other ways of giving each other pleasure. If there is any undue discomfort when intercouse is resumed, the GP should be consulted as any stitches may not have healed as they should have. Loss of muscle tone in the vagina – which has of course been stretched by the passage of the baby through the birth canal – may cause a woman to worry that she is a less satisfying lover for her partner, but postnatal exercises will help.

Sheer physical exhaustion may also be a factor in resuming sexual relations. A day of nappies, feeds and domestic routine hardly makes the new mother feel like a temptress, and she will need reassurance that, while her new role is a vitally important one, she is still a woman and an attractive one at that.

A break from the confines of the house can be helpful. Spur-of-the moment outings may now be out of the question unless the baby goes too but that does not mean that the mother should feel chained to the nursery 24 hours a day. Provided the newborn is fed and comfortable, there is no reason why he cannot be left in the care of another competent pair of hands for a few hours. It is a very good idea to accustom the baby to a change of carer from a very early age, particularly if the mother is intending to return to work once she has fully recovered from the birth. Even if the baby is being breastfed on demand, some breast milk can be expressed and left in a sterile container in the refrigerator.

Summary

Having a baby may take as long as a full year – nine months of pregnancy and a further three months of adapting to parenthood. Certainly by the time the baby reaches the age of 12 weeks the worries and uncertainties of the newborn period should be over and both parents should feel more prepared to extend their lives again. Indeed, at this time many mothers will be considering a return to work.

Caring for a young infant is an exhausting business that can involve 24-hour attention, and for a time may affect a couple's sexual relationship. Taking a break together occasionally, both from the baby and the home, may be helpful

Women who want to work after the baby is born, but do not necessarily need the company of colleagues, may find that working at home is the solution to their problem

PROBLEMS OF THE WORKING MOTHER

Millions of words have been expended in the working mother debate, but for many women the question of whether or not to work while their children are very young is academic; a job is not a matter of choice but of economic necessity. Today many families find that two incomes are required to support even a fairly modest lifestyle, and in hundreds of thousands of homes in Britain alone, the mother is the only breadwinner.

The world of work is not geared towards families. The industrial revolution brought about the removal of work from the family unit to the factory and the office, leaving the mother – who in many cases until then had been as much a productive part of the economic system as her husband – to provide the domestic support system. Some women find this caring role rewarding in itself; others prefer more tangible rewards.

The desire to work
The desire to be part of the mainstream of life, to have a role outside the home that is valuable and valued, is understood and ap-

plauded in men, but often denied to women who are mothers. The notion that nothing short of 24-hour-a-day care by the mother is adequate is still widespread. Grandparents, doctors and teacher, among others, may all be likely to ascribe any sign of unsettled behaviour in a child to the fact that the mother works outside the home. More and more women, however, are insisting on their right to work and not to be confined to the nurturing tasks alone. Many women want to work whether or not money is necessary and despite the fact that juggling work and home responsibilities is difficult. In a recent survey, four out of five of the working mothers interviewed declared that they would still want to go out to work even if they did not need the money.

The desperate loneliness and depression that can result from being shut up day after day in the home with only a small child for company has to be experienced to be fully understood. The mother feels that work is something for other people; she is merely there to attend to the needs of others. The

resentment that can build up does the mother no good at all, and the effect on the child can hardly be beneficial.

A number of studies have shown that when a mother is isolated with small children she is more inclined to be irritable and find it difficult to show physical affection; there may even be a correlation with child abuse. The isolation which leads to such an unhappy state of affairs is a peculiarly modern invention.

In returning to work while her children are still small, in insisting on her right to be considered part of the human race, the mother is reflecting the far healthier balance between family and working life that existed in pre-industrial communities where child care was a communal responsibility. The difficulty is that the network of aunts, grandparents, friends, sisters and other potential helpers who were once on hand tends to be far too widespread geographically in modern industrial societies and nothing has been found to replace it.

In this country, the lack of provision of nursery care is lamentable; in most cases finding someone to look after the child while the mother goes out to work is the major problem faced by working mothers. The various types of child care arrangements are considered in detail in the final part of this chapter, but it may be said here that the best options tend to be the most expensive and therefore are less available to women who most need to work. Many such women stagger from one informal and barely satisfactory minding arrangement to another. Yet what alternative do they have, other than giving up work and living on social security until the children are older?

The situation can only improve as more mothers of young children who enter the job market make their requirements for the provision of decent child care known, loudly and insistently.

A sense of priorities

The media often promote the idea that there is an army of supremely organised working women in high-powered jobs who are perfect mothers and hostesses and exciting lovers. The reality is, however, that most working women struggle through the week, making compromises as employees, employers, wives and mothers at almost every turn.

What the working mother needs above all else, apart from enormous will power and stamina, is an accurate sense of priorities. What those priorities are, and their order, depends very much on the individual woman, but for a high proportion of women the house seems to come firmly at the bottom of the list.

Learning to live with chaos, or at the least

with an untidy home, comes easier to some women than to others, but sensible working mothers realise that the perfectionist's attitude is a dangerous one – dangerous, that is, to the mother's health and sanity, particularly if she will not relinquish any of the responsibility for running the home. Many working mothers need to enlist the help of their partners or other members of their family, and if help is not forthcoming from these people they may have to pay someone to take over some of the responsibility.

There is no doubt that the key to combining the running of the home with a full-time job outside it lies in organization, which takes some judicious planning. For example, many working mothers find that they have become compulsive list-makers, carrying a notebook around with them in order to jot things down as they occur to them.

Getting organized on the domestic front certainly helps the working mother preserve her sanity – the sense of impending chaos that can result from simply muddling through can bring on a feeling of panic that may affect the whole family. But people do not run by clockwork, and being a good mother does not stand or fall on whether or not the child's clothes are beautifully ironed. There are times when the mother should set aside routine in favour of simply being with her partner and child.

Feelings of guilt

For many working mothers, worrying about the child while they are at work, and about work when they are with their child, is common practice, but it only produces feelings of guilt and the realisation that she is not giving her best to either, while her mind is elsewhere. Guilt is one of the most common of all maternal afflictions. Whatever the child care arrangements, however well-managed, there are times when the working mother is overcome by a wave of guilt because she is not with her child, particularly when the child is ill. Nobody likes their children to be ill, but the working mother absolutely dreads it, as she sees her carefully constructed plans of child care crumbling. Even if she is among the fortunate mothers who can afford full-time child care in her home, she is still likely to feel that it should be her, and not the nanny or nurse, who is looking after the young patient.

To avoid unnecessary anxiety at such times, working mothers should make contingency plans with their employers for these occasions, such as arranging to take any time spent in emergency care out of holiday entitlement and arranging for temporary staff to replace her when she must be absent for any length of time.

The bare essentials

The working mother does not have time for inessentials – so what are the essentials as far as the happiness of her child and partner are concerned? Her presence 24 hours a day is not necessary, as long as she makes herself available when her child really needs her, and not her substitute. It is the quality of time a mother spends with her child that is significant, not the number of hours. Mothers who work should therefore organize their day so that they spend at least several hours each evening playing with their child and attending to his or her needs, perhaps bathing or changing the baby directly before bedtime, so that the mother's face is the last image the child sees before sleep.

Children do not really care about matters such as dust or untidiness as long as they are confident that they have their parents' love and loyalty. If the mother, and father, provide those, then they will equip their child for the future. In fact, the child is more likely to grow up with a far more realistic attitude towards parenting and family life than today's parents, who may still be struggling to fit out-moded views into modern working patterns, at the expense of their own peace of mind.

Having a mother they can respect means a lot to children, particularly to girls. They see their mother as someone with the energy and initiative to do something about her life and are more likely to be more ambitious themselves as a result. Many school teachers remark on the fact that the children of working mothers are more alert and older for their age than those with mothers who are at home all day – and possibly resenting it.

When the children reach adolescence and want to lead their own life, they are not burdened with a mother who contemplates her empty nest and no longer feels she has a role. The working mother is an individual in her own right; she does not have to rely on her children for her status in society. She has her own interests outside the home, and does not need to re-live her teenage years through the exploits of her offspring.

When a woman becomes a mother she takes on an enormous responsibility, not only to care for her child's emotional and physical well being but also to provide an example of adult behaviour from which he or she can learn to adapt to the world.

At the time of writing, making the dual role of working woman and caring mother feasible is phenomenally hard work successfully achieved only by the fortunate few, with the aid of a great many helpers. Yet mothers owe it to their children and to themselves to show by example that parenting is a way into life, not out of it.

No matter how loving the mother, there may be times when she becomes exhausted and feels unable to cope, especially if she is isolated in the home with a small child day after day (far left)

FATHERHOOD

Many discussions, past and present, concerning the transition of a couple from pre-parenthood to parenthood have tended to concentrate almost exclusively on the experience and adjustments of the mother. Fathers have often been depicted as somewhat shadowy, peripheral or even comic figures in the whole process, and the impression sometimes seems to have been that, for a man, becoming a parent is somehow a less important and life-changing event than for a woman.

This tendency derived from the traditional idea of the father as that of breadwinner for the family, who had little direct involvement in pregnancy, childbirth and baby care, and the logical extension that since (according to this model) the father's role changed very little between pre-parenthood and parenthood, so he had to make less adjustment than the mother.

Over the last 25 years or so, a variety of social and economic changes, together with some scientific breakthroughs, have combined to prompt a considerable reworking of the ideas concerning the roles of men and women in society in general and of mothers and fathers in particular. Questions have also been raised about whether there are distinctive roles. Improved educational opportunities for women, combined with legal reforms and a recognition that women can perform a wide range of jobs in modern industrial societies, as well or better than men, have led to a considerable increase in female earning power. A heightened emphasis on material values, combined with a generally more tenuous employment situation, have in-

Fathers have begun to realise that the parent who has a share in child care also has a greater emotional attachment to the child and that father-infant bonding is as important as the bond formed between mother and infant

The need to communicate tenderness is essential in any loving relationship – close physical contact is one way in which a man can achieve this with his child (left and below)

creased the importance of a second income within families. Improvements in contraceptive technology and use have meant that couples are now able to plan parenthood with more precision. At the same time, there has been a recognition that the healthy emotional and psychological development of babies does not necessarily require the full-time presence of the mother, and that attachment to the father can be just as important.

New concepts of parenthood

As one of the main consequences of these changes, a far greater proportion of women are now developing careers for ten years or more prior to considering parenthood, and not surprisingly, many are resuming or expecting to resume full or at least part-time employment in these careers quite soon after childbirth. Many readers of this book will fall into this category. The inevitable corollary of this release of women – or at least improved opportunity for release – from the straitjacket of domestic responsibilities has been the release of men from being simply providers into a fuller and more active role in the home.

In the context of parenthood, these changes have produced a shift from a situation in which mothers and fathers played quite strictly defined and separate roles within the family, into one where partners have a far greater choice of options in the way they decide to share the varied and substantial demands associated with having a child, and in which the exact division of responsibilities is decided far more according to circumstances and to the aspirations and talents of the individuals concerned than on external social pressures. In short, we have moved from a situation in which mothers' and fathers' roles were quite distinct into one where these roles are to a large extent interchangeable.

This important social change has developed in a remarkably short space of time, but as yet is by no means complete. Many couples, through choice, for purely practical purposes, or perhaps because one or other of the partners is unable to escape their social conditioning, continue to conform to the traditional parental roles and to a greater or lesser extent are happy to do so; their

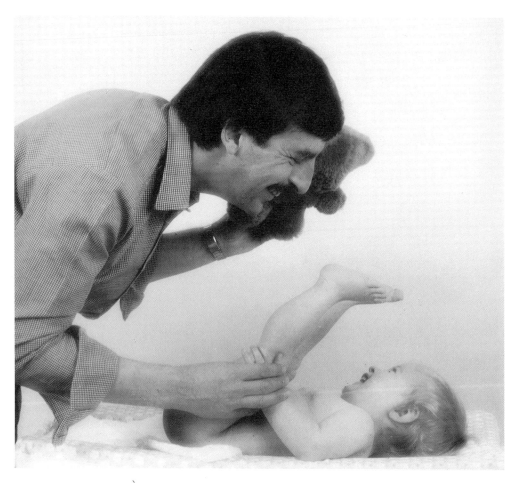

Like the new mother, the new father will learn that involving himself in all aspects of child care will often give him the opportunity to enjoy a brief but valuable interlude of play with his child

Women over thirty may be surprised to find that younger men often take an active interest in babies and enjoy babysitting from time to time

selection of each other as life-partners will often have depended on the perceived ability of the opposite number to fit into a traditional mother or father-type role. Furthermore, a complete reversal of the traditional roles (to the extent that the father takes up total responsibility for the home and baby and the mother is the sole breadwinner) has so far not become a commonly observed phenomenon.

What has become a much more common, or even typical pattern, and perhaps will be the most relevant to the readership of this book, is one in which both partners accept responsibility for all the different demands of parenthood – including care of the baby, general upkeep of the home and financial provision. This does not mean that the division of labour will be exact or will not vary from time to time: what it does mean is that each partner recognizes the right of the other to be involved in all the aspects of parenting, and also recognizes each other's right to demand and obtain assistance in any aspect as circumstances change. Much of what is discussed below assumes the modern father, who is one half of such a partnership; therefore some of the points may be less relevant to the father within a more traditional partnership.

The modern father

For the modern father who is part of a shared responsibility partnership, there are many benefits from this arrangement compared with the more traditional role. Although he may be the only partner working in the months preceding and after the birth, there will be less dependency on him as long-term breadwinner. Although he may look forward with no more enthusiasm than his partner to some of the less desirable aspects of parenthood – sleep-disturbed nights, physically and mentally taxing demands of the baby, the constraints on social activities – he realises that taking his share in coping with these stresses will have its reward in a fuller emotional relationship with the child, and the enjoyment and fulfillment this can generate. Perhaps of more importance, he realises that life with a partner with whom he is on an equal footing, with whom he will have shared experiences and interests both within and outside the home, and who is not burdened down with the monotony and frustrations of sole domestic responsibility, is potentially a considerable improvement on the traditional pattern of family life.

Possible problems

There are, however, a number of possible problems that the father may need to recognise and come to terms with. First of all, he may need to deal with any lingering anxieties concerning his self-identity. Some men will perceive that, whereas they are able to take part in most aspects of parenting, they are denied full participation in two aspects – the actual bearing of the child and breastfeeding – for which women are specifically biologically adapted. For the working father, there may thus be a feeling of unease that being fully involved in preparations for the birth and in domestic responsibilities once the baby arrives entails some net loss of identity, if taking on this role means redirecting his energies away from the workplace.

If such insecurities exist, and the father is truly intending to be a sharing parent rather than just an occasional help around the home, it is as well that they are brought out into the open and discussed with the partner at an early stage, so that hopefully, a solution can be found. Otherwise, he is likely to end up feeling either 'put upon' when called upon to take his share of domestic tasks, or reneging on commitments with possible disastrous affects on the whole partnership.

Another more practical problem for the father can be that of knowing how to be a 'good' parent. Most peoples' ideas on how to be a parent derive at least partly from memories of how their own parents coped. For the man whose own father was a somewhat distant, perhaps disciplinarian figure, only encountered occasionally in the evenings or weekends, and who intends to play a different role from this in relation to his own children, there is no model on which to rely. Advice from older male friends who have themselves recently been through the experience of be-

Not all fathers happily take on the duties of caring for the home and the baby, even part of the time. Men who have grown up in a family where the roles of male and female were strictly defined may have difficulty in adjusting to what they consider role-reversal, even if they accept the need for such a change intellectually

Particularly when the baby is very young, the mother may see herself as the primary nurturer, but if the baby is bottle-fed there is no reason why the father cannot take part in this and give the mother a much-needed opportunity to rest

coming parents can be useful.

In addition, the impact of the birth of the child can have important psychological consequences for any father. Perhaps more than any other important life event – such as leaving home, the first sexual experience, first job, or marriage – becoming a parent provides tangible proof that one has finally grown up. For the father as much as the mother, the joy and pride at the birth of the child, together with the attention and congratulations this brings from friends and family, will usually bring a great increase in feelings of self-worth and general contentment. However, these positive feelings may be tinged with feelings of depression over lost youth, or of anxiety concerning the increased responsibility. In practice, the father will have little time to mull over such thoughts as the busy schedule of looking after the baby intervenes.

The older father

Where the mother is having her first child in her 30s, often the father also will be entering parenthood at a rather older age than average – perhaps in his mid to late 30s or in his 40s or even 50s. This in itself can have both positive and negative implications for his ease of adjustment. On the one hand, greater emotional maturity is likely to be of benefit, and he may have already achieved considerable success and recognition at work, so he may find it rather easier then the younger man to divert his energies from the workplace to the home. On the other hand, if he has reached a high level of responsibility in his career, the job may make unavoidably heavy demands on his time. There are perhaps likely to be other

stresses on him as well – for example his own parents may be well into old age and require regular attention and visits.

There can be other problems for the older father. He is likely to be more set in his ways and thus adjustments required by parenthood are likely to be more traumatic; there will have been a longer timespan since his own childhood, and new ideas about fathering may seem alien to him; he may even doubt his own ability to communicate with an infant, having spent so long in a purely adult world.

The father during pregnancy

The more involved the father can be in sharing the mother's physical and psychological preparation for the birth, the less likely he is to feel excluded or shut out from the whole process, or ignored and abandoned by his partner as she becomes progressively more engrossed with the life forming within her. Instead, his involvement will provide him with the sense that the child is his as much as his partner's and that his role in the baby's creation has been much more than just a biological one.

The father can make it his business to read the same books as his partner on pregnancy and childbirth, and together they can discuss any problems envisaged and sort out the meaning of any details in the process or methods of childbirth that might seem obscure or frightening to the first-time mother. He can attend antenatal classes with her, and share in any breathing and relaxation exercises she practises, so that he realises what the difficulties are and where he can be of most help.

Family and friends – perhaps in particular his partner's mother – will often provide plenty of advice, suggestions or criticism, and he needs to stand by his partner and support her independence and self-assertiveness and let her see that he has complete confidence in her.

At various times during the pregnancy, his partner is likely to experience feelings of discomfort, nausea or tiredness, and his increased willingness to do the household chores can provide relief and prepare the way for his further involvement in this once the baby arrives. He needs also to recognise that his partner may be going through great emotional changes, partly related to the physiological changes occurring within her and the increased physical presence of the child, and that these may be displayed in various types of seemingly uncharacteristic behaviour or as overt emotional outbursts. He needs to be accepting towards these and provide comfort and the opportunity for discussion, rather than turn his back with an air of mystified resignation.

In particular, he needs to be aware that his partner may be experiencing anxieties concerning her continued attractiveness as her body changes shape and she contemplates the transition to motherhood. It is important that he lets her know that she is still desirable to him and that the transition into parenthood does not mean an end to the romantic side of their life. Lovemaking can usually continue to be enjoyed by both partners throughout pregnancy, provided it is carried out with tenderness and affection; either or both partners may develop anxieties about the advisability of sex during the later stages, but these can usually be sorted out through discussion with a counsellor. There may also be a problem of physical discomfort, particularly for the woman, but the solution to this may simply be the use of positions where weight is kept off her abdomen or to consider other forms of lovemaking without penetration.

In an increasing number of families, it is the woman who goes out to work and the father who has the major share in caring for the children and the home, but some couples find it more satisfactory to divide their time equally between work and home so that both partners have a share in each

During labour and birth

The father who frets in a downstairs room or hospital corridor while his partner delivers is largely a figure of the past. Quite apart from the natural desire of the father to be part of this emotionally charged event, his presence can be of great assistance to the mother in easing her passage, and in providing psychological reassurance (the main concern of the doctors or midwives will be with ensuring the physical health of the mother and baby). Again, his full involvement in the birth will provide a sense of having played a full part in the baby's creation.

The ways in which the father can provide support to his partner are manifold. During contractions, he can give verbal encouragement and carry her over difficult contractions by breathing with her. He may be able to ease areas of pain in the back or over the cervix by means of massage techniques learned in antenatal classes. Between contractions, he can concentrate on making sure his partner is as comfortable as possible – if only by rearranging pillows or providing sips of water. Throughout, he needs to be in close physical proximity to her, and provide frequent eye contact, firm holding and caressing.

The eventual emergence of the baby is of course a moment of great emotional significance for both parents. If the delivery is in hospital, the father can play an important role in conveying to the staff that he and his partner would like to have the baby with them as soon as possible, and be allowed an ample quiet time together to share the joy and excitement of their shared achievement, and experience the first tentative steps in forging the new bonds with the baby.

The domestic impact of the baby

Following a first-time delivery in hospital, the mother will usually remain in the hospital for a few days in order to begin her physical recovery and for breastfeeding to be established. During this time, the father will naturally want to be with his partner and baby as much as possible; however, if he is employed and is only able to obtain a few days' leave, this may be better taken when the mother has returned home and his presence may be more critically important. It can be a particularly important psychological boon to the mother if, on her return home, she finds that the father has made an effort to keep the place clean and tidy.

Once the family is reunited in the home, the enormous increase in stresses and demands brought about by the baby will become immediately apparent. Newborn babies demand almost constant attention, give relatively little in return to satisfy the parents' own needs for love and attention (which do not disappear with the arrival of the baby) and express themselves relentlessly if needs are not being met. Compared with pre-parenthood days, the overall impact on the parents' lives will be mainly in terms of increased physical work in the home, mental stress, in a generally increased amount of time spent in the home, and on the partners' finances.

Different couples will have different plans for how they intend to cope with these extra loads both in the short and long term, but whoever does what initially, it is important for both to realise that the arrangements may need to be reassessed or altered as circumstances change, or if one or other partner finds they are doing too much.

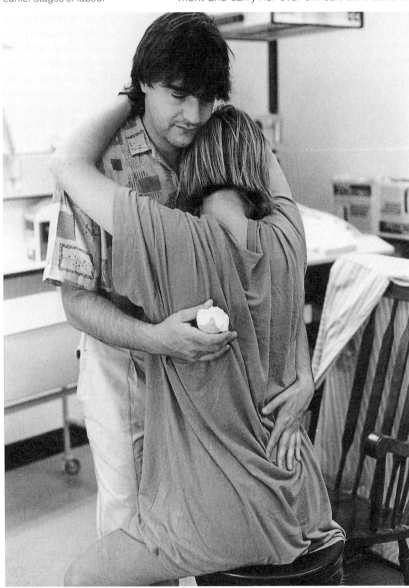

The presence of the father in the delivery room is now common practice, but he can also provide support and comfort during the earlier stages of labour

If it is planned that the mother will sooner or later return to work, and that sole care of the child while she is working will fall at least partly on the father, then his adjustment may fall roughly into three stages: an initial stage where he plays a mainly supportive role, a stage where he is assimilating the various skills required to take complete charge of the baby, and a third stage where he is able to fill in fully for his partner as circumstances dictate.

During the initial stage, which may last for several days or weeks after the birth, the mother will often see herself as the partner most intimately concerned with meeting the physical demands of the baby, virtually inevitably if she is breastfeeding; although both partners may be disturbed by the baby at night, the strain of actually getting up to feed the baby will also fall on her. Partly because of this, and partly as a result of the after-effects of the birth, she is likely to feel physically tired for much of the time. The father's main contribution during this stage may thus be to carry out as many of the general household tasks as possible – such as shopping and cooking – in dealing with visitors and telephone calls and acting as a 'buffer' between his wife and the outside world. If he is also working, his involvement in the practical side of the baby's care may be limited during this time, although he will naturally want to have his share in holding and playing with the baby, perhaps while his partner sleeps off the effects of disturbance the night before.

Some fathers will feel clumsy or awkward at first in finding out how to handle the baby, but the couple can help each other in this, and most fathers will soon find themselves engrossed in the pleasures of playing, cuddling and talking with the child, thus gradually strengthening their bond. It is of course important that the father does not monopolise the baby, thus depriving his partner of the same pleasures or ignoring her needs for love and attention.

As the mother completes her recovery from the traumas of the birth and may feel more inclined to resume a share in the domestic work, so the father at this time can begin assimilating the practical skills involved in the baby's care – changing the nappy, washing the baby, and, if a switch from breast- to bottle-feeding is evisaged, the use and sterilisation of feeding bottles. Learning such things simply requires a degree of enthusiasm and perseverance.

As the father becomes more adept at these skills, so this will increase his partner's confidence in him as a parent, and she will be released to take time off from the baby and home – an important requirement for both her

The father may initially feel clumsy and uncomfortable handling the new baby, but he should remember that his partner may experience similar feelings and that he will probably master the art of nappy changing and other chores just as quickly as she will

physical and mental wellbeing – without any feelings of guilt or anxiety.

Couples will vary in how quickly they wish to resume sex after the birth. Many will feel particularly loving towards each other in the weeks after the birth, perhaps even more so if the father has been fully involved, and will want as soon as possible mutually to reconfirm that they are still sexual beings as well as parents. There may be some physical problems with intercourse, in particular a lack of vaginal lubrication for some months, and the father may need to spend longer stimulating his partner before penetration and use a lubricant. If the mother has had an episiotomy during delivery, she may well not want intercourse for some weeks, and may feel some pain or discomfort on penetration for several months.

Lifestyle adjustments

Whatever the father's exact share of responsibilities in the home, it is likely that he will be spending more time there than hitherto. If he is working, obviously the more paternity leave he can obtain the better, although in some cases leave may not be possible or financially viable.

Often, the major sacrifice will need to come from time previously devoted to pastimes outside the home. Prior to becoming parents, the couple may have spent some of their non-working life apart, pursuing different interests. With the arrival of the baby, the absence of either partner for long periods in the evenings or at weekends can be a bone of contention, not only tying the other down to the home, but also denying them participation in his or her own pursuits. Each partner needs to acknowledge the other's right for time off. Since men are perhaps slightly more likely to have an outside interest in which neither partner nor baby can be involved, it will often be the father who needs to make the main adjustment.

Social activities and relationships are also likely to undergo an upheaval. Often, relationships with friends who have recently also become parents and who have shared problems and interests to discuss will strengthen. However, constraints on going out imposed by the baby, and possibly by finances, can lead to a weakening of ties with other social companions, and the father may need to recognize the possibility of some estrangement from his male companions.

Summary
Fathers will often see their main role as breadwinner for the family, but today they are likely also to be more involved in the domestic side of parenthood, and this may require more adjustment from pre-parenthood days than was once the case. The father's closer involvement in child care can have many benefits both individually for father, mother and child and for the couple's relationship. In particular, a more flexible approach to the division of labour may make the parents better adapted to deal with crises and stresses.

THE SINGLE MOTHER

The stigma that once attached to a single mother and her child is largely a thing of the past, but women who choose to bring up a child on their own should not underestimate the difficulties that lie ahead

The woman who decides to have a child without the support of a partner will face many problems, but it must be said that these have often been overstated. Although some of the legal rights and obligations of the single mother differ from those of a married couple and their children, they are nevertheless legal rights and they exist to give a measure of protection to both mother and child.

Several generations ago, the illegitimate child and his or her mother were virtually unprotected by law.

Currently, in some Scandinavian countries there is no such thing as illegitimacy; many women choose to have children on their own and many couples opt for parenthood outside marriage, but, in law, their rights, duties and obligations and the status of the child differ in no way to those of married parents and their children. We are moving nearer to that situation in Britain; although illegitimacy is still a legal fact and stigma may still cling to the single mother and her child, this is decreasing. The rights of an illegitimate child now differ only slightly from one born in wedlock.

Rights of the parents and child

A baby must be registered within 42 days of his or her birth. Registration establishes the child's right to citizenship and all the necessary entitlements of the welfare system. The date and place of birth, the names and surnames of the mother and the child's sex and names will all be recorded. A married couple have a joint responsibility to register a birth and the birth certificate would then include the name and occupation of the father. A single mother, however, has sole responsibility for this registration – the father of her child cannot do so on his own. Neither can he insist that his name is included on the birth certificate. Similarly, unless there is an affiliation order in force, naming him as father, his name cannot be entered as father without his agreement.

As well as having these rights, the single mother can choose the baby's surname. Even if the father's name is on the certificate she can give the baby her own surname. (Since there is no law relating to surnames, a married woman can do the same.) Furthermore, even if the father has denied paternity, is not subject to an affiliation order and has refused to be named on the birth certificate, the mother can still choose to give his surname to the child.

Within the first year of the baby's life the mother can re-register the baby's surname, either if she has married the child's father or changed her mind about giving the baby her own or the father's name.

There are two types of birth certificate: a long and a short version. The short certificate does not include full details about the parents; the long one does. A short certificate therefore effectively conceals the fact that the child is illegitimate. Both types have equal legal validity. If the mother feels that the stigma of illegitimacy might distress the child later in life when a birth certificate must be shown – such as prior to marriage or when applying for a mortgage or passport – she might wish to choose the shorter version.

The father of the illegitimate child has no rights at all over the child. He can apply for custody, but it would only be granted in the most extreme and exceptional cases. Successful affiliation proceedings would, however, make him bound to contribute towards the maintenance of his child, but not towards the upkeep of the mother. Even if he were making regular payments, he still would have no right to dictate how the child is to be brought up or educated. If the mother refuses to acknowledge his paternity there is no equivalent of an affiliation order for men. He cannot establish his paternity without the woman's consent and co-operation.

Illegitimate children can now inherit from their fathers even if he has not specified that they should. If, in his will, a man leaves his property to his children, this blanket statement is assumed in law to include illegitimate as well as legitimate sons and daughters. Even if his will names only legitimate children to specifically exclude children outside of marriage, a child could claim against the estate if it could be shown that a 'substantial contribution' had been made to the child's upkeep. However, there can be no claim against the estate of any other member of the father's family, such as grandparents, unless the will of that family member names or specifies the illegitimate child.

If the mother dies, the father of her child would still have no automatic rights, even if he had been paying maintenance or has been under an affiliation order. Only if he had obtained custody of the child would he become the legal guardian. Single parents, even more than couples, would do well to make sure that their children are protected in such an eventuality by leaving a will naming a guardian.

Babies can have their own passports, although more usually they are included on

Assuming the role of both father and mother requires some mental adjustments and the learning of new skills, but with time most single parents learn to cope very well

one or both of their parents' passports. The father of an illegitimate child cannot make this addition without the mother's consent.

The child of the single mother

There are various beliefs about the harmful effects that single parenthood has on the child. Before these are discussed two points about illegitimacy should be noted. First, it must be stressed that illegitimacy does not necessarily imply single parenthood. Sixty-three per cent of illegitimate births are registered jointly by both partners and 48 per cent are registered by two parents sharing the same address. Second, studies purport to show that illegitimacy puts children at a social, educational and personal disadvantage. However, it can be shown that it is less the illegitimacy of the child or the solitariness of the parent that creates this situation than the poverty that often goes with such status. Single parents represent 58 per cent of families on supplementary benefit. When studies are adjusted to allow for the financial position of each family, the differences between illegitimate children or those with single parents and children with a traditional background or who are adopted are less than one might think.

There are several arguments that might be levelled against a woman's decision to become a single parent. The commonest arguments are: that a single mother does not give her child a role model on which to learn how to establish a heterosexual relationship; that she deprives the child of a masculine influence – especially important if she has a son; that she marks the child with the stigma of illegitimacy and leaves it with a poor self-image; that she deprives the child of a second adult to turn to, and deprives herself of a helpmate; and that she condemns her child to poverty or to having a working mother who is never at home when needed.

All of these points are debatable. It is certainly true that children take their parents and their parents' relationships and behaviour as role models. The child of violent parents is at risk of growing up accepting that force is a legitimate way to express feelings. Parents who show affection easily and are open and frank with their children about sexual matters are likely to instil very different beliefs than those to whom sexual matters are taboo.

To a society that accepts that the traditional two-parent, two-child family is the best medium for continuity, the growth of a different pattern can appear to be a threat. Obviously the child of a single parent will grow up without the automatic assumption that the only way for one adult to live is with another. But children do not learn their social patterns from the family alone. If this were so, we would all copy our parents' lifestyle slavishly. Yet children from large families have a single child and vice versa; children of heterosexual parents find ther sexual orientation is to members of their own sex and homosexual

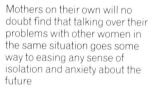

Mothers on their own will no doubt find that talking over their problems with other women in the same situation goes some way to easing any sense of isolation and anxiety about the future

women may bring up children who choose to be heterosexual.

One of the greatest fears about single parenthood is that by leaving the child to brought up by the member of one sex, the child will be subjected to an unbalanced gender influence. This may have been a reasonable fear in the days when human traits were seen as rigidly divided between the masculine and feminine. If women alone were allowed to be emotional and caring, conciliatory and gentle, and men had exclusive rights to be strong and assertive and having a part to play outside the home, then it would be obvious that children with only one parent would probably lose out on many influences. Is this still a reasonable fear? Boys brought up by single mothers do not become effeminate or homosexual any more than girls become ultra-feminine or unable to relate to men.

One of the major changes of the last few years is in the recognition of a range of human emotions and behaviour patterns that, instead of being artificially parcelled out between the sexes, can be part of any individual's personality. Thus sons and daughters can learn the value of both self-assertion and gentleness from a parent who works outside the home as well as sharing the home. Such a family may well produce more rounded personalities than the traditional home that still divides abilities and emotions by sex rather than by individual talents and feelings.

A major distress that can be experienced by the child and the single mother is the social stigma of illegitimacy. Both adult and child may come under pressure from family and neighbours for being different. It is true that there are still people who consider sex outside marriage a sin, and who will show their disapproval by refusing to speak or forbidding their own children to have contact with what they see as a bastard. However, as one in eight children have only one parent, due to death, divorce or separation as well as illegitimacy, such prejudices are becoming the exception. More worrying, perhaps, in a society which still sees the presence of a father as desirable, is the child's own self image. Some children of single mothers fantasize that the father might have left or refused to acknowledge them because of something they have done, or that they have failed to come up to expectations. Others are convinced that their own identity is linked to the personality of the missing father and feel betrayed and lost without some knowledge of him.

Women bringing up children on their own certainly can lack the support of another adult. Yet it can be argued that in some partnerships the second adult demands more than they give or offers no advice or help whatsoever. While it can be desirable for children to be able to elicit more than one point of view, two parents with widely disparate opinions can leave a child worried and

One criticism often levelled against single mothers is that they are unfairly exposing their male children only to feminine attitudes and emotions. Yet such traits as gentleness and tenderness are not the exclusive property of women and deserve to be more widely recognised as preferable characteristics of both sexes

Gingerbread is just one of the organisations set up to help single parents and their children

insecure rather than intellectually stimulated. Children, however, do need more than one adult to turn to, but even the child with two parents can prefer to take his or her worries and questions to a trusted adult outside the immediate family circle. The single mother might accept or even encourage this, rather than feel threatened by it.

Possibly the greatest danger to the single mother and her child is that the mother may see her relationship with the child as resembling more the close intimacy of two adults than of parent and child. In some ways the child will benefit enormously from being given the trust and responsibilities usually accorded to adults; yet the time will come for them to become independent. At such a time both parent and child can experience excessive pain and a sense of betrayal that accompanies separation.

If, at some point in the child's development, the mother decides to live with another adult, the child could resent the person who appears to take their principal place in her affections. Conversely, a child can be deeply hurt when

the mother's relationships with other adults fade or break up, particularly if the child has had an opportunity to make his or her own friendship with the people concerned. The other view of this is that the child can learn to be more self-sufficient and self-confident by seeing that adults are capable of being independent and do not always need another person to support them. Given that the women's unconscious intention in having a child was not to produce a substitute partner to her own design, the closeness of the relationship can enrich both the mother and the child.

The final accusation levelled against single parents is that their selfishness will condemn a child to a life of poverty, or to being a neglected, latchkey child as the mother takes on the role of breadwinner. It is true that one parent families are over represented among families on supplementary benefit or family income supplement. However, neither of these are a necessary concomittant of single parenthood, nor do they only occur in families of single mothers. Last but not least, neither are automatically a blight on a happy and normal development: If, at the relatively mature age of 30 onwards, you are choosing single parenthood or it has chosen you, it is likely that you would be prepared to put a considerable amount of thought and care into your future. Whether you will choose to stay at home on benefits or take employment full- or part-time in your home or at a place of work, you will assess what will be the best option for you and your child. The fact that you are making an informed decision and taking this step because you really want a child, suggests that in spite of the drawbacks, you have a good chance of succeeding.

Getting help

Women who choose to become single mothers and find they are happy in this role may still find it useful to get in touch with other parents in the same situation. It is possible that things may go wrong and there are several specialist organisations that offer advice and support to parents on their own. (Details for getting in touch with the organisations mentioned below are given on p 146.)

One Parent Families exists to help and advise single parents. They are always willing and available to answer any questions and sort out problems. The organisation is also a pressure group, lobbying on behalf of single parents. They also publish leaflets and pamphlets with current information about how to make the best of adverse legal, financial and emotional circumstances.

Gingerbread is a specialist organisation that has a network of local self-help groups run entirely by single parents for single parents. Their aim is to put such families in contact with one another and to encourage friendships. Their groups and advice centres are located throughout England and Wales, but for single parents who live in remote areas they run a pen-friend scheme. Gingerbread also run a holiday service. There is a clear need for specialist holidays of this type which offer single parents the opportunity to share the care of their children, meet others in the same situation and have some time free to please themselves while their children are cared for safely.

The single mother over thirty
Whether single motherhood has been chosen or thrust upon you, you are probably at the best age to manage the task of bringing up a child on your own. You are beyond the stage when unrealistic hopes and inexperience will prevent you from coping with most difficulties, and yet not too old to enjoy the new life that you have created.

Most of the apparent problems of single motherhood can be said to be caused by the mother who is too young, too inexperienced and too hurt to be able to function adequately and be happy in her role. The woman who enters single motherhood with her eyes open and with some experience of life is just as likely as a more conventional couple to bring up a well-balanced and happy child and enjoy doing so.

CHILDMINDING

Whether you plan to stay at home or return to work, there will be times when you need someone else to take care of your child. Initially, the full-time mother may feel that casual arrangements – with friends, neighbours or relatives – will meet her needs. But, like the working mother, she may soon discover that an organised and regular system is more than a luxury and is a necessity.

There are people and services that can and will look after your child, for periods ranging from a few hours a week to the entire working day. The type of service you choose will depend on your needs and what you can afford to spend. However, you need not necessarily be limited in your choice by lack of money. A modicum of imagination and persistence can make up for a tight budget. The choice of childminding services are described in the following pages.

A nanny or mother's help
Properly speaking, a nanny is a woman who has been through a nursery nurse's training course and is qualified to take on the full-time care of a child. This professional status means that they are not usually expected to do household duties other than those directly concerned with child care. If you want someone to do the housework as well, you would need to look for a mother's help. A mother's help may have a good deal of experience but will lack a nanny's formal qualifications.

Nannies and mothers' helps generally live in and would require their own separate accommodation in the house. Hours would be by arrangement and you would probably want to agree to a certain number of evenings when you could go out. Since you would be employing your help for more than 16 hours a week, there are certain obligations you would have under the Employment Act, so an agreement over working conditions, pay, hours, holidays and notice would have to be discussed fully and put in writing.

Since this is possibly the most complete arrangement, it can also be the most expensive. If you cannot afford to take on a nanny or mother's help fulltime, you might consider sharing one with one or two other mothers in the area. The nanny could board with one family and divide her attention between you

Having a nanny is probably the most satisfactory form of childminding for couples who work, but it is also the most expensive. However it is possible to share a nanny with one or two other families, and this may be a suitable arrangement for some

Au pairs will look after the children and do light housework, but they should only work a maximum of five hours a day. For women who work full time this will only be suitable if someone else can take charge of the children for the remaining hours they are away from the home

and the others, sometimes taking two sets of children at the same time.

Nannies can be found through specialist agencies. Alternatively, you could place an advertisement in a local or national paper or magazine. Mothers' helps can sometimes be contacted through a job centre. *The Lady* is probably the recognised market place for nannies and mothers' helps of all levels. Some branches of the National Childbirth Trust organise nanny sharing.

Au pairs

While a nanny or mother's help is a professional employed by you to do a job, the underlying concept of the au pair arrangement is that the au pair is supposed to live as a member of the family. Indeed, the official definition of one is that she is a young woman, allowed to remain in Britain for a maximum of two years, living as a member of the family in order to learn English. Au pairs are only supposed to work for a maximum of five hours a day, doing light duties which can include both housework and child care. In return, you should offer full board and enough pocket money to enable her to pursue her studies and to have a reasonable social life. Male au pairs are now more common and the same rules apply to them.

You cannot expect that having an au pair will allow you to go back to full-time work unless you combine their help with another form of childminding. Unless you have contacts abroad, the best way to obtain an au pair is through specialist agencies. The system, relying as it does on goodwill on both sides, rather than a formal employer and employee relationship, is open to abuse. The better agencies will try to ensure that both the family and the girl are suitably matched and protected.

Private nurseries

There are several types of private nurseries. They can either be run as a commercial concern or by local community groups or one of the large children's charities. Since proper care for young children demands a maximum of three children to each staff member, a well-run private concern is likely to be quite expensive. As such, nurseries do need to come up to certain legal requirements, and to meet regulations concerning staff and facilities, they often need to make a high charge to show any profit. For this reason, they are few and far between, and many will not accept children below the age of two. Community-run nurseries will be a less expensive and more flexible alternative, but not only do they

usually have long waiting lists, they also necessarily demand that parents involve themselves in the running of the group.

Some of the large children's charities, such as Dr Barnardos, the Church of England Children's Society or the National Children's Homes, run volunteer nurseries. However, there are very few of them available and, rather than taking complete charge of the child, may expect you to stay and take part in activities. They offer a break from isolation instead of of a place to leave your child.

Both types of nurseries can be found by asking at the local library, the doctor's surgery or community centre. If you cannot find one or all your local groups are full, you might like to consider getting together with other parents in the vicinity and establishing one yourself or employing people to do so for you. Your local authority has a statutory responsibility to register all services that look after children under five years of age for more then two hours a day, without parents being present and outside the child's home. This applies to all nurseries, whether private or run by the local authority, and to all childminders offering their services for pay. In theory, the local authority should be able to give you a list of everyone available, although in practice they are not always equipped to do so.

Council nurseries

Council nurseries are run by the local authority and you can find out if one can take your child by contacting the Social Services Department. The nurseries are free but you might have difficulties since places are limited. Priorities are always given to working single parents or families where hardship of various kinds mean that nursery provision is desperately needed. If you think that you should qualify, a letter from your doctor, health visitor or social worker would help your case. In some situations, councils are prepared to pay for private care, where a child would qualify for a council nursery place but none is available.

Crèches

It is an indictment of our attitudes to parenthood that crèches are not a routine part of working life, but still a rare facility offered by a very few enlightened employers. Crèches can range from a custom-built and professionally staffed unit financed fully by a firm, to a makeshift group established and run by employees, where the organisation has only, and sometimes grudgingly, allowed the use of an empty room. Of all the options, a crèche at your workplace can be the most convenient for parents and the most efficient for em-

Council nurseries are free but places are very difficult to find, quite simply because the demand exceeds the supply. At the moment, priority is given to parents facing hardship; those who think they might be eligible should obtain a letter from their doctor or social worker and contact their local Social Services Department

ployees. For instance, the parent does not have to add the journey to a nursery or a minder to their ordinary travel time and can attend immediately to a sick or distressed child, rather than leave work to do so. If he or she is so disposed, breaks can be spent in the child's company and, at the end of the day, there would be no need to dash off to meet strict child-collecting times.

While it may not occur to most managements to offer a crèche, especially in firms with a predominately male workforce, the arguments for increased employee efficiency are convincing. If you or your partner's firm does not provide one, it might be worthwhile asking the union representative to press for the establishment of a crèche. If the firm's argument against it is a purely economic one, you and your colleagues could consider meeting costs yourself if a room can be found.

Childminders
For those without the financial opportunity to afford live-in help or a private nursery, or those unable to get a council nursery place, a childminder is the most popular alternative. Childminding can vary from an *ad hoc*, casual

arrangement whereby a friend, neighbour or relative looks after your child when you go shopping, to a full five-day week, eight or nine hours a day paid service. Legally, if anyone other than a relative looks after your child for more than two hours a day for payment, they are childminders and should be registered as such with the local authority. Even if this is an informal arrangement that has grown up with a friend, registration is a legal requirement and anyone who offers themselves as a childminder should have the local authority certificate. This registration is there for your protection as it enables health visitors to call and check up on the facilities offered by the childminder. The Social Services Department will have a list of local childminders and will also let you have a standard agreement form for working out hours, payment and other matters, such as meals for your child.

The National Childminding Association can give you further information.

Play groups and mother and toddler groups
Play groups and mother and toddler groups offer the full-time mother and her child a chance to be with other mothers and children

Play groups and mother and toddler groups provide women and their children with the opportunity to get away from home and socialise with others. They are particularly useful for mothers who spend most of the day on their own

outside the home, and for the mother to have the occasional few hours to herself. Both types of group are voluntary and run by the mothers themselves. The Pre-School Play-groups Association has many branches and will put you in touch with your local group, or advise you how to form a group yourself. Mother and toddler groups are often run by local church or community organisations. Depending on the agreed system, your group may allow you to drop your child off for a session in return for your taking a share in running the group. However, you may be expected to remain at all times, but this at least will allow you the chance to meet other parents.

Babysitting

Babysitters can be found by word of mouth, advertisements in the local press or cards in the newsagent or post office. Some local secondary schools can also help, especially those that offer parentcraft or child care on the curriculum.

Alternatively, there may be a baby sitting club in your area. Parents take turns babysit-ting for one another in return for having one of the other parents babysit for them. This system is more easily operated when there are two parents in a family – one to go to a fellow member's home and the other to mind their own child. However, single parents can join if they are able to take their own child with them when they babysit, or have the other child in their own home.

Using childminding facilities

Although children need security and stability in their upbringing, there is no evidence to support the view that a child's mother is the only one who can give this properly. Leaving a child in a series of overcrowded and inade-quately staffed facilities will obviously produce an unhappy, confused and emotionally or physically underdeveloped child. However a nursery or minder who offers continuity and the type of stimulation and affection needed by all growing children will produce better results than an isolated, harrassed and bored mother. As long as certain guidelines are borne in mind when seeking a childminder both mother and child will benefit.

Since whoever looks after your child in your absence will have a profound influence on them and shoulder enormous responsibilites, you do need to be certain that they are able to fulfill their role. Do not feel embarrassed at wanting to interview individuals and to ask for references. In the case of a nursery or childminder, it is perfectly reasonable to insist on seeing the facilities during the day so that you can assess whether other babies and

children already being looked after appear to be happy. Even if the carer is a personal friend, it is wise to discuss all the details of payment, expected and special duties, hours of work, holiday and sickness arrangements, and to put these in writing so that there will be no misunderstandings.

It has been said that the most profound discovery made by the growing child is that he is a separate entity to his mother. Many mothers can testify to the fact that mothers have to accept that their children have a life separate from them, and can and should make relationships and share experiences with other people. In seeking help with the care of your child, you will be allowing him to make emotional links with other people, but you should be prepared to find this painful to some degree. However annoying it is to you, your child will benefit from learning how to make friendships with others, and, in small ways, will learn how to gain a measure of independence. Considering the fact that at the age of five, your child will be expected to spend the better part of the day in school with his peers and a new group of adults, it is obvious that some form of child care before then will help both of you to face this new stage with cheerful anticipation rather than with dread.

A crèche is probably the ideal solution for the working parent, but like many other childminding facilities there are not many of them. Employers may seem reluctant to provide them, but if there appears to be a demand for child care facilities at your place of work it might be worth approaching the management – it may well be that the idea had not occurred to them

Chapter 5

THE CHILD IN THE FIRST YEAR

- Early child development
- Common illness and problems in the first year

The first year of life is a time of rapid physical, emotional and mental growth. Particularly with the first-born, parents find the rate at which their child grows remarkable and often surprising: they also discover the joy of watching the baby learn about his or her environment and how to adapt to it and change it. Yet the first year of life may also be attended by minor problems which, although common, can be distressing for the new parents.

Many parents worry about whether their child is developing normally; although in the early years at least, development occurs in a natural sequence of events, there are no definite ages at which the baby can be expected to have gained a specific level of development. It is therefore important for parents to realize that comparisons with other babies of the same age can often be inappropriate and misleading; as an example,

parents with more than one child can usually relate how each of their children differed from the others at the same age, in behaviour, temperament and development. However, as explained in the following pages, child development is not something that should be left to nature alone: parents can play an extremely useful role in encouraging their child to achieve in all areas of growth.

Often too, the baby's health is a particular cause for parental concern. It would be very rare, indeed for a baby to reach his first birthday without having had at least one of the minor complaints that so often occur in young infants, so illnesses such as a cough or cold are to be expected and should not cause undue concern when they occur. The commoner illnesses of young infants are outlined and identified in the final section of this chapter, together with information about their treatment.

EARLY CHILD DEVELOPMENT

Successful rearing of a baby requires a blend of sound knowledge with emotional responsiveness. A wholly intellectually planned rearing programme pursued rigidly should be avoided, as should one based soley on emotional instinct.

Parents learn a lot from their first baby. Frequently heard comments are 'I never realized babies behaved like this'; He does many things I didn't expect'; and 'I learn something new about him every day.' Babies do many things which seem unusual or unexpected to their parents and yet are perfectly normal and natural. Uncertainty about what is normal, however, can cause anxiety. In this situation do not hesitate to seek advice. Friends and relatives who have children will come forward with advice which may be sound and reassuring, but conflicting opinions may confuse or fail to dispel anxiety. In such circumstances it is best to consult the health visitor, doctor or paediatrician. However, while valuing the advice received, do not become entirely dependent on outside counsel: trust yourself. Babies do best when they sense their parents are confidently enjoying their new situation

and are looking forward to the changes and demands of the years ahead. Good rearing leads to optimum development.

Babies develop enormously in the first 12 months. They grow. As an approximate guide, weight at one year will be about two and a half times the birthweight, and length about one and a half times. During the first year the baby also changes from a dependent being who responds automatically, to an individual who is aware of his or her surroundings and who moves about and controls his own actions.

As well as knowing what changes will occur, it is helpful for parents to understand why they occur. They will then be able to enjoy their baby more and also help him to develop.

When the baby presents a problem, parents want to know about it and have it dealt with as soon as possible. In the sections which follow, descriptions are given of the baby's first year to give this information and guidance. In many cases precise figures for the development of various activities have not been given, as babies vary and not all develop in the same way and at the same time. To give

Learning to handle and manipulate objects is an important stage in an infant's development, and as with all phases of learning the baby will benefit from the interest and encouragement of parents

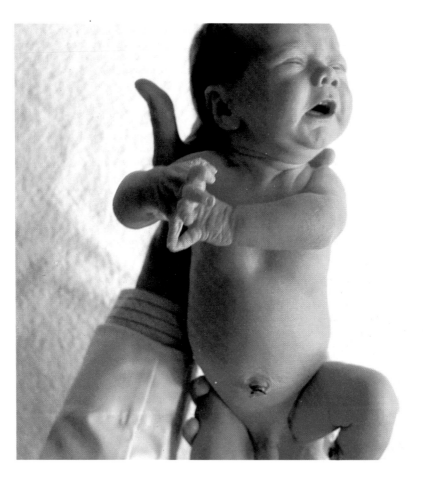

First impressions are always terribly important, and so is the first opportunity the parents have to closely examine and delight in the uniqueness of their newborn

a definite time can be misleading and cause unnecessary anxiety. Some books state dogmatically that babies sit up at six months and cut their first tooth at seven months; parents then feel worried when their baby reaches these ages without sitting or having a tooth. When precise ages are quoted in books about child development they refer to the *average* age, when infants achieve a particular stage of development. Some babies will achieve the ability earlier and some later than the stated age. Remember that children vary; they have their individual rate of development, and it is this which makes them so fascinating. As the parents get to know their baby they feel proud that he is growing in his own particular way.

First impressions

As soon as the baby is born the mother wants to hold him close and look at him face to face. He may have left the uterus, but he is still a part of her, and this early contact reinforces the bonds between mother and baby.

After this first close contact the parent or parents will look at him carefully. What is he like? Has he all his fingers and toes? Why does he look so wrinkled? These are just some of the many questions which come to mind

and have to be answered satisfactorily. The baby will then be examined by a paediatrician. Some doctors like to examine the newborn in front of the mother, and the father also when possible. The parents are able to see all that is done and realize that babies can be lifted, turned and pushed about, and are not delicate individuals who have to be kept in cotton wool. The doctor may explain what he or she is doing during the examination, answer any questions, and explain and demonstrate some of the interesting and useful reactions of babies. Older mothers on the whole are better able than younger ones to request that the doctor carries out the examination of the baby in their presence, and to make sure they start off with all their questions answered and discussed.

When a baby is born he is already a well developed and complex individual, and ready for life in the outside world. At this early stage his responses are largely automatic and follow definite patterns. Some of these responses are useful aids to his rearing. For example, the area around the mouth is sensitive to touch. A light touch at one side will cause the mouth to open and the head to turn to that side. When the baby is lifted to the breast for a feed the contact of his cheek with the breast will set off this reaction and his open mouth will turn to take the nipple. If he is bottle-fed light stimulation of the corner of the mouth just beforehand will make it easier to introduce the teat of the bottle. Gently making use of this automatic response (the rooting reflex) promotes easier feeding. Hasty forceful attempts at feeding which ignore this response lead to inadequate entry of the nipple into the mouth and subsequent soreness.

Another automatic reaction which is enjoyable to demonstrate is called the stepping response. When the baby is held upright and the soles of his feet are allowed to touch a firm surface he bends his legs in alternate stepping movements. This is not walking, as the baby cannot yet support his own body in the upright position, but it shows that his nervous system is prepared for the development of walking which occurs at about 12 months.

Other first impressions of the baby are that his life is dominated by sleeping, waking, feeding, elimination and changing. When sleeping he will usually lie on his back or front; sleeping on one side is a later development. Laying the baby on his back is the long standing traditional way and it does mean you see his face as soon as you look into the cot. Laying him on his front is increasingly popular, largely to reduce risks from vomiting.

Either method is reasonable, and some mothers like to give their babies experience of both positions. In babies who show a preference for one or the other position their parents follow this guide.

At the early stage it is to be expected that parents will have disturbed nights, but after a night feed the baby should settle down again. Continued restlessness should raise the question of adequacy of the feed or some other cases of disturbance.

Should babies waken or be wakened for their feed? Rigid time-based methods of feeding which required that babies be wakened at the time of their feed are not currently popular. A more relaxed and flexible approach is preferred. Babies soon settle to a routine if the issues are approached with common sense. If the baby wakens and is clearly hungry it is reasonable to feed him, but sometimes a period of wakefulness before feeding is acceptable. If the baby seems to be sleeping longer than expected, then gentle, gradual wakening can be tried.

Feeding is an important part of a baby's day, not just because of the nutritional aspects, but because of the cosy interaction with parent or other carer. Pleasurable feeding sessions help a baby's development. The closeness, firm support, warmth, pleasant smiles and soothing tones from the parent all add to the satisfaction of filling the stomach.

Gently stroke the side of a newborn baby's mouth and he will turn his head and move his lips as he tries to get his mouth around the finger. This is the rooting reflex that makes the baby instinctively take the nipple into his mouth when put to the breast. Shortly after birth the newborn is capable of carrying out a number of actions which he will not truly aquire until later in his development. 'Walking' is one of them

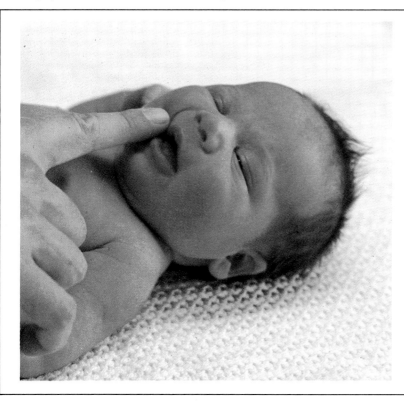

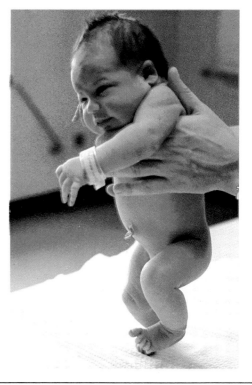

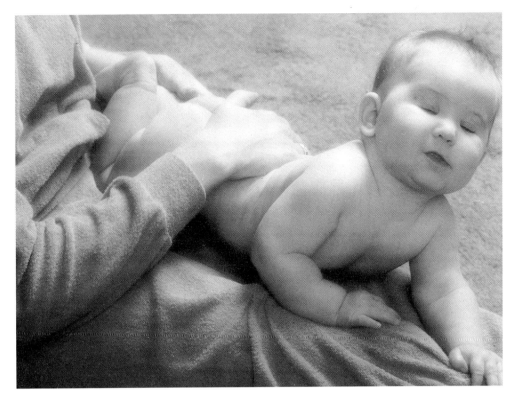

Feeding is an important part of the baby's day and is crucial not only to his physical but also his emotional development (far left)

The momentary periods when the baby breaks off feeding and leaves and re-enters this comfortable situation are valuable developmental experiences.

A steady head

If it is free to do so the head of the newborn baby flops about according to the position of the baby. Consequently a steadying hand is needed behind the head when the baby is lifted and moved. Gradually, the head will become firmer. When the baby is laid on his front he will begin to raise his head, at first for a few moments and then for longer periods. Later, he will not only raise his head but also push his chest up with his forearms and then with his extended arms. When a baby who is lying on his back is raised to a sitting position, his head has to be supported at first, but as time passes he can steady his own head. Make a practice of talking to and smiling at the baby when you go towards him; you will gradually notice that he not only gets excited in response to your overtures, but also begins to attempt to raise his head. The ability increases until he can be raised to a sitting position without support for his head, which is now firm and steady on his shoulders. It seems sensible that head control should be encouraged to develop early. The baby needs to learn about his new world as soon as possible, and he does so with his eyes and ears which function best when the head is firm and steady. Also, a steady head makes feeding easier.

At birth, the eyes and ears are well developed structually, and newborn babies can see and hear. The old wives' tales that say they cannot are quite wrong. As the weeks go by the baby's responses to sounds change. At first sudden noises may startle him, but this reaction lessens and he soon begins to listen. The mother's voice usually becomes especially familiar, and it is very pleasing to her when he smiles as he hears it.

Control of the eye movements seems to develop first in the horizontal plane. As the baby learns to look at nearby objects and then to follow them with his eyes as they are moved, the ability appears first with sideways movements and later with up and down movements.

Although the baby is beginning to listen and look around, his world is still very small and circumscribed. He needs his mother or carer near at frequent intervals, such as when he is fed or changed. At all these times he needs to see the carer's smiling face and hear her voice. A baby's face is a delight to watch. Expressions come and go. In the early weeks they are often put down to 'wind', but as the second month begins a genuine voluntary smile should appear in response to overtures.

The baby is learning about his nearby surroundings as much as he can, so simple toys, noticeable by their bright colours and

Initially, the newborn's head will need to be supported, but gradually the neck muscles that control it's steadiness will become firmer, and when placed on his stomach he will eventually be able to raise his head and look about him. From now on he will be more able to take in what is going on around him. In the first few months the baby becomes more aware of sounds, as well as faces that he begins to recognise. When approaching a young infant, talk to him as you come towards him. He will soon respond to the familiar sound of your voice and reward you with a smile

shiny surfaces, or the pleasant sounds they emit, can be placed nearby for him to see and hear. This is the time for giving the baby many cuddles. It will not spoil him; he will benefit from all the stimulation.

Gathering in

Arms are too useful to be allowed to continue the aimless movements of the newborn period. They gradually come under control, so that by six months of age babies can reach out for an object voluntarily, can grasp it and bring it towards themselves.

The sequence of changes is as follows: the aimless movements of the newborn period get less; the hands which were fisted much of the time initially relax and open more often. The arms extend towards the direction in which the baby is looking. The nervous system is responsible for this action and it appears to be an excellent preparation for the next steps in development. With the head turned to one side, the baby will see a nearby object. The nervous system makes the arm extend in that direction and one day the arm will touch the object; the baby is being made to see and to touch an object at the same time. Visual and touch sensations are beginning to be co-ordinated and the baby is learning that something he sees can also be touched. Gradually the accidental touches

turn to purposeful ones. The hand then comes into use. The palm and fingers fold over an object and grasp it.

When the development has reached this stage, the drive from the nervous system to make the arm extend in the direction that the baby is looking lessens, and the arms are brought back towards the body. The baby has now reached a point where he can see a nearby object, reach it, grasp it and bring it back. Once back, what to do with it? He might look at it, put it in his mouth, or even begin to pass it to the other hand. Mouthing of objects is commonly seen around five or six months. It is not because the baby is teething; it is a means of learning about the objects he retrieves.

Both arms work similarly, so it is easy for them to come towards the body at the same time and for the hands to meet together. This meeting of the hands sets the scene for gradually passing an object from one hand to the other. Watching a baby learn to use his hands to gather in objects is a fascinating pastime. Sometimes before he can take hold of an object with his hands he will look at it fixedly as if taking hold of it with his eyes. Understanding this aspect of development gives an idea of how the baby can be helped.

Do not get cross because he is messy and is mouthing objects – it is part of his learning.

Place objects where he can touch them. A few small boxes he can knock with his hand are more useful than an elaborate mobile out of reach. Use objects of different textures. He is just learning about the world and needs to know there are more things than smooth slippery plastic toys. Things that are rough, squeezy, furry and noisy can all be considered.

An expanding world

A baby's world gradually expands as his sensory awareness increases. In the early months he learnt about his nearby world by looking at and taking hold of objects and then bringing them back to inspect them and mouth them. He could not learn about objects at a distance by touch because his arms are not long enough. Now however his eyes and ears detect stimuli from a distance and with his marvellous brain he learns that objects he sees at a distance are like similar objects he has grasped and mouthed. In other words he learns to contrast and compare and to identify likes and differences.

Babies learn to identify familiar pleasant sounds and to listen for them and pick them out from the extraneous background noises. Do not make it difficult for your baby. Let him hear some sounds repeatedly so he can become familiar with them – mother's own voice particularly, and perhaps a few favourite rattles and musical boxes. Interesting everyday domestic sounds are useful stimuli, and should not be obscured by a lot of meaningless background noises such as a blaring radio.

Not only do babies learn to listen to sounds they like, but they become increasingly skilful in finding where they come from. When about

When the baby has learned to reach out and grasp an object he will proceed to the next stage of bringing it towards him and then putting it into his mouth. Mouthing is a way of learning about the shape and texture of the object he holds, so it should never be discouraged
From gathering objects in to himself, the baby will learn to pick up objects and give them out to others. At this stage the activity of picking up and offering will be repeated over and over again, much to the delight of the child (top left)

3-4 months old a baby will turn his head towards the side from which a sound comes. Within another six months he learns to locate the source with pin-point accuracy. The range of visual interest gradually increases. This is demonstrated when testing the vision of babies. In the early months the test is done within a few feet of the baby, otherwise the object is beyond range and the baby ignores the test stimuli. As the months go by the stimuli is moved further away but still evokes responses from the baby.

As the range of visual recognition extends, the eyes begin to work together and binocular vision develops. Consequently, any failure of the eyes to move in unison, which occurs with a squint, should not occur after the first few months of life; if it does occur it needs attention. A squint should not be ignored in the hope that the baby will grow out of it.

Although auditory and visual functions develop to take in a wider world, babies can understand their environment only because the brain develops appropriately at the same time. This may sound complex, but examples of it happening may be seen as the baby plays. Watch when he takes an object such as a small wooden brick in one hand and a similar one in the other hand. He looks first at one and then the other. He may move them in his hands to feel them. He knocks them together. He is beginning to learn to compare them and to learn that two similar objects can exist in different places.

By now baby will be spending some of his time in a high chair. Watch what he does with his toys. At first anything which falls to the floor will be ignored. In time, however, (around eight or nine months) he will look to see where the toy he dropped has gone to – he is beginning to realise that it continues to exist even when it leaves his hands, and that it is the same object even when it has rolled away out of his reach. These are remarkable things for a baby to learn, so when he tries to reinforce his learning with a little experimentation by throwing his dinner from the high chair on to the floor, one should not get too cross with him.

By this stage the baby is interested in toys both in his hands and at a distance. Small balls and bricks which roll and can be dropped will be of interest. Mobiles and colourful objects around the room will absorb his attention. Paralleled with his increasing awareness of the world around him he has an urge to become mobile.

Moving about

In the early months the baby stays where he is put. He may roll or change his position a little, but he stays more or less where he is placed. During all this time you could leave him and return when you thought it necessary or when he did something to demand your attention. However, there comes a time when circumstances change and he leaves you. He will creep or squirm away a few feet and look back to see your reaction to his daring move. From this time onwards he is going, increasingly, to determine his own activities. This should be regarded as an important step in the development of his emotional maturity and independance. It may come as a shock to realise this separation as a manifestation of his independant will. Also, work now increases because he no longer stays in one place.

Babies show different patterns of achieving mobility and reaching standing and walking. A baby who spends much of his time on his front may move about quite early by squirming and scooting (pulling or pushing himself on his tummy with his arms) and then may get on his hands and knees and pull himself to an upright position. A baby who initially spends much time on his back seems to become more familiar with a sitting position from which he may fall forward on to his hands and crawl, or pull himself up to standing. A few babies begin moving about in the sitting position. This bottom shuffling is not abnormal, but babies who show this pattern of early

At three or four months of age the baby's visual awareness will have increased, and he will be fascinated by bright colours and objects that move. A mobile will retain his interest for a considerable period (right) Once the infant can support himself on all fours there will be no holding him. He will no longer have to rely for entertainment on things within his reach – he can go and get them (below)

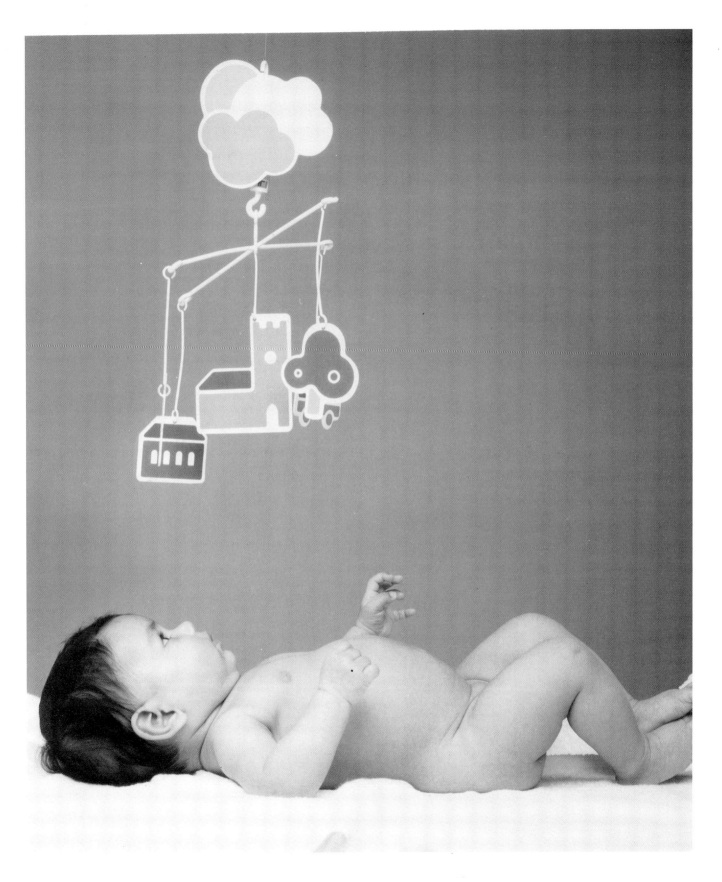

WHEN TO SEEK ADVICE – THE WARNING SIGNS

Parents should seek advice if they notice any of the following:
☐ the baby is excessively sleepy or restless
☐ the baby is excessively floppy or stiff
☐ the baby has reached three months and is not holding his head steady or smiling in

response to overtures
☐ the baby has reached six months and is not reaching out
☐ the baby has reached nine months and is not sitting alone or taking weight on his legs

when held up, or passing objects from hand to hand
☐ the baby has reached 12 months and is not moving about or trying to stand
☐ the pupils of the baby's eyes look opaque or white
☐ the baby's eyes turn and squint, especially when over six months

☐ the eyes show shaking movements
☐ the baby does not seem to hear you
☐ the baby does not respond to your voice or other sounds, or loud noises etc
☐ the baby fails to vocalise or chortle or begin to imitate sounds as he gets older

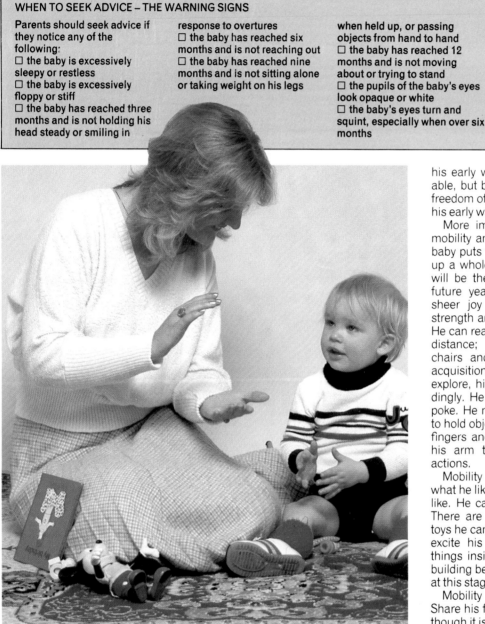

his early walking attempts are more acceptable, but best of all the baby should have the freedom of the room to explore and to practise his early walking efforts.

More important than the development of mobility and walking is the use to which the baby puts these new abilities. They can open up a whole new range of experiences which will be the mainstay of his development in future years. The ability to move provides sheer joy and pleasure. It also increases strength and the baby is now able to explore. He can reach those objects which he saw at a distance; he can find out what is behind chairs and inside cupboards. Just as the acquisition of mobility gives him the power to explore, his manipulative skills expand accordingly. He uses his index finger to point and poke. He no longer uses a crude hand grasp to hold objects but can take them between his fingers and thumb. He is beginning to twist his arm to achieve screwing and turning actions.

Mobility means that he can go towards what he likes and away from what he does not like. He can make choices, and he does so. There are many suitable toys for him now: toys he can pull and push and roll; toys which excite his exploratory drive; and toys with things inside to take out and put in. Simple building beakers and posting boxes are useful at this stage.

Mobility is a great thing in a child's life. Share his fun and enjoyment with him – even though it is a lot of work.

Parents are always delighted when their baby begins to imitate their facial expressions or actions. It is a marvellous moment when the child learns to copy an action he sees someone else doing, such as clapping hands

motor development are later than average in walking.

Babies vary in the way they get to standing, and once standing when holding on to objects, show varying degrees of confidence to move about and to step off on their own. Suitably placed sturdy tables and chairs are a great help at this stage. A stable (weighted if need be) push-cart or toy animal on wheels is a useful asset. The use of baby bouncers in which babies sit and bounce when their feet touch the ground should be avoided. Baby walkers which support the baby as he makes

Letting you know
A baby does not hesitate to let you know what he wants – loud and clear – and he requires instant attention. You soon come to recognise the distinctive cries of hunger, discomfort and temper. Even earlier there will have been opportunities for communication between the mother and baby, beginning with the initial spontaneous response as they look at each other face to face. Thereafter, there are many opportunities for communication. One of the advantages of starting a family a little later is that mothers have had experience of life and

have become aware of the many types of interpersonal communication.

A baby is full of expression; his movements give a clue to his feelings – greater when he is excited and restless and less when contented and somnolent. Listen carefully to his vocalisations – they are not just simple sounds. Much meaning can be conveyed by inflection, intensity and duration.

It is hoped that more mothers will come to realise that their babies are not just passive bundles to be fed and changed and made comfortable. Babies are very aware of their mother's actions and they respond to them. In fact, little interchanges occur in which babies respond to or even imitate their mothers and mothers respond to them, and on occasion may imitate the baby. This complex interchange between mothers and their babies which has been revealed by recent research applies especially to vocalisations. Do have time for your baby and do enjoy sharing experiences together. Career and work conflicts have to be considered but time which can be set aside for the baby will be well worthwhile. From the baby's point of view, the stimulation will promote his development. From the parents' point of view, they will come to know a fascinating individual.

When should you worry?

Most babies thrive and develop well; just a few have serious problems and if this is the case mothers will want to know about it as soon as possible. Although most babies are fine and well there are many occasions when questions and worries may arise which turn out to be due to conditions which respond

Learning to walk is a tricky business – it is a question of co-ordination and balance. No wonder both parents and child find those first independent steps such a wonderful achievement

spontaneously and are not serious issues. So, although all mothers have concerns from time to time, the likelihood is that they are not due to serious problems.

Parents should not hold back from seeking advice for fear of being thought to be fussing or anxious or wasting the doctor's time – this does not help the baby. It is preferable for a doctor to see 20 mothers and reassure 19 of them that their worries are unwarranted so they do not miss the 20th who may have some important problem.

COMMON ILLNESSES AND PROBLEMS IN THE FIRST YEAR

Every young child is bound to have an illness at some stage in early life. Such events are full of anxiety for the parents and misery for the child, but in most cases the problem is easily dealt with and recovery is quick

Some 40-60 per cent of the average pediatrician's time is given to well-children visits. This can have a positive influence on the parent-child relationship when social, physical and emotional health can be stressed. However, much time is also devoted to children suffering from illnesses.

Some of the common illnesses that occur in the first year of life are discussed below. Many of these can be dealt with by the family doctor, whose advice should be sought whenever the parents feel that the condition requires professional help. He or she can then make referrals where necessary,.

In many cases a call to the GP will reassure parents and alleviate any fears. In others, a home visit or a visit to the surgery will be necessary. Where appropriate, guidelines are given in the following pages to help parents assess the severity of a condition, but it must be stressed that no precise time for seeking help can be given, as symptoms can vary enormously. The best advice is if in any doubt, consult the doctor.

Circumcision

Circumcision is the removal of the foreskin from the penis. It is mainly performed for religious reasons and is seldom necessary for medical reasons.

If the operation is required for religious reasons it should be performed within the first or second week of life, when a simple surgical device can be used. This is less traumatic for the child and less painful than if left to an older age.

Circumcision is only performed under the National Health Service for medical reasons, but some maternity units can arrange for a baby to be circumcised while in hospital for a small fee, or will be able to advise parents of private facilities in their area.

Colic

Colic can be defined as intermittent unexplained crying during the first three months of life that reaches a point where parents become concerned. Colicky babies are usually well fed, healthy, and happy between crying spells. If the crying becomes continuous and severe, an organic cause, such as acute infection, should be ruled out.

When the baby cries, he usually draws his knees up to his abdomen. This posture is a non-specific reaction to crying at this stage, and does not mean that the baby is suffering from stomach cramps or abdominal pain. There is no scientific evidence that gastro-intestinal spasm or indigestion are major factors in the cause of colic. Likewise, cow's milk allergy is unlikely to explain increased crying in babies. There are no studies to date which link cow's milk with colic.

In most cases, however, careful physical examination by the family doctor is essential to relieve the parent's fear of a physical illness. The doctor will also want to rule out the presence of acute otitis, anal fissures and tears and constipation, which can often cause pain in the first weeks of life.

Colic usually begins towards the end of the first month, but often during the first fortnight. Crying occurs intermittently but may continue for up to two hours at a time. Although colicky crying can occur at any time of the day, most babies have their most difficult period before or after the evening feed. Some 10-15 per cent of infants develop colic at some stage. In most cases it resolves spontaneously by three months of age and sometimes earlier.

There is an increased rate of colicky babies in first-born children, which suggests that parental inexperience is a main factor. Babies can recognise that they are being held in secure or tense arms and can sense the emotional state of the mother and the emotional atmosphere in the home.

Parents who are angry, shout at the baby or handle him roughly can accentuate the problem. The continuous nerve-wracking crying can lead to emotional exhaustion and sleep deprivation in the mother. At this point the condition has become a vicious circle that can permanently damage or impair the mother-child relationship.

Treatment for colic usually entails reassurance and rest for the mother and comfort for

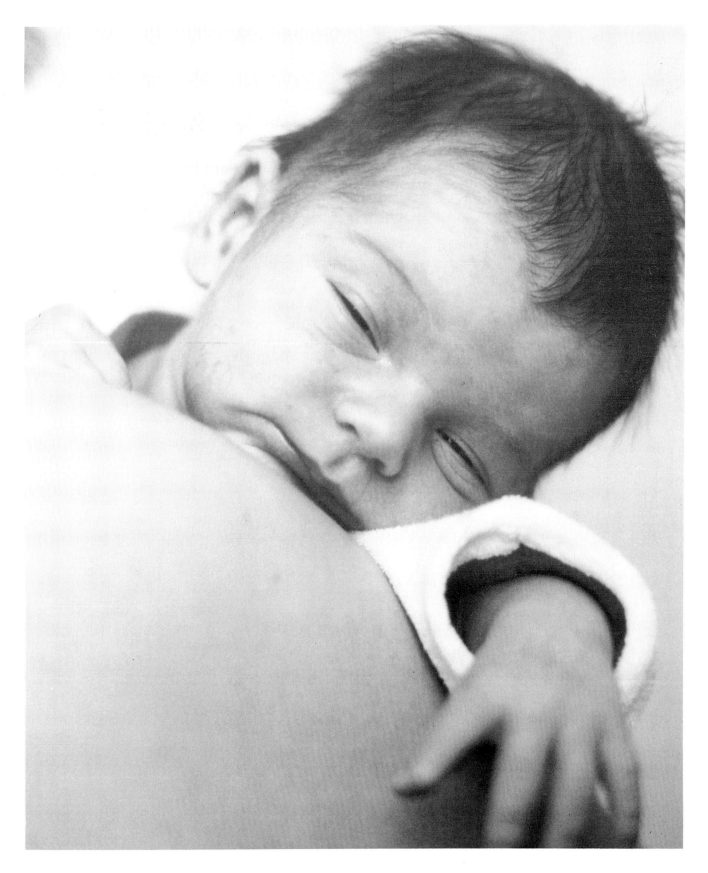

the baby. The latter can be provided by gentle rocking and physical contact during crying spells, by the mother or father carrying the baby in a front harness for three hours a day when the baby is not crying, and by the use of a pacifier. Elimination of over- or underfeeding of the baby and daytime sleeping for more than three consecutive hours may also be required.

In addition to reassurance, the mother should be urged to get help from relatives and friends, both in caring for the baby and in routine tasks such as housework. She should also be persuaded to talk about her feelings towards the baby, which in some cases will be ambivalent.

Providing drugs for infantile colic has many shortcomings. Dicoclymine, which was effective in eliminating colic in some 60 per cent of cases, is no longer prescribed as there were reports of respiratory collapse, breath holding and seizure in infants under six months of age given the drug. Other medications have very little effect.

Colicky babies respond most effectively to physical contact and gentle motion. The role of crying in precipitation of child abuse requires special vigilance on the part of paediatricians, health visitors and GPs; intervention in cases of colic can be an important preventive step.

Conjunctivitis

Conjunctivitis is the most common eye problem in young infants. It is usually caused by a bacterial, viral or fungal infection. Less frequently, it may result from an allergic reaction or a physical or chemical irritation. Symptoms are redness of the white areas of the eyes (conjunctiva), irritation, a discharge of pus and the eyelids sticking together following sleep.

The condition requires medical treatment. If it is caused by an infection then care must be taken to ensure that the baby's face flannels and towels are not used by other members of the family as the infection is contagious. The doctor will prescribe suitable antibiotic eye drops, which usually should be applied every four hours when the infection is in its acute stage. Treatment should continue for a few days after the symptoms have subsided.

Conjunctivitis does not damage vision.

Coughing and wheezing

Other than in the immediate neonatal period, coughing and wheezing occur throughout childhood. In the first year of life the common conditions causing these symptoms are acute bronchiolitis, wheezy bronchitis and inhala-tion of secretions or a foreign object.

In all these conditions the baby is usually under one year of age, has a short history of a cold (two to four days) and then develops a fast respiratory rate – in excess of 40 breaths per minute – that is associated with feeding difficulties.

Expert advice is needed to differentiate between bronchiolitis and wheezy bronchitis and even then it can be difficult to distinguish between the two. The bronchiolitic baby is usually much younger and has rather distended and over-inflated lungs. Drugs have little effect on the condition but most babies respond to a warm, moist environment when lying in a semi-recumbent position. If the baby has sucking and feeding problems a tube can be passed into the stomach to keep the baby properly hydrated. Broncho-pneumonia may follow but this is rare. It can be treated with antibiotics.

A baby with acute wheezy bronchitis is usually an overweight, plump nine- to ten-month-old baby who shows very little distress even though he is audibly wheezing. There may be a family history of disorders such as asthma or allergies, and the baby may have had infantile eczema some months earlier. Drugs may improve the condition but the routine oral drugs used for older children with asthma are almost always ineffective.

Wheezy bronchitis is thought to be part of the asthma syndrome and many babies will continue to have further attacks during their early years. Fortunately, the majority appear to lose all their symptoms well before puberty.

Inhalation of foreign objects or mucus is less frequent in the first year but should be considered when a baby who was previously quite well starts to cough, wheeze and then vomits. Paroxysmal coughing with vomiting suggests the possibility of whooping cough. Both conditions require the attention and advice of a doctor.

Cradle cap

Babies often get flaky patches or crusts of skin on their scalp, mainly around the softened area on the top of the head (the anterior fontanelle). Although it may look unsightly it is not a sign of poor hygiene and should not cause concern. It is caused by secretions from the sebaceous glands in the skin.

Cradle cap, or scurf, usually subsides when the baby is three or four months of age. Mild cases can usually be treated by frequent cleansing of the whole head with a mild baby shampoo. More severe encrusted lesions may require the application of olive oil. This should be left on overnight to soften the crusts which can then be removed easily.

Colic usually begins at the end of the first month of life and may continue until the baby is three months old. The reason for its onset is not known, but a relaxed and comforting attitude on the part of the carer will often alleviate the symptoms

Croup

Croup syndrome consists of inspiratory noises, called stridor, and cough. The illness usually arises without warning and can be distressful for both baby and parents.

The noise is caused by obstruction of the upper airway due to a variety of inflammatory conditions that narrow the airway. Occasionally an inhaled object can cause the same noise.

Croup can take two forms: viral croup, the most common, and bacterial croup, which is probably the more serious of the two. Viral croup is most common in the first years of life and predominantly occurs in early winter. An upper respiratory tract cold, runny nose and cough usually precede the croup by several days. This is sometimes accompanied by a fever.

Treatment for viral croup should be given by a doctor, but the mist generated by running a hot shower with the bathroom doors closed will often give relief until the doctor arrives. If the stridor persists and the child is becoming distressed, he or she will be admitted to hospital for a few days. Most babies do not progress beyond the stage of a cough, stridor and minimal increase in breathing rate, and the illness usually resolves completely within a week.

Bacterial croup usually affects the older child and the peak age of incidence is around three years. The course can be rapidly progressive and therefore the child must be admitted to hospital. Young children may have a high fever and respiratory distress as well as difficulty in swallowing. Intensive hospital treatment is often required for this.

By far the commonest cause of persistent stridor is a floppy infantile larynx. There is no anatomical abnormality for this exaggerated softness of the larynx. The cause is an indrawing, or sucking in of the trachea during inspiration. This often only occurs when the child cries or becomes excited. If the infant does not have respiratory distress when calm and the stridor does not get worse, no investigation or treatment is necessary. Symptoms usually subside by the end of the

first year. However, parents should be aware that the noise will probably be exaggerated when the child has a cold.

Earache

The usual causes of pain in the ear are otitis media or a local infection such as a boil in the outer ear; a foreign body might also cause pain.

Acute otitis media is an infection of the middle ear, which usually occurs in association with an upper respiratory infection caused by a virus. Young children are most commonly affected and the condition may sometimes occur even in the newborn infant. In this condition the eardrums bulge, causing severe pain, subsequent irritability and difficulty in sleeping. A common symptom of the disorder in young children is that they frequently tug at their ear. In some 20 per cent of cases, the drum ruptures spontaneously and pus is discharged. This can make examination of the ear difficult, but by analysing the discharge the offending organism can usually be identified so that the appropriate treatment can be given. With treatment, complications such as mastoiditis are rare, although temporary hearing loss is common. Permanent defects are unusual.

Not all earache is caused by otitis media. Mumps, toothache, foreign bodies or injury to the ear may also cause a child to complain of earache. No matter what the cause, the child who complains of earache should always be seen by a doctor.

Fever of unknown origin

It is often impossible to be certain about the cause of fever in the first few days of illness, unless a specific and localising diagnosis can be made on the basis of the illness's history, clinical findings and X-ray investigations. In the first five days of an illness a fever is most likely to be due to an acute infection. Viral infections rarely cause fever beyond seven to ten days, although inadequately treated or untreated bacterial infections with fever can last for many weeks.

In those children with fever who are not critically ill, a specific diagnosis cannot always be made, but a virus-like illness is assumed. Most of these are characterised by fever, constant irritability, refusal to eat and vomiting.

The doctor should ask the parents about recent family history, contacts, pets, drugs and recent immunisations, and especially overseas travel. A child who only has a fever does not justify an antibiotic, on the basis that it might be a bacterial infection, in which case the antibiotic will have no effect. An investigation after a full physical examination will usually guide the doctor to the right diagnosis. The doctor may prescribe medication to reduce the fever, especially as convulsions can sometimes occur in infants with a high temperature.

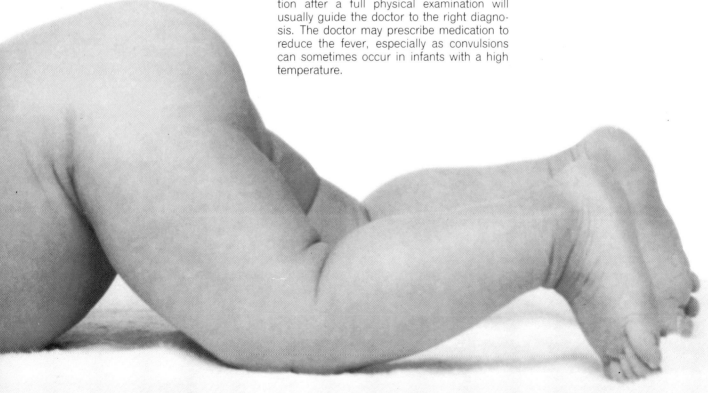

Hernias

Two types of hernia, or rupture, may occur in young babies: umbilical and inguinal. An umbilical hernia occurs when the intestines protrude through a weak muscle in the umbilical ring, or navel. The resultant swelling protrudes even more when the baby cries because crying increases pressure within the abdomen. An umbilical hernia is unsightly but is not serious and will usually disappear in a year or so. However, if it persists surgical treatment will be necessary.

An inguinal hernia appears as a lump in the region of the groin; it is caused by the protrusion of the intestine through the abdominal cavity. This type of hernia can occur at any age, including the newborn period, and is more common in boys than girls. In boys it may be associated with an undescended testicle. The hernia is usually a painless swelling, varying in size and becoming more distended when the baby coughs or cries. In some cases it causes vomiting and distension of the abdomen.

Any unsual swelling in the region of the scrotum or groin requires medical attention. As the hernia may become strangulated if left untreated, surgery is usually necessary soon after diagnosis.

Immunization

All childhood immunizations are planned to prevent specific infectious diseases or their toxic manifestations. Therefore, to achieve maximum effectiveness, the vaccine must be administered to an appropriate population at the appropriate time in life when the infant is immunologically susceptible and has not been exposed to the natural disease. Each immunization should be viewed as a balance between the risk of that disease in the individual and population as a whole, and the potential adverse effects of the procedure.

Administration of vaccines is not without intrinsic risk. For every product used there are expected side effects and occasional adverse

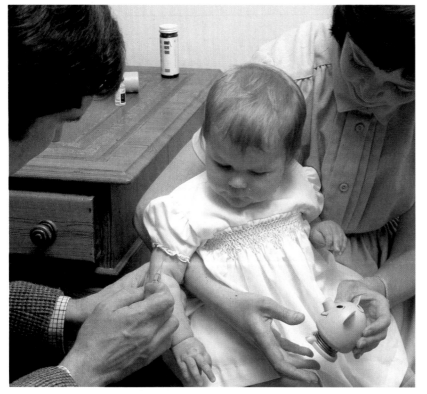

Triple vaccine is given at three months, repeated twice in the first year, and again on entry and leaving school

Immunization against diphtheria, whooping cough and polio have resulted in a dramatic drop in the number of cases

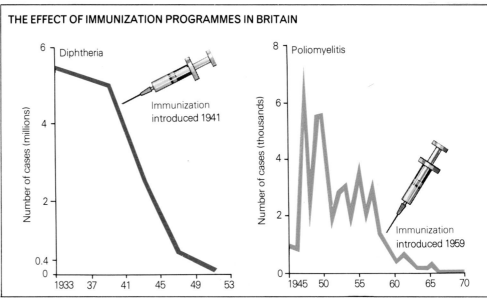

THE EFFECT OF IMMUNIZATION PROGRAMMES IN BRITAIN

Diphtheria — Immunization introduced 1941 — Number of cases (millions): 6, 4, 2, 0.4, 0 (years 1933, 37, 41, 45, 49, 53)

Poliomyelitis — Immunization introduced 1959 — Number of cases (thousands): 8, 6, 4, 2, 0 (years 1945, 50, 55, 60, 65, 70)

reactions. The parents therefore should be informed of the risks of immunization and also informed about the risks of the natural illness. Many specific routine procedures exist nationally but most countries differ considerably in their programmes.

At all times, only healthy children should be given vaccines. Febrile (feverish) illnesses, incubation of an infectious illness and any active infection are contraindications to immunisation. Minor non-febrile illnesses should not prevent the vaccine from being given. An infant who constantly appears to have a minor upper respiratory tract infection or allergic rhinitis (inflammation of the membrane lining the nose) has little or no risk from vaccination. Avoiding immunization of infants or children on the basis of such conditions frequently results in them not completing the full course, as the child does not return regularly for care and injections.

Vaccines have been developed against many infectious diseases. Only a limited number of these have general application in the United Kingdom. The choice of what is given rests on careful evaluation of the disease concerned and the benefits and potential side effects to be expected from the vaccine. Therefore, on the one hand, measles vaccination is highly recommended because it provides valuable long-term immunity with minimal side effects. The unmodified natural disease can be much more serious, with both nervous and breathing complications.

Mumps, on the other hand, although unpleasant, is usually mild with only occasional serious complications; the vaccine therefore has a low priority and is not among the officially recommended immunizations for infants in the United Kingdom. The Joint Committee on Vaccination and Immunization last revised the immunization schedule in 1978. A modified schedule for routine immaunization is given below.

Diptheria and tetanus immunization is safe and has an excellent record. The major controversy at present in the United Kingdom still relates to the whooping cough vaccine. In the early 1970s there was a high degree of compliance with the official schedule for whooping cough immunization. Eight out of every ten children born in 1971/72 received the vaccine in the following two years. It was at

SCHEDULE FOR ROUTINE IMMUNIZATION		
Age	Vaccine	When given
0-1 year	*DPT and oral polio (first dose)	3-12 months
	DPT and oral polio (second dose)	After interval of 6-8 weeks from the date of the first injection
	DPT and oral polio (third dose)	After interval of 6-8 weeks from second injection but may be extended to 4-6 months
1-2 years	Measles vaccine	Soon after the child's first birthday
4-5 years	†DT and oral polio (booster)	At least 3 years after completing basic course

*DPT – Dipheria, whooping cough and tetanus
†DT – Diptheria and tetanus

After the introduction of vaccination the number of cases of whooping cough dropped dramatically. In recent years there has been an epidemic due to the vaccine controversy, although compared to the disease the vaccine is relatively safe

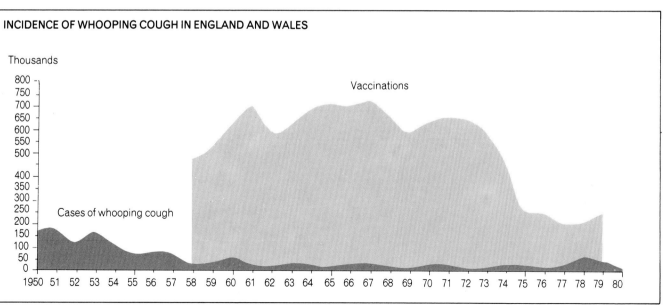

INCIDENCE OF WHOOPING COUGH IN ENGLAND AND WALES

Thousands

Vaccinations

Cases of whooping cough

800 750 700 650 600 550 500 400 350 300 250 200 150 100 50 0

1950 51 52 53 54 55 56 57 58 59 60 61 62 63 64 65 66 67 68 69 70 71 72 73 74 75 76 77 78 79 80

When the polio vaccine is given to a tiny baby it is made up into a syrup, then squeesed from a dropper into the baby's throat

this time that concern was growing about the safety of the vaccine.

There had always been a lingering suspicion of some link between the administration of the vaccine and the subsequent occurrence of brain damage. A paper published in 1974 reporting this association caused a dramatic fall in the number of vaccines requested, with the result that only three out of every ten children born in 1976 had been immunized two years later. Recent available data indicates that only half of the nation's newborn children are protected against whooping cough.

The attributable risk of neurological disease starting within a week of whooping cough immunization in infants who are neurologically normal is calculated to be 1 in 310,000 immunizations. This is equivalent to approximately 1 in every 100,000 children receiving the full recommended course of three injections.

The assessment of risk against benefit in the field of vaccination has to be a continuous process because of the steady flow of new data relating to both vaccine safety and disease significance. In regard to whooping cough, the recent reporting of the results of a Japanese trial of a potentially safer vaccine is awaited with interest. Evidence regarding the protective efficacy of this vaccine against all whooping cough serums will be critical. A universally safe vaccine is urgently required.

The United States, despite its litigious reputation, maintains very high rates of whooping cough immunization, mainly because the State Health Authorities require evidence of immunization before entry into school is permitted.

Jaundice in the newborn

Jaundice is a condition found in a large number of newborn infants. It is caused by the accumulation in the blood of a substance called bilirubin, which is a by-product of the normal disintegration of red blood cells. Bilirubin is usually excreted from the liver into the intestine in bile. The presence of bilirubin in the blood causes the characteristic yellow tinge to the skin and whites of the eyes.

Jaundice may be either physiological or pathological in origin. In the former case the baby appears well and feeds normally and the

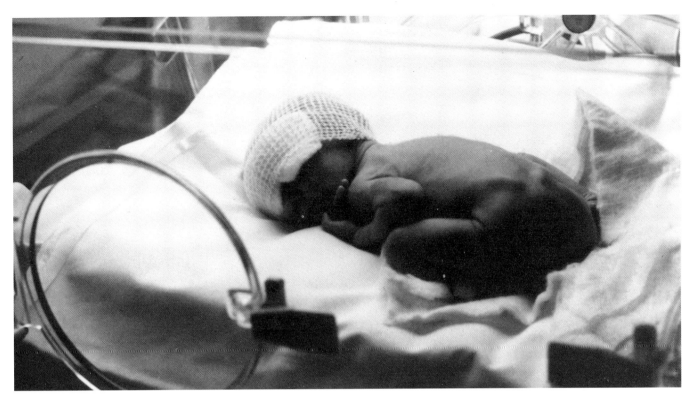

level of bilirubin in the blood is not usually very high. In most cases the condition does not require any specific treatment as the basic problem is immaturity of the liver which will correct itself around the fourth day of life. However, if the bilirubin levels are high enough, phototherapy, or exposure to ultraviolet light, is the best treatment. It effectively reduces the levels of bilirubin.

Pathological forms of jaundice are caused by conditions such as blood group incompatability, drugs administered to the mother in labour, inherited defects of the red blood cells and infections of the liver. Each of these requires accurate assessment of the causative factor so that a decision can be made on how best to manage the problem. With the introduction of phototherapy and exchange transfusion, severe complications from jaundice have now become rare. However, this does depend on giving appropriate treatment early, so parents who suspect that their child might have jaundice should consult their doctor immediately.

Rash in the nappy area

The commonest form of nappy, or diaper, rash seen in the neonatal period is perianal excoriation. The skin around the anus is red and raw, in an area on both buttocks but not usually touching the anus itself. The main cause of this type of rash is contact between

faeces and the skin. It is commoner in babies fed on cow's milk formulas. The most effective treatment is to expose the area at reasonably warm room temperatures. Applications of cold cream may help to relieve the rash.

Cutaneous candidiasis, or thrush, occurs most frequently in the warm moist intertriginous areas – those areas where the skin surfaces are in opposition, for example in the folds of the groin. The red lesions characteristically have sharp margins and individual spots occur beyond the margins. This type of infection, caused by a yeast fungus, candida, is not superimposed on an existing dermatitis as in the case of other wet lesions, but is rather a primary infection by candida that is present in the intestinal tract. This type of thrush often follows shortly after an attack of oral thrush, or monilia.

Atopic dermatitis is a more generalised skin disorder that may first become apparent in the nappy area, especially in the infant over eight weeks of age. The eruption is markedly red and frequently infected. Psoriasis may have its onset in the nappy area in the first year of life.

The successful treatment of eruptions in the nappy area requires accurate assessment of the various possible causes, so parents should consult their doctor about any rash in the area.

In treating inflammatory lesions it is best to avoid ointments, as they aid the retention of

A jaundiced newborn baby may be treated with a powerful light. This is painless and helps break down the bilrubin causing the condition. Bandages protect the baby's eyes

sweat. The doctor may prescribe a dusting powder with an antifungal agent, or, in the case if candidial nappy rash, give an oral medication, since yeast in the gut is probably the primary source of infection.

As mentioned above, the warm humid condition in the area is an important contributing factor. Frequent nappy changes, and leaving the nappy off for long periods each day are advisable. Parents should also ensure that when changing nappies they clean the nappy area thoroughly.

When the rash has subsided, prevention of a recurrence requires continued attention to the nappy area. Always make sure that the area is properly dried after washing. The skin should be protected from irritants by applying zinc oxide paste or other non-irritating creams.

Squint

Approximately five per cent of children have a squint, or strabismus. However, infants usually do not develop co-ordinated eye movements until approximately four months of age, so what appears to be a squint in the first few months of life may be due only to lack of control of the eye muscles.

Infants with a squint have an eye that deviates in one of the following ways: downwards, inwards, outwards or upwards. Any child over the age of three months who has such a deviation that persists for several weeks should be seen by a doctor. Early treatment may include wearing an eye patch over the good eye to strengthen the eye in which the muscles are weak. In many cases this will correct the fault, but in others surgery may be necessary to lengthen or shorten the eye muscle.

Sucking blisters

At birth, the lips shows a demarcation line where the mucous membranes meet the skin. A few days after birth the surface of the lip is thrown up into folds or cushions called sucking callouses, or blisters. These are not actually callosities due to pressure or friction. They represent a blister base with inflammatory borders. Such blisters probably result from vigorous sucking in-utero. They need no medication and disappear in time without complications.

Teething

Teething is a cause of anxiety for most parents, and in some cases there is a tendency to blame many common ailments that occur at the same time on the develop-

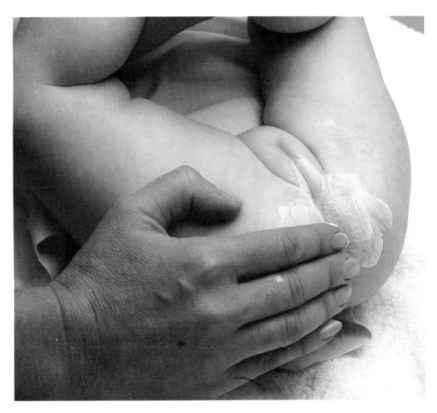

ment of the first teeth. Normally, however, the only symptoms of a tooth erupting are a small bump on the gums, excessive dribbling and perhaps a red cheek. Teething does not cause colds, fever, diarrhoea and so on, and if these occur during teething medical advice should be taken.

The first teeth begin to come through at about six months of age, but this varies from one child to another, and any delay beyond this does not indicate retarded physical development. The approximate age at which the different types of teeth develop and their sequence is as follows:

6 months – 2 lower central incisors
2 upper central incisors
2 lateral incisors in each jaw
18 months – 4 molars
18-20 months – canine teeth
24 months – back molars

The baby's first teeth are very important and therefore dental hygiene is vital. Avoid giving the baby sweet foods and drinks. The teeth should be cleaned following each meal; when the baby is small use a piece of gauze wrapped around your finger and then gradually encourage the child to use a toothbrush. Regular visits to the dentist should begin at the age of two and a half years.

Zinc and castor oil ointment has a soothing effect on skin made sore by nappy rash

Babies find relief from teething by mouthing a teething ring or similar object (left)

Giving a baby solid foods too early can cause him to vomit

It is not necessary to pat a baby on the back to wind him; merely hold him upright at the end of a feed so that the air in the stomach rises above the fluid contents

presence of bile (a green-coloured fluid) or blood in the vomit should be regarded as possibly due to intestinal obstruction. In this case the child should be referred for specialist advice.

The main feature to observe in a young baby who is vomiting is weight gain. If there is a history of vomiting over a prolonged period and the child's weight is average or above average, organic disease is unlikely. Organic disease is much more likely if the child is underweight. Examination of the possible sources of disease or infection should be looked for in the ears, kidneys and abdomen. Unexplained vomiting may also be caused by drugs or other toxic substances, and this possibility should always be considered.

The commonest non-organic cause of vomiting is excessive wind, especially when a breastfed baby sucks too long on the mother's breast. Too small a hole in the teat is invariably the cause of excessive wind in a bottle-fed baby.

Many doctors and nurses, when faced with a baby who cries and vomits, or has other symptoms, advise the mother to change from one dried milk to another. It is rarely, if ever, necessary or advisable to make this change. A rare metabolic problem may be the only exception.

Giving solids to a baby before he can chew often causes him to vomit. Six to seven months is the most likely time when babies begin to chew, so the parents should thicken feeds rather than give solids. Some mothers force their infants to take certain foods which they think might be good for them, or compel the baby to take more than he needs, with the result that vomiting ensues. Vomiting is rarely due to the eruption of teeth.

Vomiting

Most, if not all, babies vomit at some time, but some tend to vomit much more than others. Almost all normal healthy babies regurgitate some milk after feeds, usually by expelling the food while bringing up wind. The difficulty lies in deciding whether the vomiting should be regarded as within the range of normal, or whether it should be investigated as a symptom of disease.

There are many causes to consider when assessing the child, but innocent vomiting (posseting), intestinal upsets and infections are the commonest.

When vomiting is frequent and excessive the doctor may consider the possibility that it is due to an organic problem. If the amount brought up is small and the child is well – taking food avidly and gaining weight – it is unlikely that an organic disease exists. The

Wind and winding

The term wind refers to air that is trapped in the stomach; its precise cause is unknown but it is partly due to the baby swallowing air during a breast or bottle feed. In western societies, much is made of winding babies following or during a feed, to the extent that some babies are not allowed to sleep until they make the requisite noise.

At the end of a feed a baby should be held upright so the air in the stomach rises above the level of the fluid contents, thus allowing the air to be expelled easily. If the wind is not passed after a few minutes the baby should be placed in the cot on his stomach.

It is not advisable to try to actively wind the baby by rubbing or patting the back, or to wind the baby until fully fed – otherwise the problem may be made worse if the baby cries and thus swallows more air.

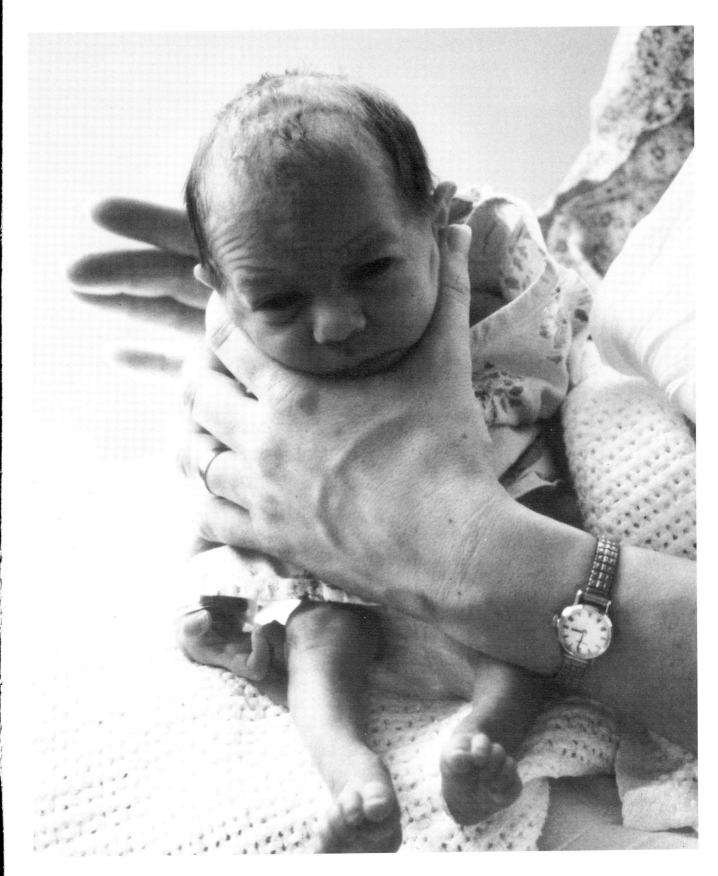

HELP AND ADVICE

BREASTFEEDING

ASSOCIATION OF BREASTFEEDING MOTHERS
131 Mayow Road, Sydenham,
London SE26 4HZ
Tel: 01-778-4769
Advice for breastfeeding mothers (24-hour telephone service). Organizes support groups locally and advises on setting up similar groups

LA LECHE LEAGUE
BM 3424, London WC1 3XX
Tel: 01-404-5011/01-242 1278
An organization established to help and advise mothers who want to breastfeed. Queries answered by phone; free leaflets available (enclose stamped addressed envelope) giving details of local groups

FERTILITY, GENETICS AND TERMINATION

BROOK ADVISORY CENTRES
Listed in local directories.
Give help and advice on contraception, pregnancy tests and coping with unplanned pregnancies

NATIONAL ASSOCIATION FOR THE CHILDLESS
318 Summer Lane, Birmingham,
BR19 3RL
Tel: 021-359-4887
Offers help and advice to infertile couples on a self-help basis

SICKLE-CELL SOCIETY
c/o Willesden Hospital, Harlesden Road, London NW10 3RY
Tel: 01-451-3293
Information on sickle-cell disease. Provides a free information pack about the disease and trait

PREGNANCY AND BIRTH

ACTIVE BIRTH CENTRE
18 Laurier Road, London NW5 1SG.
Tel: 01-267-3006.
Provides a full service for women and their partners from conception to the child's first year. Yoga-based exercise classes, posture and massage, weekend workshops and post-natal mother and baby groups featuring 'baby gymnastics'

INDEPENDENT MIDWIVES
c/o Melody Weig, 65 Mount Nod Road, London SWI6 2LP
Offers women home birth and continuity of care (private)

THE MISCARRIAGE ASSOCIATION
18 Stoneybrook Close,
West Bretton, Wakefield,
West Yorkshire WF4 4TP
Tel: (0924) 85515
Nationwide service providing information and support for women who have had a miscarriage. Send stamped addressed envelope for details and free leaflets

CAESAREAN SUPPORT NETWORK

c/o Sue Johnson, 11 Duke Street, Astley, Manchester M29 7BG
Tel: 0942 878076
A nationwide network providing advice and support for women who may need a Caesarean or have already had one

NATIONAL CHILDBIRTH TRUST

9 Queensborough Terrace, London W2 3TB
Tel: 01-221-3833
An organization whose aim it is to help mothers and fathers to cope with pregnancy, birth and early parenthood. Offers antenatal classes in the last three months of pregnancy, counselling on breastfeeding and literature on all aspects of pregnancy and birth. Details about local branches, antenatal teachers and breastfeeding counsellors available from the London office

PRE-PREGNANCY CARE

FORESIGHT

Mrs Peter Barnes, The Old Vicarage, Church Lane, Whitley, Surrey GU8 5PN
A private organization offering health and dietary advice based on blood and other tests

PARENTS AND CHILDREN

THE ASSOCIATION OF POST-NATAL ILLNESS
Institue of Obstetrics and Gynaecology, Queen Charlotte's Maternity Hosptial, Goldhawk Road, London W6
Offers advice on coping with post-natal depression and other illnesses. Send stamped addressed envelope for free leaflet

ASSOCIATION FOR SPINA BIFIDA AND HYDROCEPHALUS
22 Upper Woburn Place, London WC1H OEP
Tel: 01-388-1382
Support for parents of children with spina bifida or hydrocephalus

CHILD POVERTY ACTION GROUP
1 Macklin Street, London WC2B 5NH
Tel: 01-405.5942
Provides information on social security and other benefits (housing, education, health and so on)

COMPASSIONATE FRIENDS
6 Denmark Street, Bristol BS1 5DQ
Tel: 0272-292778
An organization of bereaved parents offering support to other bereaved parents

DOWN'S CHILDREN ASSOCIATION
4 Oxford Street, London W1N 9FL (other branches throughout the British Isles; see local directory)
Advice for parents of Down's syndrome children on their education and training. Details can be obtained by sending a stamped addressed envelope

GINGERBREAD
35 Wellington Street, London WC2E 7BN
Tel: 01-240-0953
Self-help organization for one-parent families offering advice, help and information

NATIONAL CHILDMINDING ASSOCIATION
204/206 High Street, Bromley BR1 1PP
Tel: 01-464-6164
Membership of childminders, carers and parents whose aim it is to improve the conditions of care for children

NATIONAL COUNCIL FOR ONE-PARENT FAMILIES
255 Kentish Town Road, London NW5 2LX
Tel: 01-267-1361
Advice, help and information for single pregnant women and single parents on matters such pregnancy, finance, legal rights and benefits

PRE-SCHOOL PLAYGROUPS ASSOCIATION
Alford House, Aveline Street, London SE11 5DH
Tel: 01-582-8871
Association of mothers-and-toddlers groups, playgroups and the people who run them. Branches throughout the United Kingdom

THE SPASTICS SOCIETY
12 Park Crescent, London W1N 4EQ
Tel: 01-636-5020
Support for parents of handicapped children

STILLBIRTH AND NEONATAL DEATH SOCIETY
Argyle House, 29-31 Euston Road, London NW1 2SD
Tel: 01-833-2851/2
Support for bereaved parents. Information on national network available by phone or post

Front cover credits:
Maternity clothes courtesy of Mothercare, branches throughout the UK.

Furniture courtesy of the Reject Shop, Kings Road, London SW1.

Picture by Adrian George (limited edition) from a selection at Artbeat, 703 Fulham Road, London SW6.

149

INDEX

Numbers in *italics* refer to captions and illustrations

CREDITS

Picture credits